VEGETARIAN COOKING

A COMMONSENSE GUIDE

MURDOCH BOOKS

CONTENTS

THE VEGETARIAN ADVENTURE

People can be drawn to a vegetarian diet for a variety of reasons. Some have ethical or health concerns, for others it is a matter of religious belief. But the decision to eat this way could just as easily be an aesthetic or culinary one: vegetarian cooking offers huge scope for creativity and can be gastronomically sensational. For so many reasons, a vegetarian menu is now first choice for people of all ages and lifestyles.

The vegetarian choice

The variety of ingredients, abundance of dishes and sheer scope that vegetarian cuisine offers for creative cooking and eating are often overlooked by confirmed meat-eaters. For many in the developed world, flesh foods such as meat, chicken and fish have for a long time formed the centrepiece of most meals. This tradition has led to a diet often lacking in variety—as well as a beneficial balance of nutrients—and often overloaded with unhealthy saturated fats. A diet that overemphasises meat is a product of affluence, and not necessarily a good one.

Many people have recognised an imbalance in their way of eating and are modifying the amount of flesh foods included in their diets. The discovery of vegetarian food often begins in this way. As people gain confidence, experiment more and discover the pleasures of cooking vegetarian foods—the wealth of flavours, textures, colours and aromas—they often welcome increased vitality and say goodbye to weight problems. Other benefits people report include clearer skin and less constipation, and many choose to abandon eating meat and fish altogether.

The term 'vegetarian' is often used quite loosely. Some people call themselves vegetarian (or semi-vegetarian) while still eating a little fish or chicken and no red meat. Many just exclude all meat and fish from their diets. Vegans, on the other hand, exclude all flesh foods, as well as all animal products such as milk, cheese, eggs and honey. Most vegetarians, however, are lacto-ovo vegetarians who still eat eggs and dairy products.

Meatless meals need never be bland or boring. They offer enormous variety, stimulating the imagination and sometimes offering the opportunity to learn new cooking skills. Vegetarian cuisine offers the cook great scope to be inventive.

About this book

This book features recipes using no flesh foods. It is not specifically a vegan cookbook in that eggs, butter, milk and cream are used liberally. However, there are plenty of recipes that are suitable for vegans, or can be modified to suit.

This is not a diet book, health food book or one that offers strange vegetarian substitutes for a meat-centred diet, with recipes for bland imitations of meatloaf or burgers.

This is a cookbook that is simply designed to expand the menu of possibilities, to show that one can simultaneously be a connoisseur of good food, a fine cook and a vegetarian. The recipes are for anyone who loves preparing, serving and eating good food. All the delights of richer foods are available for vegetarians—for instance there are plenty of luscious desserts to be sampled here!

This chapter contains an overview of basic nutritional principles relating to the vegetarian diet so you can be confident of balancing your nutritional needs. In particular it also introduces the concept of the vegetarian 'food pyramid', which can help guide you through your shopping and menu decisions.

At the end of this chapter is an extensive glossary of ingredients used in this book, drawing from the great food cultures of Asia, Europe, the Mediterranean and the Middle East.

Back to basics

Many people who have discovered the joys of vegetarian eating are unaware of a few dietary pitfalls which they could easily avoid with a little knowledge. With the increasing popularity of vegetarian food, and despite a high level of awareness of the facts about nutrition, there are still gaps in many people's knowledge about how to get the most out of their diet.

Filling in these gaps can enhance the vegetarian experience and make it beneficial as well as enjoyable. If you were raised as a vegetarian, you are probably already in the habit of making sure all your nutritional needs are met, but for those making the transition from eating flesh foods, or even to eating substantially less of them, there are a few important basics to bear in mind.

- It is perfectly possible, and not at all difficult, to live a healthy life eating only vegetarian foods. The key is to ensure variety in the diet: eat as many different kinds of food as possible and all the essential nutrients that the body requires will be available.
- It is a common mistake to think in terms of 'substituting' the nutrients provided by meat, fish or poultry. A little knowledge, awareness and enthusiasm for trying new things, plus a willingness to broaden your culinary repertoire to include delicious vegetarian dishes from all over the world, is more important than any specialised scientific knowledge about nutrition.

- If you include grains, pulses, vegetables, fruit—and providing you're not a vegan, eggs and dairy food—in your diet, you'll be covering all the nutritional bases.
- Many studies have shown that populations enjoying a diet that is high in unrefined foods and fibre and low in salt and sugar have a lower incidence of blood pressure problems, heart disease, bowel disease (including cancer), diabetes and gallstones. Unrefined whole foods are best in this regard.
- It is important that the produce you buy be as fresh as possible so that the nutrients have not had time to deteriorate. For this reason, as well as for economy, it is a good idea to get into the habit of shopping and eating seasonally, when fruit and vegetables are at their best and cheapest.
- Similarly, it is wise to freeze some fruits and vegetables when they are in season. If you make sauces from tomatoes and red capsicums (peppers), and purées from berries and stone fruits, you can enjoy the bounty of each season throughout the year.

Is it safe for children?

Children thrive on a vegetarian diet—in fact, many make the choice for themselves at quite an early age. When planning meals for vegetarian children, the principle of maximising the number of different kinds of food in the diet is even more vital. Most of the nutritional needs of children will be met this way, but there are a few important things to remember. Pulses, eaten at the same meal with grains, nuts or seeds, provide complete protein, which is an absolute necessity for children. This is not as daunting as it may sound: baked beans on toast; lentils and rice; a falafel sandwich; red kidney bean chilli with tortillas or tacos are all examples of popular meals providing complete protein.

Growing children need foods rich in the many nutrients their bodies require; they also need more fat in their diet than adults. There are lots of healthy sources of dietary fat for children, including peanut butter, avocado, cheese, yoghurt and nuts. Most children enjoy these foods anyway, which means there is really no excuse for resorting to nutritionally empty foods such as cakes, chocolate, or fried takeaways.

Make sure your children eat a good breakfast, avoiding sugary, processed cereals. If you start them off eating home-made muesli and wholemeal (whole-wheat) toast, you'll set up a pattern that will benefit them all their life.

A special note for vegans

Vegans—those who eat only foods of plant origin, and no animal products such as dairy and eggs—can obtain all their nutritional needs with just a little planning. Some extra care is needed with vegan children, as their needs are slightly different. Again, variety is the key. Vegans need to be especially vigilant about eating a variety of foods from the four plant food groups every day:

- grains in the form of bread, cereals, pasta and rice
- pulses, nuts and seeds including peanut butter and tahini, beans of all kinds (including baked beans), chickpeas, soy products (tofu, tempeh, and soy milk that has been fortified with calcium and vitamin B12)—especially for children
- vegetables
- fresh fruit and juices.

Vegans need to take special care that they do not miss out on vitamin B12, as the usual sources in a lacto-ovo vegetarian diet are eggs and dairy products. Supplements may be necessary, although fortified soy milk is a good source.

Calcium can be found in soy milk, as well as some green vegetables, sesame seeds and tahini, almonds, and breads and cereals fortified with calcium.

The iron which is found in meat and which lacto-ovo vegetarians can obtain from eggs can come also from pulses, soy products, green vegetables, breakfast cereals, dried fruits, nuts and seeds— provided you eat a wide variety of these. The amount of iron available from these foods is maximised if you eat them with foods that are rich in vitamin C, such as oranges or blackcurrants.

It is important to remember that children need more fat in their diets than adults to provide them with energy for growth. Vegan children can thrive if they obtain their dietary fat from foods such as peanut butter and nuts, vegetable oils, tahini and avocados.

Snack foods can include dried fruit, nuts, seeds and fresh fruit juice.

THE VEGETARIAN FOOD PYRAMID

It is just as possible to have a poor diet eating exclusively vegetarian foods as it is eating excessive animal products. The vegetarian food pyramid is a good starting point if you want to check whether your current diet is adequate. Its underlying principle is simple: it shows food groups in the form of a pyramid, with those that should comprise the bulk of your diet forming the base of the pyramid, and those to be consumed more sparingly at the top.

Eat most

- Grains: wheat, rice, barley, corn, oats, rye, millet, buckwheat
- Foods made from grains: pasta, bread, wholegrain breakfast cereals
- Fruit and vegetables

Eat moderately

- Dairy: milk, yoghurt, cheese
- Pulses: peas, beans of all kinds, lentils
- Nuts
- Eggs

Eat least

- Sugar, honey, sweets
- Butter, cream, margarine, oils
- Alcohol, tea, coffee

Navigating the food maze

Meal planning becomes easier if you make a habit of using the food pyramid as a guide. Your daily diet should be stacked with the staple foods from the 'eat most' group: fruit, cereals and toast for breakfast; bread or bread rolls, salads or cooked vegetable dishes and fruit for lunch; pasta or rice-based main course for dinner with fresh bread or rolls, and more fruit for dessert or snacks.

Small amounts of dairy foods from the 'eat moderately' group can be part of the day's meals (unless you are a vegan): yoghurt with breakfast or lunch, a little cheese with lunch or dinner. Dinner can include filling dishes and hearty soups made from dried beans or lentils, as well as tasty egg dishes. Nuts are great for snacking.

The 'eat least' category means exactly that—a small amount of butter or margarine on your breakfast toast, a little virgin olive oil with your salad or to stir-fry the onions for the evening meal, the occasional glass of wine with dinner. A sugary treat is fine if it isn't a regular occurrence, and tea and coffee can be enjoyed in moderation.

You can balance the nutritional content of the day's meals so that the overall pattern satisfies the food pyramid guidelines. Compensate for an unavoidably fatty lunch, for example, with an evening meal made up of vegetables, grains and fruit.

Eating out can be a trap, so keep the food pyramid in mind when ordering food and to compensate for any imbalances when preparing food for yourself at home.

Easy does it

Changing the habits of a lifetime is not something we can do overnight. If your usual diet doesn't bear much resemblance to the food pyramid, you can move gradually towards a healthier way of eating. Don't worry if every meal is not perfectly balanced. You can correct the proportions over the course of each week as you adjust to buying and cooking healthier foods and experiment with new dishes. Replace refined foods with whole foods, and high-fat dairy products with reduced-fat versions. Check labels for salt, sugar and fat content, and for food additives. Have fun making your own versions of soups, sauces and even breakfast cereals, rather than buying the ready-made product. This way you can control what goes into your body.

Children generally enjoy healthy eating. Pastas, fruit, yoghurt, peanut butter, cheese, milk and nuts are usually popular. The difficulties only arise if you are trying to change bad habits: doing it gradually is best.

Menu planning

Aim to shop and eat for health, using the food pyramid as a guide. Buy several different kinds of rice, couscous, a variety of pastas, lots of breads (freeze loaves and flatbreads if you have room), breakfast cereals and interesting flours.

Replenish your store of fresh produce regularly, but do it systematically. Shop with some idea of your meal plans from week to week to avoid wastage. Taking advantage of enticing seasonal produce by buying up big is pointless if fruit and vegetables languish at the bottom of your refrigerator while you think of a way to use them. Vary your choices as much as possible to keep your diet interesting and to maximise the nutritional benefits.

Buy cheeses, milk, yoghurt and eggs regularly, but plan how much you are likely to need to avoid overloading on dietary fat.

Tinned foods are an essential pantry item: tinned beans of every variety are great time-savers if you don't want to soak and cook your own. Tomato pastes and tinned tomatoes are invaluable; also keep olive oils—extra virgin for flavour, lighter grades for cooking—on hand. Bottled sauces such as pesto, basic pasta sauces and chilli sauce are versatile flavour enhancers.

CARBOHYDRATES

Carbohydrates are vital for energy. The critical importance of complex carbohydrates in a good diet cannot be overstated.

Carbohydrates occur in the form of starches and sugars from grains and their products (flour, bread and pasta). They are also found in potatoes, pulses and to a lesser degree nuts, as well as in fruits and sugars. There are probably still people who think potatoes are fattening, but fortunately we now have a far greater awareness of the benefits of loading our diet with pasta, rice, breads, cereals and, yes—potatoes. It is difficult to eat too much carbohydrate—usually excess flab comes from eating too much fat rather than too much carbohydrate.

There is a whole array of delicious grain foods that have only relatively recently become part of the Western diet: couscous, buckwheat, quinoa and hybrid grains like triticale, which is bred from wheat and rye and has a deliciously nutty flavour—try it instead of or as well as rolled (porridge) oats in home-made muesli. Take advantage of these more unusual grains to add variety to your menus.

Many different rices are also readily available now: fragrant basmati and jasmine rice; pearly arborio, essential for the perfect risotto; and wild rice (an aquatic grass), which, although expensive, is available in more economical mixtures and makes a delicious—and nutritious—change.

The fibre component of carbohydrate foods is another bonus. The less processing the food has undergone, the more of it there will be. The presence of fibre in complex carbohydrates allows the energy from sugars to be used by the body at an even rate, whereas refined sugars hit the bloodstream rapidly and are quickly used up, leaving energy levels depleted. This is why you may feel elated and then lethargic in quick succession after eating sugary foods. Complex carbohydrates, with their sustained release of energy, provide more stamina over a longer period.

Foods rich in complex carbohydrates include:

- breads
- potatoes
- rices
- wheat
- barley
- corn
- buckwheat
- rye
- dried beans
- lentils
- bananas
- pasta.

These foods, as we have seen, also form the basis of the vegetarian food pyramid.

A word about sugar

Cane sugar is valueless in terms of vitamins and minerals. Excessive amounts also interfere with the body's ability to metabolise fat. If you eat lots of sugar, the fat you eat will be stored more readily as body fat instead of being burned off with physical activity.

Few people, however, are going to eliminate sugar entirely from their diets as they simply enjoy the taste too much. Like all good things, sugar is fine in moderation. A delicious pudding or sweet treat enjoyed on a special occasion does no harm. It is when these foods displace other more nutritious ones that problems arise.

Sweet tooths can always indulge in fruit, where sweetness comes bundled up with fibre and other nutrients. Fruits are also more filling than other sweet foods so there is less danger of overeating.

FIBRE

Fibre is essential for bowel health, but nutritionists say most Westerners don't consume anywhere near the recommended daily intake of 30 g (1 oz). A good vegetarian diet is replete with many different types of fibre.

Fibre includes the cellulose and gums in fruit and vegetables. Animal products do not contain any fibre at all—there is none in dairy foods, fish, poultry or meat, despite their sometimes chewy texture. A well-balanced vegetarian diet, on the other hand, is rich in fibre. Among other things, fibre acts as a broom in the bowel by moving food along at such a rate that the potential for problems is minimised. It prevents constipation and lowers the risk of bowel cancer and other intestinal problems.

Because different types of dietary fibre have different functions, again it is important to vary the diet as much as possible. Some types of fibre (mainly from fruit and vegetables) help lower blood cholesterol. It is not enough—as was the fad at one time—to simply heap spoonfuls of unprocessed bran onto your breakfast cereal. Apart from some uncomfortable consequences while the body adjusts to the unfamiliar onslaught of fibre, unprocessed bran contains large amounts of phytic acid, which inhibits the uptake of iron. Since vegetarians need to maximise their intake of iron from sources other than meat, this is to be avoided. It's a good rule to include some fibre-rich foods in every meal.

Foods rich in fibre include:

- dried beans and peas
- fresh green beans and peas
- cabbage
- carrot
- potatoes (especially in their jackets)
- spinach
- corn
- cereals such as oats and wholegrain wheat
- products made from wholegrains, such as wholemeal (whole-wheat) bread
- dried fruits
- fresh fruit (especially apples, bananas and oranges), but only when you eat the whole fruit and don't just drink the juice.

PROTEIN

Protein is essential for cell growth, tissue repair and to manufacture the substances that help protect us against infection.

Nobody needs huge amounts of protein from any source, but everybody does need some. Growing children and pregnant women need a little more protein than other people.

It is easy to get too concerned about protein. The truth is that most people in Western societies eat far more protein than they need, and if there is too much protein in the diet it is simply converted to body fat. Affluent communities very rarely produce a case of protein deficiency, even when the members are otherwise careless of their nutritional needs and live on too much takeaway food, for example. The real problem is too much fat, sugar and salt.

Deriving protein from vegetable sources has a distinct advantage: foods such as legumes and grains have a high fibre content that is beneficial for bowel health and also puts the brake on overeating.

Food combining and 'complete' protein

Protein is made up of 23 different amino acids, substances that combine to make what is termed a 'complete' protein. The body breaks down complex proteins from food into these simpler units and uses them to build up proteins of its own.

Amino acids occur in different combinations and proportions in various foods. The body can make most amino acids itself if the diet is adequate. However, eight essential amino acids can't be made by the body and can only be obtained directly from food. Some foods have these eight essential amino acids in almost the right proportions for the body to use immediately.

Protein from animal sources—meat, eggs, cheese, fish, poultry, milk, cheese and yoghurt—provides all eight essential amino acids and is considered 'complete'.

Although cheese and eggs are complete proteins, overloading on these sources of protein will introduce too much fat into the diet, so vegetarians need to look beyond these to supply their dietary protein needs. This is where food combining comes in.

Pulses and grains contain some but not all of the essential amino acids, and they also contain *different* essential amino acids. If a pulse is eaten with a grain—for example, if rice is eaten with beans—the body combines the different amino acids contained in each to form a complete protein. These foods don't even have to be eaten at the same time—within a few hours of each other will do.

Most vegetarians are aware of the importance of obtaining protein from a range of sources. Food combining needn't be complicated: by following a few simple principles you can invent a delicious way of eating. The proteins in dairy products, nuts and seeds, pulses and grains are complementary, so eating foods from two or more of these groups together makes plenty of protein available to the body.

In many societies, ways of combining complementary proteins have naturally evolved in the indigenous diet. Think of

dal and rice, beans and corn, hummus and pitta bread—all are combinations of a pulse and a grain. Other common combinations include:

- peanut butter sandwiches on wholemeal (whole-wheat) bread
- baked beans on wholemeal toast
- split pea soup and a bread roll
- brown rice and chickpeas
- rice and tofu
- corn tacos with red kidney beans
- lentil patty on a wholemeal bun
- pasta and cheese
- muesli with milk
- vegetable pies: potato, spinach
- muesli with nuts and seeds
- chickpeas and couscous.

Tempeh and tofu, wheatgerm and oatmeal come pretty close to being complete proteins, the only non-animal products to do so. This is why they are so highly valued by vegetarians.

Vegans can obtain all the protein they need by eating a wide range of foods of purely vegetable origin.

Sources of protein

- Dairy: cheese, milk, yoghurt
- Nuts and seeds: sunflower, sesame, pepitas (pumpkin seeds), pecans, Brazil nuts, hazelnuts, almonds, walnuts, cashew nuts, pine nuts
- Pulses: peanuts, peas, beans, lentils, soya beans and soya bean products such as tempeh and tofu
- Grains: rice, oats, corn, wheat/flour products, pasta, couscous, rye, barley

Eating foods from at least two of the above groups together will make more protein available to the body. There is no need for complex mathematical calculations—making sure you eat a varied diet will ensure you get enough protein.

VITAMINS AND MINERALS

Vegetarians who combine food to obtain their protein can still miss out on some essential nutrients that meat-eaters obtain easily. The most important of these are vitamin B12 and the minerals iron, zinc and calcium.

Including dairy foods and eggs in the diet will generally ensure enough protein, calcium, iron, vitamins and minerals are supplied. Vegans, however, need to take particular care.

For maximum nutrition, freshness is important when buying fruit and vegetables. Most nutrients are retained quite well in snap-frozen products, although the flavour may not be as good.

Taking vitamin and mineral supplements is a waste of time if your diet is inadequate as the body cannot use them effectively in the absence of the right kinds of foods.

Vitamins

The body needs vitamins from the B group to metabolise food and to allow proper functioning of the nervous system. These vitamins come from wholegrain cereals, bread and pasta, nuts and seeds, peas, beans, leafy green vegetables, potatoes, fruits, avocados and yeast extract.

Vitamin B12, found in dairy foods, eggs, yeast extract, alfalfa, seaweeds and fortified soy milk, is essential for red blood cells and nerve cells. If there is one vitamin vegetarians are going to be deficient in, it will be this one.

Vitamin B1 (thiamin) is found in soya beans, wheatgerm, sunflower seeds, Brazil nuts, peas and beans.

Vitamin B2 (riboflavin) is obtained from milk products, mushrooms, soya beans, leafy green vegetables, almonds, prunes and dates.

Vitamin B3 (nicotinic acid) is contained in mushrooms as well as sesame and sunflower seeds.

Vitamin B6 (pyridoxine) is found in currants, raisins, sultanas (golden raisins), bananas, sunflower seeds and soya beans.

Folic acid is found in leafy greens, oranges, walnuts, almonds and avocados.

Vitamin C is essential to protect against infection, for healing, and to help the body absorb iron from foods. It is found in leafy green vegetables, tomatoes, capsicums (peppers), blackcurrants, oranges, strawberries, kiwi fruit and papaya.

Vitamins A, D, E and K are fat-soluble vitamins found in foods such as milk, butter, cheese, margarine, vegetable oils, nuts and seeds. Deficiencies in these vitamins are rare.

When exposed to sunlight, the body makes **vitamin D**, which is needed to allow the absorption of calcium into the bones. **Vitamin A** is needed for good eyesight, healthy skin, hair, nails and mucous membranes, and for resisting infection. It is found in dairy foods, green and yellow vegetables (especially carrots), and in apricots, red capsicums (peppers), parsley and spinach. You can see it would be difficult to develop a deficiency in a normal vegetarian diet. **Vitamin E** is an important antioxidant guarding against cell damage, and **vitamin K** helps the blood to clot.

Vegetarians should not need to take vitamin supplements, except on medical advice. The key is variety: a well-balanced vegetarian diet will supply all the vitamins you need.

Minerals

Iron is needed for the formation of red blood cells. One of the biggest potential problems for vegetarians—particularly for women—is iron-deficiency anaemia. A varied vegetarian diet provides enough iron if it includes pulses, most especially lentils and soya beans; wholegrains and products made from them, and nuts and seeds such as pistachios, pepitas (pumpkin seeds) and sesame seeds.

Dark, leafy green vegetables, brewer's yeast, wheatgerm, egg yolks, dried fruits (especially apricots and prunes) and seaweeds are also good sources of iron.

Signs that you may not be getting enough iron include tiredness and lethargy, paleness and shortness of breath.

Calcium is needed for good teeth and bones and for the healthy functioning of the muscles (including the heart) and nerves. Cheese is rich in calcium, as are milk, yoghurt and cream. It's worth remembering, if you are concerned about the amount of fat in your diet, that low-fat and skim versions of dairy products have the same amount of calcium as the full-fat form. Eggs contain calcium as well.

For vegans, there are many non-animal sources of calcium. One of the richest is sesame seeds, which can be sprinkled on cereal or salads, or used in the form of the ground paste tahini, an essential ingredient of hummus. Soya beans contain calcium, as do flour, figs and other dried fruits, almonds, sunflower seeds, dark green vegetables, broccoli, brewer's yeast, carob, molasses and seaweeds. Vegans need to eat these foods to avoid becoming deficient in calcium.

Women have a greater need for calcium and should be aware of this from early adulthood. Getting regular supplies of calcium fortifes their store of dense bone for the years after the menopause. At this time of life, osteoporosis, a painful and sometimes crippling deterioration of the bones, is a very real possibility if dietary calcium has been inadequate in earlier years. Osteoporosis can be prevented but not cured.

Zinc is needed by the body for growth, healing, and metabolising protein and carbohydrates. Signs of a zinc deficiency include white flecks on the nails and skin problems. Sources of zinc include oatmeal, wheatgerm, cheese, skim milk, brewer's yeast, dried figs, peanuts, nuts, sesame seeds, pepitas (pumpkin seeds), corn, peas, mangoes, spinach and asparagus.

Magnesium is also necessary for metabolising carbohydrates. It is soluble but not damaged by heat, so it's a good idea to save the water in which vegetables are cooked for making stock or sauces. Magnesium deficiencies are rare. Fresh fruit and vegetables, nuts and seeds, brewer's yeast, wholegrains, dried fruits, pulses and soya beans all contain some magnesium.

Iodine, needed for the functioning of the thyroid gland, is only required in tiny amounts and is present in iodised salt and seaweeds.

system. It would be harmful to try to eliminate all fat from the diet, but eating a variety of foods will supply plenty without any special effort.

Healthy fats

Dietary fat comes from two sources: animals and plants.

Sources of animal fats that vegetarians (but not vegans) can use include butter, cheese, cream, yoghurt and egg yolks.

Plants provide oils and the hard vegetable fats (such as margarine) that are made from them. Fats containing essential fatty acids and that occur in foods containing other nutrients (such as olive and other vegetable oils, nuts, seeds, avocados, grains) are a better source of fat in the diet than the saturated fat used for making fried takeaway foods, cakes, biscuits (cookies), chocolates or ice cream.

THE FAT TRAP

Meat-lovers who give meat a central place in their diet face one pitfall a vegetarian largely avoids: eating a lot of saturated fat, which has unhealthy effects on the body.

However, it is important for vegetarians to remember that there are plenty of non-meat sources of saturated fat, and these are best eaten in moderation. One example is coconut oil, which is used in many commercial baked goods. Coconut cream and tinned coconut milk used in many curries is another.

Children need more fat than adults to help them grow, but they can obtain it from a range of nutritious vegetarian foods including milk, avocados, peanut butter, yoghurt and cheese.

Everyone needs some fat, as fatty acids are essential for the formation of cells in the body, especially those of the nervous

Kinds of fat

Saturated fats solidify at room temperature. Most animal fats are saturated, including lard, butter and dripping. Saturated fats are thought to raise the level of a harmful type of cholesterol in the blood and also lower the amount of a beneficial type of cholesterol. They are also thought to be implicated in some cancers.

Polyunsaturated fats, on the other hand, lower the overall amount of cholesterol in the blood. They are found in vegetable oils such as safflower, sunflower, corn and soya bean oil. Polyunsaturated fats are liquid at room temperature but can be chemically processed into margarines.

The effects on the body of eating a lot of polyunsaturated fats are still being investigated. It used to be thought that they had a beneficial effect on the amount of cholesterol in the blood, but it is now known that this effect is indiscriminate and reduces 'good' cholesterol as well as 'bad' cholesterol.

Margarine in the diet in large amounts is thought to contribute a kind of fatty acid implicated in heart disease. Large quantities of polyunsaturated fats can also oxidise to form free radicals in the blood. These are responsible for tissue damage and contribute to the formation of plaque on the artery walls. Eating lots of fruit and vegetables reduces this effect as these foods contain antioxidants.

Monounsaturated fats have recently come into favour, for a number of reasons. When it began to be noticed that people in countries like Spain and Italy had a lower incidence of heart disease than those of other nations, it was recognised that the so-called 'Mediterranean diet' is high in olive oil and low in dairy fats.

Large amounts of monounsaturated fats occur in olive and canola oils. These kinds of fats reduce the levels of 'bad' cholesterol and increase 'good' cholesterol, protecting against heart disease. In addition, populations using olive oil as the main fat in their diets have been shown to have lower rates of breast and bowel cancer, although the exact reason why this should be so is still being investigated.

Watch out for hidden fats

Different kinds of fat usually occur in foods in combination. More important than worrying about which kind of fat you are eating is being aware of the overall amount of fat in your diet. This means being conscious of hidden fats in foods such as pies, crisps, chocolate (and carob) bars, cakes, biscuits (cookies) and other commercially produced, ready-to-eat foods. Many people worry about the sugar in these foods and forget about the fats.

Eating out a lot and eating takeaway foods and commercially produced snacks can easily lead to excess fat in the diet. A good guide is to aim at getting only about a quarter of your total daily kilojoules from

fat, or to eat about 30–40 grams (1–1½ oz) of fat per day if you are a woman or child, and 40–60 grams (1½ –2 oz) if you are a man. Very active adults and teenagers need about 70 grams (2½ oz) a day, and athletes and those engaged in heavy physical work 70–80 grams (2½–2¾ oz).

There also hidden fats in many innocent-looking 'health' foods, for example toasted muesli, which contains a lot of vegetable oil. Avocados and nuts are also high in fat and should be eaten in moderation. Remember also that foods labelled 'low cholesterol' are not necessarily low in fat.

The body only needs small amounts of fat, and nobody eating a Western diet is ever in danger of suffering a fat deficiency. However, it is just as important for vegetarians as it is for meat-eaters to be aware of how much fat they are eating.

Vegetarians can sometimes be under the illusion they are eating a healthy diet simply because they have eliminated meat with its hidden and not-so-hidden fats. But unthinkingly loading up on cheese, cream, sour cream or even vegetable oils is just as hazardous for health.

Excessive amounts of fried food will lead to weight gain, whether these foods are fried in animal or vegetable fats. The only difference is that a vegetarian eating lots of food fried in, say, olive oil—and not burning up these added kilojoules with increased physical activity—will gain weight, but without increasing their blood cholesterol levels in the way a meat-eater who consumes lots of saturated fat will.

If you are concerned about your weight, it is more important to be aware of the *amount* of fat in the foods you eat on a daily basis than to try counting kilojoules from all sources, as was done in the past. Excess kilojoules from fat are readily stored as body fat, whereas those from cabohydrates, for example, are made available to the body as energy.

VEGETARIAN 'HERO' FOODS

Some foods have been called the 'heroes' of a vegetarian diet because they are rich sources of certain essential nutrients which meat-eaters obtain in abundance. Including these foods regularly in your diet will help ensure you avoid any deficiency problems. The amount of nutrients contained per 100 g (3½ oz) of each 'hero' food are also given below.

Almonds are a good source of monounsaturated oil, dietary fibre and vitamin E.
– Protein: 20 g
– Calcium: 250 mg
– Iron: 3.9 mg
– Zinc: 3.8 mg

Dried apricots contain beta-carotene (the plant form of vitamin A), fibre and vitamin C.
– Calcium: 67 mg
– Iron: 3.1 mg
– Zinc: 0.8 mg

Eggs supply iron, phosphorus, protein and vitamins A, B12 and D.
– Protein: 13 g
– Calcium: 43 mg
– Iron: 1.8 mg
– B12: 1.7 ug

Lentils contain protein, fibre, complex carbohydrates, B vitamins, potassium, magnesium and zinc.
– Protein: 6.8 g
– Calcium: 17 mg
– Iron: 2 mg

Cheese, milk and yoghurt provide calcium, phosphorus, protein and vitamin A. Milk and yoghurt retain the B vitamins which are removed in the processing of cheese.

Cheddar cheese
- Protein: 26 g
- Calcium: 720 mg

Milk
- Protein: 3.3 g
- Calcium: 120 mg
- B12: 0.5 ug

Yoghurt
- Protein: 5.8 g
- Calcium: 195 mg
- B12: 0.5 ug

Parsley contains many vitamins, minerals and antioxidants, and is rich in calcium and iron.
- Calcium: 200 mg
- Iron: 9.4 mg

Rolled (porridge) oats are a good source of protein, thiamin, niacin, iron, fibre and carbohydrate.
- Protein: 10.7 g
- Iron: 3.7 mg
- Zinc: 1.9 mg

Sesame seeds are rich in calcium and contain vitamin E, magnesium, phosphate and zinc.
- Protein: 22 g
- Calcium: 62 mg
- Iron: 5.2 mg
- Zinc: 5.5 mg

Soya beans have the best-quality protein of all pulses, some B vitamins, polyunsaturated fat and fibre.
- Protein: 13.5 g
- Calcium: 76 mg
- Iron: 2.2 mg
- Zinc: 1.6 mg

Spinach contains most of the vitamins and minerals normally found in meats.
- Calcium: 53 mg
- Iron: 3.2 mg
- Zinc: 0.6 mg

Sunflower seeds are rich in protein, vitamins, minerals and trace elements.
- Protein: 22 g
- Calcium: 100 mg
- Iron: 4.6 mg
- Zinc: 6.4 mg

Tempeh and tofu provide magnesium, calcium, phosphorus, iron and protein.

Tempeh	Tofu
- Protein: 19 g	- Protein: 10 g
- Calcium: 142 mg	- Calcium: 128 mg
- Iron: 5 mg	- Iron: 1.4 mg
- Zinc: 1.8 mg	- Zinc: 1 mg

Wheat bran is an excellent source of soluble fibre, iron, thiamin, niacin and zinc.
- Iron: 12 mg
- Zinc: 4.7 mg

Yeast extract is a concentrated source of B vitamins, minerals and protein.
- Protein: 24 g
- Iron: 3.7 g
- Zinc: 5.1 mg
- B12: 5 ug

Recommended daily intakes

Protein: 55 g (men), 45 g (women)
Calcium: 800 mg
Iron: 7 mg (men), 12–16 mg (women)
Zinc: 12–16 mg
Vitamin B12: 2 ug

Women who are pregnant, breastfeeding or over 54 years of age require different amounts of these nutrients.

A FEAST OF FLAVOURS

One of the great joys of vegetarian eating lies in its versatility. It's an opportunity to take exotic detours through some of the world's most wonderful cuisines, broadening your menu options and expanding your cooking skills. The limitations of the traditional meat-and-two-veg diet will soon become obvious!

Many cultures feature a strong vegetarian component and some are exclusively vegetarian, having evolved this way of eating for economic as well as religious reasons. These cuisines are the source of delicious, nutritious dishes that any cook can easily master.

Some dishes are classic examples of efficient and tasty food combining. From Mexico we get tortillas and beans; from the Orient, tofu, tempeh and rice; from the Middle East, hummus with lavash or pitta bread; from North Africa and the Mediterranean, couscous and chickpeas.

When you don't have to make meat, chicken or fish the centrepiece of your meals, mealtimes become much more interesting and it becomes much easier to serve food buffet-style. Many ethnic cuisines actually demand this way of serving and eating, offering platters of complementary dishes from which people help themselves, adding accompaniments of their choice.

With vegetarian food you can break all the rules. You can serve first courses as main courses, mains as starters, or make a soup the star of your meal. Many exotic vegetarian dishes can be served as either a side dish, main course, light meal or snack.

All you need is a little knowledge, a few interesting ingredients, and some thought about complementary flavours and textures. You will then discover that it is really quite impossible to be bored by vegetarian food!

Wake up your tastebuds

The incomparable flavours of fresh whole foods can be enhanced with spices and condiments such as harissa, chilli powders and pastes, and curry spice mixtures. Herbs are also indispensable, while pickles, chutneys, sauces, mustards and relishes can be used to dress up any number of dishes.

Certain herbs and spices go particularly well with certain foods:

- basil with tomatoes and cheeses
- cinnamon, cardamom and cloves with yoghurt, cream and milk dishes
- cloves with oranges
- chives in soups, dips, salads, sandwiches and sauces, and with eggs, potatoes and cheese
- dill in salads, egg dishes and with potatoes
- chopped herbs with pasta and rice dishes
- ginger with carrots
- lemon grass in rice dishes and Asian-style sauces
- lemon thyme in salads and with cooked vegetables
- oregano and marjoram with eggs, in salads and marinades, and with cauliflower and tomatoes
- mint with potatoes, rice and in tabouleh
- paprika with eggs, cheeses and in casseroles
- parsley in salads and with tomatoes
- rosemary with eggplant (aubergine), tomatoes and zucchini (courgette)
- sage in bean, cheese and egg dishes
- garlic is brilliant with just about anything savoury!

Consider colour and texture as well as taste and nutritional value. Serve a pasta bake with a salad or crisp-textured greens such as asparagus or snow peas (mangetout) to lend extra colour and crunch. Make simple vegetable dishes and salads more interesting and nutritious by sprinkling them with chopped nuts or seeds—try a mixture of pepitas (pumpkin seeds) and sesame seeds tossed in soy sauce and roasted in the oven (it will keep for months in the refrigerator in an airtight jar). Include lots of interesting breads when serving vegetarian foods, including flatbreads such as lavash, chapattis, rotis, poppadoms, tortillas and pitta.

Stock up the pantry before you begin to roam through the varied world of vegetarian cookery. This will ensure you will always have the necessary ingredients for a successful dish and you won't need to compromise on flavour.

Most supermarkets these days stock a huge variety of the items you will need, but don't forget to explore delicatessens, food markets and Asian and other ethnic food stores for condiments and more unusual ingredients.

The recipes in this book are grouped into basic chapters, from which you can browse and plunder at will. Enjoy experimenting and giving recipes your own individual twist. We hope this book inspires you on your gastronomic journey through some of the world's great vegetarian cuisines!

THE VEGETARIAN KITCHEN

Vegetarian cookery opens up a whole world of flavours, drawn from all corners of the globe. Many of the different grains, herbs, spices and vegetables used in this book are readily available from supermarkets, but some may require an exploratory trip to a speciality food store, good greengrocer or health food shop. Experimenting with different ingredients introduces variety into the diet—and variety is, after all, the spice of life!

Banana chilli This large, long chilli has a slight banana shape and a waxy yellow skin that turns red when fully ripe. The flavour is sweet and mild. It is also sometimes called a sweet banana pepper and is sold in some supermarkets and greengrocers.

Barley is a starchy grain that is especially wonderful in winter soups. As the soup cooks, the barley starch helps thicken it, while providing flavour, texture and creaminess. It is also a good alternative to rice for a winter risotto. Most barley is milled to some degree to make it edible. Pearled barley has had the outer husks removed and is brownish in appearance. You'll find it in health food stores and supermarkets.

Besan (chickpea flour) is a pale yellow, finely milled flour made from dried chickpeas. Used in Indian cooking to make batters, doughs, dumplings and pastries, it has a slightly nutty aroma and taste. It is unleavened, so produces a heavy texture.

Betel leaf This delicate green leaf, also known as wild betel leaf or *char plu*, is commonly eaten raw in Thai cuisine, where it is often used as a base or a wrapping for small appetisers. The leaves are sold in bunches in Thai or Asian speciality shops.

Black rice This glutinous rice owes its colour to the layer of bran left intact on the grain which colours the rice as it cooks, resulting in a purplish-black rice. It is mainly used in sweet dishes in Thailand and the Philippines and is available from Asian food stores.

Bocconcini (fresh baby mozzarella cheese) These are small balls of fresh mozzarella, often sold sitting in their own whey. A smooth, mild, unripened cheese originally made from buffalo milk but now usually made from cow's milk, bocconcini is soft and springy to the touch and has a milky taste. Drained and sliced, it can be used in salads, as pizza or bruschetta toppings, and in pasta dishes. Cherry bocconcini is a smaller bite-sized version. Both are available from delicatessens and some supermarkets.

Bok choy (pak choy), also known as Chinese chard and Chinese white cabbage, has fleshy white stems and leaf ribs and green flat leaves. It has a slightly mustardy taste. Separate the leaves, wash well and drain. The white stems can be sliced thinly and eaten raw. Look for firm stems and unblemished leaves. A smaller type is known as baby bok choy.

Borlotti (cranberry) beans This large, slightly kidney-shaped bean is a beautifully marked pale, pinkish brown with burgundy specks. Popular in Italy, borlotti beans have a nutty flavour and are used in soups, stews and salads. They are sometimes available fresh, in which case they take about 30 minutes to cook, but they are also available dried or tinned.

Brioche is a light, sweet French-style bread flavoured with eggs and butter. Its rich colouring and fine texture make it ideal for breakfast dishes and for desserts. It is sold in most bakeries and some large supermarkets.

Broad (fava) beans can be eaten whole when they are very young, but are more commonly sold as large, flat beans which need to be shelled like peas. The beans are then cooked and peeled of the outer tough skin to reveal delicate bright green beans. They are a good bean for Mediterranean dishes. When fresh beans are not in season, frozen shelled beans can be bought from most large supermarkets.

Brown rice still has its bran and germ intact. Generally speaking, it has a nuttier, stronger flavour than white rice, and is more nutritious. It is available in long- and short-grain varieties. Short-grain rice is generally stickier and is the best choice for puddings, sushi and rice balls, where its stickiness is an advantage. Long-grain rice tends to remain separate and is preferable for savoury dishes such as fried rice, pilaff or on its own.

Brown rice vinegar is a perfect choice for Asian-inspired dressings and pairs well with sesame oil. It is lovely with sushi and is also good for pickling.

Burghul (bulgur) Popular throughout the Middle East, and also known as cracked wheat, burghul is a key ingredient in tabouleh. You can buy these wheat kernels either whole, or cracked into fine, medium or coarse grains. They are pre-steamed and pre-baked and require little or no cooking, but are generally soaked before using to soften them.

Buttermilk This cultured, low-fat dairy product is made from skim milk and milk powder and has a tart taste. It is often used in baking as a raising agent and can be found in cartons in the refrigerated section of most supermarkets.

Cannellini beans These small, white, kidney-shaped beans are also known as Italian haricot beans or white kidney beans. Mildly flavoured and slightly fluffy in texture when cooked, they are good all-purpose beans for use in soups, casseroles, stews and salads, and are available fresh, dried or tinned.

Capers These are the pickled green buds of a shrub which grows wild in many parts of the Mediterranean. Capers have a sharp, sour taste and are sold in seasoned vinegar or packed in salt, which needs to be rinsed off before use. Salted capers have a firmer texture, better flavour and are often smaller than those preserved in brine. Baby capers are also available; generally, the smaller the caper, the better the flavour.

Cardamom This very aromatic spice of Indian origin is available as whole pods, whole seeds or ground. The pale green oval pods, each up to 1.5 cm (⅝ inch) long, are tightly packed with sweetly fragrant brown or black seeds. When using whole pods, lightly bruise them before adding to a dish.

Cavolo nero, or Tuscan cabbage, is especially popular in Italy and is a staple of Tuscan peasant cuisine. Rich in nutrients, it has tall stalks and long, narrow, crinkled very dark green leaves that curl attractively into scrolls at the edges. Unlike spinach and silverbeet (Swiss chard), it benefits from long, slow cooking to bring out its tangy, almost sweet flavour. It is lovely in pasta, soups such as minestrone, with beans or lentils, or as a side dish.

Chickpeas are one of the world's most versatile and popular legumes. There are two kinds of chickpea: the large white garbanzo and the smaller brown dessi. Some of the most popular Middle Eastern dishes, including hummus, have chickpeas as their basis. They can be boiled, roasted, ground, mashed and milled and are available dried or tinned. They are excellent for dips, stews and salads, and work well with curry flavours.

Chinese black vinegar This rice vinegar is sharper than white rice vinegars and is traditionally used in stir-fries, soups and dipping sauces. The Chinese province of Chekiang has the reputation for producing the best black vinegars.

Chinese broccoli, also known as Chinese kale or gai larn, has smooth, round stems sprouting large dark green leaves and small, white flowers. The juicy stems, trimmed of most of their leaves, are the bit most commonly eaten. Chinese broccoli has a similar flavour to Western broccoli, but without the characteristic large flower heads.

Chinese cabbage, also known as celery cabbage and napa cabbage, has a long shape and closely packed broad, pale green leaves with wide white stems. It has a delicate mustard-like flavour.

Chinese rice wine (also called shaoxing or shao sing) is made from glutinous rice and is similar to a fine sherry, being amber-coloured with a rich, sweetish taste. It adds flavour and aroma to a variety of Chinese dishes and is also used in marinades and sauces. Dry sherry can be substituted, but grape wines are not suitable.

Choy sum, also known as Chinese flowering cabbage, is slimmer than bok choy (pak choy) and has smooth green leaves and pale green stems with clusters of tiny yellow flowers on the tips of the inner shoots. The leaves and flowers cook quickly and have a light, sweet mustard flavour; the stems are crunchy and juicy.

Coconut cream is extracted from the flesh of fresh coconuts and has a thick, almost spreadable consistency. It is very rich and sold in tins alongside coconut milk. If you can't get hold of it, use the thick cream off the top of a couple of tins of coconut milk instead. Pour the milk into a jug and leave it to settle — the cream will separate out at the top.

Coconut milk is extracted from fresh coconut flesh after the cream has been pressed out and has a much thinner consistency than coconut cream. It is sold in tins in most supermarkets. Once opened, the milk or cream does not keep, so freeze any leftovers. (Coconut milk is not the clear, watery liquid found in the centre of fresh coconuts—this is known as coconut water or coconut juice.)

Coriander (cilantro) Also known as Chinese parsley, all parts of this aromatic plant—seeds, leaves, stem and root— can be eaten. The leaves add an earthy, peppery flavour to curries, and are used in salads and as a garnish; the stems and roots are ground for curry pastes. Dried coriander is not a suitable substitute.

Couscous is a grain made from semolina and coated with wheat flour. In North Africa, couscous is used in much the same way as rice is in Asia—as an accompaniment to meat and vegetable dishes. Traditionally it is steamed in a couscousière. Today, most large supermarkets sell instant couscous, which cooks in 5 minutes.

Crème fraîche A naturally soured cream that is lighter than sour cream, crème fraîche is available from gourmet food stores and some large supermarkets. Sour cream can usually be used as a substitute.

Cumin This small, aromatic pale brown seed has a warm, earthy flavour. In its ground form cumin is an essential component of curry pastes and many other spice mixes. Black cumin is smaller and darker than common cumin and sweeter in taste. Cumin's flavour is more pronounced when it is dry-roasted in a pan or oven, then ground in a spice grinder.

Curry leaves These small, shiny, pointed leaves are from a tree native to Asia and have a spicy curry flavour. They are available from Asian grocery stores and larger supermarkets. They are not edible, so remove them from dishes before serving.

Daikon Much used in Japanese and Chinese cooking, this carrot-shaped white radish can be up to 30 cm (12 inches) long, depending on the variety, and has a similar taste and texture to ordinary radish. Daikon contains an enzyme that aids digestion.

It is added to stewed dishes, thinly sliced as a garnish, or grated and mixed with finely chopped chillies and used as a relish. It is also sold pickled in a solution of soy sauce. The leaves can be eaten raw in a salad or sautéed. Daikon is available from most large supermarkets or Asian grocery stores. Select firm and shiny vegetables with unscarred skins.

Dried black fungus Also known as cloud ear fungus or wood ears, this tree fungus has little flavour of its own, but is valued for its crunchy texture. It is most commonly available in its dried form, which looks like wrinkled black paper. Before use, soak in warm water for 15–30 minutes, or until the fungus swells to about five times its size.

Dried Chinese mushrooms, also known as Chinese dried black mushrooms, grow on fallen decaying trees. Their distinctive woody, smoky taste is intensified by the drying process. They are rarely eaten fresh.

Dried rice vermicelli are thin translucent noodles. They need to be soaked in hot water until tender, then drained thoroughly before being used in stir-fries and soups. Small bundles of unsoaked noodles can be quickly deep-fried until they expand, then used as a garnish.

Eggplant (aubergine) Native to Asia, eggplants come in a variety of shapes, sizes and colours. Tiny pea eggplants are small, fat, green balls which grow in clusters, and can be bitter in flavour. They are used whole in Thai curries or raw in salads. Slender eggplants, also called baby and Japanese eggplants, are often used in curries, where they readily absorb flavours; the common large purple eggplant used in Mediterranean and Middle Eastern cooking can be substituted.

Enoki mushrooms are pale, delicate mushrooms with long, thin stalks and tiny caps. They are very fragile and need only minimal cooking. They are quite bland in

flavour but have an interesting texture and appearance so are ideal for blending with other mushrooms.

Fennel A white, large-bulbed vegetable with a feathery green top, fennel can be gently braised or baked, or finely shredded and eaten raw in salads. It has a soft aniseed flavour. The seeds are used as a spice.

Fenugreek An important ingredient in Indian cooking, the dried seeds from this plant of the pea family are small, oblong and orange-brown. They are usually gently dry-fried, then ground and added to a curry paste; in Sri Lanka a few seeds are often used whole in seafood curries. Use sparingly, as the flavour can be bitter. Pungently flavoured fenugreek leaves are cooked in vegetable dishes or ground as part of a tandoori marinade.

Feta cheese A soft, white cheese ripened in brine, feta was originally made from the milk of sheep or goats, but is often now made with the more economical cow's milk. The fresh cheese is salted and cut into blocks before being matured in its own whey. It must be kept in the whey or in oil during storage or it will deteriorate quickly. Feta tastes sharp and salty and can be eaten as a starter, cooked or marinated. Bulgarian feta is not as sharply flavoured as the traditional Greek variety. Feta is available from delicatessens and most supermarkets.

Filo pastry (also called phyllo) is a paper-thin pastry made from flour and water. It is used widely in Eastern Mediterranean countries in both sweet and savoury dishes. The paper-thin layers are lightly buttered and stacked to make sweets such as baklava, or several layers can be rolled up to enclose a filling.

Fontina cheese is a rich cow's milk cheese from the alpine region of Italy. It varies in flavour according to its age. Young fontina is semi-soft, with a mild, creamy and somewhat nutty taste; mature Fontina is hard and more pungent in flavour. With a milk fat content of around 45%, it melts well but is also a great table cheese.

French shallots are small, round or elongated onions that grow in clusters and have thin, papery brown skins and a mild onion flavour. They are sometimes called eschallots. *See also red Asian shallots and shallots.*

Fresh egg noodles are made from egg and wheat flour and are pale yellow. Before use they need to be shaken apart and cooked in boiling water until tender and then drained well. In addition to their traditional use in chow mein, Chinese stir-fries and short soups, they are now used in recipes from many other parts of Asia. Fresh egg noodles are sold in a range of widths. The noodles are dusted lightly with flour before packing to stop them sticking together. Store them in the refrigerator.

Fresh rice noodles are made from a thin dough of rice flour. This is steamed, giving it a firm, jelly-like texture, then lightly oiled and packaged ready for use—the pearly white noodles need only to be rinsed in hot water to loosen and separate them, then drained. They come in thick or thin varieties, or in a sheet that can be cut to the desired width. Rice noodles are used in stir-fries or added to simmered dishes near the end of cooking. Store them in the refrigerator.

Fried Asian shallots These are very thin slices of red Asian shallots that have been deep-fried until crisp. They are used as a crunchy, flavoursome garnish, and can be added to peanut sauce. They are sold in packets in Asian grocery stores.

Galangal root is similar in appearance to its close relative, ginger, but is a pinkish colour and has a distinct peppery flavour. Use fresh galangal if possible as it has a better flavour than slices of dried galangal, but take care not to get the juice on your clothes or hands, as it stains. Ground dried galangal is also known as Laos powder.

Garam masala is an Indian spice blend which usually includes cinnamon, black pepper, coriander, cumin, cardamom, cloves and mace or nutmeg, although it can sometimes be made with mostly hot spices or with just the more fragrant spices.

Garlic chives Also known as Chinese chives, these thick, flat, garlic-scented chives are stronger in flavour than the slender variety used in Western cooking. They are particularly prized when topped with the plump, edible flower bud.

Ginger This spicy-tasting root, used fresh, is an indispensable ingredient in every Asian cuisine. Look for firm, unwrinkled roots and store them in a plastic bag in the refrigerator. The brown skin is usually peeled off before use. Ground ginger cannot be substituted for fresh.

Goat's cheese is a soft, fresh cheese made from goat's milk. It has a slightly acidic but mild and creamy flavour.

Golden syrup A golden-coloured syrup that has a thick consistency similar to honey. It is used to flavour puddings and other sweet recipes. Dark corn syrup can usually be substituted.

Gow gee wrappers are round, thin pieces of dough used to wrap bite-sized savoury fillings. They are made from wheat flour. When filling them, work with one wrapper at a time and keep the others covered with a damp tea towel (dish towel) so they don't dry out. They are sold in packets in Asian food stores and some supermarkets.

Gruyère cheese A firm cow's milk cheese with a smooth texture and natural rind. It has a nutty flavour and melts easily, making it perfect for tarts and gratins.

Haloumi is a salty, semi-firm sheep's milk cheese. It has a rubbery texture which becomes soft and chewy when the cheese is grilled or fried. It is available from delicatessens and most large supermarkets.

Haricot beans There are many types of beans that belong to the haricot family, including cannellini and flageolet (white or pale green beans), and also navy beans, which are famously used in baked beans. In Europe and the United States, haricot are also called white beans.

Harissa is a spicy, fiery chilli paste widely used in North African cooking. It is delicious with tagines and couscous, or can be added to soups, salad dressings, marinades, pasta sauces, casseroles and dried bean salads for a flavour hit. You can buy harissa from speciality food stores.

Hoisin sauce A thick, red-brown Chinese sauce made from soya beans, garlic, sugar and spices, hoisin sauce has a distinctive salty, sweet–spicy flavour, with a hint of garlic and Chinese five-spice. It is used in cooking and as a dipping sauce.

Hokkien (egg) noodles, also known as fukkien and Singapore noodles, are thick, yellow, rubbery-textured noodles made from wheat flour. They are packaged cooked and lightly oiled and need no preparation before use—simply stir-fry or add to soups or salads. Store them in the refrigerator.

Jerusalem artichokes No relation to the globe artichoke, these small tubers are in fact a cousin of the sunflower. Their sweet earthy flavour makes them ideal for use in soups and purées.

Kecap manis Also known as sweet soy sauce, this thick, dark, sweet soy sauce is used in Indonesian cooking as a seasoning and condiment, particularly with satays.

Kefalotyri cheese A very hard, scalded and cured sheep or goat's milk cheese with a mild flavour. Its use depends on its age. When young, it is a table cheese; at six months old, it is used in cooking; and when more mature, it makes an excellent grating cheese. Parmesan or pecorino cheese can be substituted.

Lemon grass This long, grass-like herb with fragrant stems has a citrus aroma and taste and is very popular in Thai cuisine.

Trim the base, remove the tough outer layers, then finely slice, chop or pound the white interior. For pastes and salads, use the tender, white portion just above the root. The whole stem—trimmed, washed thoroughly and bruised using the back of a heavy knife—can be added to simmering curries and soups (remove before serving). Dried lemon grass is rather flavourless.

Lentils A large range of lentils (often called dal) are eaten throughout the world. Tiny blue-green lentils—the most famed being the French 'puy' lentils—are small, hold their shape well and can be used in place of brown lentils. Brown lentils are larger than a green lentil, with a strong, deep, astringent taste. They hold their shape well, but can easily be puréed. Red lentils are small and a vibrant orange colour and break down easily when cooked. They are great in soups, and to help thicken dals and pâtés. Black lentils (also called caviar or beluga lentils) are less common than other varieties. They can be interchanged with green or brown lentils in recipes.

Light soy sauce is thinner and lighter in flavour than regular soy sauce and pale golden in colour. It is suitable for soups, vegetable dishes and dipping sauces.

Mace is a spice ground from the fine, bright red membrane that envelops the nutmeg seed. It has a similar flavour to nutmeg, but is softer and more delicate. It features in savoury and sweet dishes and is often used in the spice blend garam masala.

Makrut (kaffir lime) leaves Native to South-East Asia, this variety of lime tree has fragrant green leaves and bears a dark green, knobbly fruit. The leaves and fruit zest are added to curries and other dishes to give a citrus tang (the fruit is not very juicy and is seldom used). Remove the coarse central vein from the leaves before tearing or shredding them. Leaves and fruit are available fresh from Asian food stores; leftover fresh leaves can be frozen in airtight plastic bags. Fresh young lemon leaves and strips of zest from a standard lime can be substituted, but the flavour will not be quite the same.

Maple syrup A rich brown syrup obtained from the sap of certain Canadian and American maple trees.

Marsala A fortified wine from Marsala in Sicily that comes in varying degrees of dryness and sweetness. Dry marsalas are used in savoury dishes and enjoyed as an aperitif. Sweet ones are suitable for use in dessert dishes such as zabaglione and are also served with desserts.

Mascarpone This heavy, Italian-style set cream is used as a base in many sweet and savoury dishes. It is made from cream rather than milk, so is high in fat. It is sold in delicatessens and supermarkets.

Mirin is a sweet and subtle golden-coloured rice wine used in Japanese cooking. It is added to salad dressings, marinades and glazes, is mixed with soy sauce to make teriyaki sauce, or used as a seasoning in long-simmered dishes. True (unprocessed) mirin is fermented, producing enzymes and lactic acid bacteria traditionally valued for good health. It is available from Asian grocery stores, health food shops and most supermarkets. Sweet sherry can be substituted.

Miso A staple of the Japanese diet, miso is a protein-rich, thick, fermented paste made from fermented soya beans, salt and other ingredients, such as wheat, rice or barley. Miso contains all eight essential amino acids and a protein content of 12–20%. It also contains vitamin B12, so vital for vegetarian diets; unpasteurised miso is also a rich source of live lactobacillus. Like yoghurt, miso is a 'living' food as it contains beneficial bacteria and enzymes which are destroyed by boiling. For this reason it is best added as a flavouring at the end of cooking. Miso comes in a wide variety of colours, including red (genmai),

brown, light brown, yellow and white, each having a distinctive flavour and varying in texture from smooth to chunky. Lighter coloured miso is usually milder and sweeter. Genmai miso is made from brown rice and has a light, sweet taste. It adds flavour and depth to soups and stews, and is great as a spread. White miso, which is actually a pale yellow colour, is the fermented paste of soya beans, salt and either rice or barley. It has a sweet, mellow taste and a relatively low salt content. Miso is used in soups, sauces, marinades and dips and is available from Asian grocery stores and health food stores.

Mozzarella cheese is a smooth, fresh white cheese with a mild, slightly sweet flavour and a distinctive ball-like shape. It is traditionally made from buffalo milk, but is now often made with cow's milk. Used as a table cheese as well as in cooking, it melts well and is a great pizza topping. Fresh mozzarella can be found in most delicatessens and is usually sold packed in whey. Buffalo mozzarella is considered the best.

Mushroom soy sauce is a dark soy sauce enhanced with the addition of mushroom essence. It has a deep, rich flavour and can be substituted with regular soy sauce.

Mustard seeds have a sharp, hot flavour that is tempered by cooking. Both brown and yellow seeds are available, although brown mustard seeds are more common.

Natural vanilla extract is derived from vanilla beans. When using vanilla extract, ensure it is made from real vanilla and is not labelled 'imitation' vanilla extract or essence, which is completely artificial. The flavours are quite different, with imitation vanilla having a harsh, nasty aftertaste.

Nori is an edible seaweed sold in dried, paper-thin sheets commonly used in Japanese cooking. Nori sheets can be plain or roasted. Before use they can be toasted lightly over a naked flame to freshen and produce a nutty flavour. Store it in an airtight container or in the freezer. Nori is sold in most large supermarkets and Asian grocery stores.

Oats are a good source of protein, calcium, B vitamins and fibre. They are one of the few grains that do not have the bran and germ removed during processing and are higher in unsaturated fats than other grains. Rolled (porridge) oats are the most common form.

Orange flower water is an essence distilled from the blossoms of the bitter Seville orange. It is used extensively in Eastern Mediterranean countries to perfume pastries, puddings, syrups and drinks.

Oyster mushrooms Also called abalone mushrooms, these beautifully shaped, delicately flavoured mushrooms are usually white or a pale, greyish brown, but can also be pink or yellow. They are wonderful in stir-fried or creamy pasta dishes.

Palm sugar (jaggery) Made from the boiled-down sap of several kinds of palm tree, including the palmyra palm and the sugar palm of India, palm sugar ranges in colour from pale golden to deep brown. It is sold in hard cakes or cylinders and in plastic jars. Palm sugar is thick and crumbly and can be gently melted or grated before being added to sauces or dressings. It can be found in Asian grocery stores and large supermarkets. Soft brown sugar can be substituted.

Pandan leaf This fragrant leaf of a type of pandanus tree is widely used in South-East Asian cooking to flavour rice dishes and sweets. It is sold in Asian grocery stores.

Papaya This large tropical fruit can be red, orange or yellow. It is sometimes erroneously called a pawpaw, but is actually part of the custard apple family.

Parmesan cheese A hard cow's milk cheese widely used in Italian cooking, either grated and added to dishes, or shaved as a garnish. Always buy parmesan in a chunk and grate it as you need it, rather than use ready-grated. Parmigiano Reggiano, from Parma in Northern Italy, is considered the finest parmesan available.

Pecorino cheese One of Italy's most popular cheeses, with virtually every region producing its own variety, pecorino is a hard, strongly flavoured cheese made from sheep's milk. It is quite similar to parmesan cheese in flavour.

Pecorino pepato is a pecorino cheese to which black peppercorns have been added, giving a peppery bite.

Pickled ginger Japanese pickled ginger is available from most large supermarkets. The thin slivers of young ginger root are pickled in sweet vinegar and turn a distinctive salmon-pink colour in the process. This soft pink colour is often exaggerated to a hot pink colour in commercially produced ginger, which has had food colouring added. The vinegar is an ideal additive to sauces where a sweet, gingery bite is called for.

Polenta Also known as cornmeal, these ground, dried corn kernels are a staple in Northern Italy. Polenta is available as both a coarsely and finely ground meal, and is most often made into a thick, savoury porridge and flavoured by mixing in butter and parmesan cheese. After it is cooked, it can also be spread into a thin layer in a dish, then allowed to set before frying or grilling and being served with vegetables or with toppings as a starter.

Pomegranate molasses Also sold as pomegranate syrup or concentrate, this is the boiled-down juice of a sour variety of pomegranate. It has an unusual bitter-sweet flavour and is used in sauces and dressings. It is available from Middle Eastern speciality stores. The closest substitute is sweetened tamarind.

Porcini mushrooms, called ceps in France, are highly prized in European cooking for their flavour and are especially good in risottos and omelettes. In appearance they are creamy brown, with thick, rounded caps. They are more commonly available dried than fresh; you'll find dried porcini in most delicatessens and speciality food stores. Dried porcini have a strong flavour and should be used sparingly. Soak them first in warm water, then rinse them (you can strain the soaking water and add it to stocks and risottos).

Potato starch noodles, also known as Korean vermicelli, are long, fine translucent dried noodles. Cook in rapidly boiling water for about 5 minutes or until plump and gelatinous; overcooking will cause them to break down and become gluggy.

Preserved lemons These are whole lemons preserved in salt or brine, making their rind soft and pliable. They need to be rinsed before use, and only the rind is used— the bitter, salty pulp should be scraped out and discarded. They are used in North African cuisine to flavour couscous and tagine dishes. They are available from many delicatessens.

Provolone A golden yellow Italian cheese with a glossy rind, provolone is often moulded into a pear shape before being hung to mature. When young, provolone is mild and delicate and often used as a table cheese. As it matures, the flavour becomes sharper and it can be used for grating. Provolone is often smoked.

Quinoa Pronounced 'keen-wah', quinoa is a grain native to South America. Greatly revered by the ancient Incas, who called it 'the mother grain', quinoa boasts the highest protein content of any grain and is especially valuable for vegetarian diets as it contains all eight essential amino acids, and is also rich in B vitamins, calcium and vitamin E. It is a wonderfully versatile grain with a delicate flavour, and requires only a short cooking time. Quinoa makes a great base for salads and hearty sauces and is an ideal substitute for brown rice, having a similar nutty flavour. It is available from health food stores.

Red Asian shallots These small reddish-purple onions grow in bulbs, like garlic, and are sold in segments that look like large cloves of garlic. They have a concentrated flavour and are easy to slice and grind. If unavailable, substitute French shallots or brown or red onions. *See also French shallots and shallots.*

Red kidney beans are wonderful in slow-cooked dishes. They have a deep, strong flavour and are a source of fibre, iron, potassium and several B vitamins. They are especially good in nachos.

Rice flour is ground from short-grain rice. It has a fine, light texture and is used in noodles, pastries and sweets, and gives a crunch to fried foods if used in a batter or as a coating.

Rice noodle sheets are flat sheets of fresh rice noodles, sold in Asian grocery stores. The sheets can be cut into strips to make a rough noodle, or wrapped around cooked ingredients to make tasty little parcels.

Rice stick noodles are short, translucent flat noodles. They need to be soaked in hot water until soft, then cooked briefly in boiling water until just tender. They are then ready to use in stir-fries and soups. They are also sometimes used in salads.

Rice vinegar Made from fermented rice, this vinegar comes in clear, red and black versions. If no colour is specified in a recipe, use the clear vinegar. Clear rice vinegar is sweeter and milder than its European counterparts or the darker, sharper-flavoured Chinese black vinegar. Diluted white wine vinegar or cider vinegar can be substituted.

Ricotta cheese can be bought cut from a wheel or in tubs, in normal and low-fat versions. The wheel tends to be firmer in consistency and is better for baking, as is the ricotta with the higher fat content. If you are only able to obtain the tub ricotta for baking, drain off the excess moisture by letting it sit for 2–3 hours in a sieve lined with muslin (cheesecloth).

Risoni is a small rice-shaped pasta. It is ideal for using in soups, where it absorbs the other flavours of the dish.

Risotto rice There are several varieties of risotto rice. Of these, arborio is the best known and most commonly available. A short-grained, plump rice imported from Italy, arborio is used in both sweet and savoury dishes, and is particularly suited to risotto because the grains absorb a lot of liquid and become creamy, but still retain their firmness. Vialone nano and carnaroli are two other types of risotto rice you might come across.

Rocket (arugula) This fast-growing salad green, also known as rugula or roquette, is native to the Mediterranean. It is a rich source of iron and its peppery flavour increases as the leaves grow. Wild rocket has smaller, more delicate leaves and is perfect in salads.

Rosewater is a distilled essence, extracted from rose petals, used in the eastern Mediterranean region to perfume pastries, drinks, fruit salads and sweets such as Turkish delight.

Saffron threads The thread-like stigma of a violet crocus, saffron is the world's most expensive spice because of the intricate work involved in extracting it from the flowers. Thankfully, only a small amount is needed to impart its vivid yellow colour and subtle flavour to food. The colour and flavour varies greatly according to the origin and quality. Saffron is available as bright orange threads (sealed in small glass jars or tiny plastic packets) or ground into powder, but the latter is often adulterated with dyes and is generally of lesser quality.

Sambal oelek This is a hot paste made from fresh red chillies mashed and mixed with salt and vinegar. It is used as a relish in Indonesian and Malaysian cooking, and can be used as a substitute for fresh chillies in most recipes.

Semolina is the product obtained from milling durum wheat. Semolina can be coarse, medium or fine and is used for making pasta, gnocchi and some puddings and cakes. Fine semolina has smaller grains and is available from gourmet food stores.

Sesame oil is available in two varieties. The darker, more pungent type is made from roasted sesame seeds and comes from China, while the paler, non-roasted variety is Middle Eastern in origin.

Shallots are small onions that grow in clusters and are joined with a common root end. They have thin, papery skin and a mild onion flavour. *See also French shallots and red Asian shallots.*

Shiitake mushrooms are closely related to the Chinese black mushroom and are the most commonly used mushroom in Japan. They are grown on the bark of a type of oak tree, have a rich smoky flavour, and are used fresh and dried. The fresh mushroom has a fleshy, golden-brown cap, white gills and a woody stem. Meaty in texture, they keep their shape well when cooked. Dried shiitake are often sold as dried Chinese mushrooms.

Shimeji mushrooms have a small brown cap, long pale stalk and delicate flesh. They grow in clumps, from a single short, thick stem. They are eaten cooked rather than raw, where they lose their slight bitterness and take on a nutty flavour. They are lovely in soups and stir-fries. Before using, cut the very end off the stem, then separate the stalks.

Shoyu A fermented soy sauce, similar to tamari, shoyu is used in Japanese cooking as a flavour enhancer. It has a noticeably stronger fermented taste than tamari and contains wheat. Traditionally, shoyu was the liquid pressed from miso paste.

Sichuan peppercorns are made from the dried red berries of the prickly ash tree, native to Sichuan in China. The flavour is spicy-hot and leaves a numbing aftertaste, which can linger for some time. Dry-fry and crush the berries for the best flavour. Japanese sancho pepper is a close relative and may be used instead.

Silverbeet (Swiss chard) is often confused with spinach. The large, crinkly leaves have more texture than spinach and are suited to longer cooking because they don't collapse like spinach. Both the leaves and stems can be eaten, but need to be blanched before being braised, gratinéed or used as pie fillings.

Snake (yard-long) bean Also called a long bean, this legume grows wild in tropical Africa, where it probably originated. Growing to 38 cm (15 inches) long, with a crunchy texture and similar taste to green beans, it comes in two varieties: pale green with slightly fibrous flesh, and darker green with firmer flesh. To use, simply snip off the ends and cut into bite-sized pieces. Stringless green beans can be substituted.

Soba noodles A speciality of northern Japan, these thin, beige-coloured noodles are made from buckwheat (and sometimes wheat flour). They are usually sold dried, and some are lightly flavoured with green tea or beetroot. They are cooked in simmering water, then rinsed in cold water and served either hot in a broth, or cold in noodle salads.

Somen noodles are fine, wheat-based Japanese noodles, commonly sold dried and in bundles. Before use, cook in boiling water for 1–2 minutes, then rinse in cold water. They are available from Japanese speciality stores, large supermarkets and health food stores.

Soy sauce is made from fermented soya beans, a roasted grain (usually wheat, but sometimes barley or rice) and salt. Dark in colour and with a rich, salty flavour, it is an essential flavouring in many Asian dishes.

Soya beans are high in protein, but are rarely served on their own as they have very little flavour. They are used to make tofu and tempeh.

Spring onions (scallions) Also sometimes called green onions, these are immature onions which are pulled before the bulb has started to form and are sold in bunches with the roots intact. Discard the roots and base of the stem, and wash well before use. Spring onions add colour and a mild onion flavour and they need little cooking.

Star anise The dried, star-shaped seed pod of a tree native to China, star anise adds a distinctive aniseed taste to long-simmered dishes. It is available whole or ground.

Sticky (glutinous) rice can be long- or short-grained, and has a high starch content a little like arborio. It comes in black, white and even red varieties, and is the essential ingredient in sticky rice puddings.

Sumac is a peppery, sour spice made from dried and ground sumac, a reddish berry with a sour, fruity flavour. Sumac is the fruit of a shrub found in the northern hemisphere and is used in Middle Eastern cookery. It is sold in most large supermarkets and Middle Eastern speciality stores.

Sun-dried tomatoes It was the Italians who came up with the idea of preserving summer's tomato harvest for the winter months by drying them in the sun. Today these chewy, intensely flavoured tomatoes are sold either dry and loosely packed, or in jars in oil. The dry variety need to be rehydrated before use—to do this, soak them in boiling water for about 10 minutes. If buying sun-dried tomatoes in oil, choose the variety in olive oil as you can use the oil for cooking to add extra flavour to your dish. Semi-dried (sun-blushed) tomatoes have not been dried to the same extent as regular sun-dried tomatoes and have a softer texture and flavour.

Swiss brown mushrooms have a stronger flavour and texture than the common mushroom. Larger specimens are called portobello mushrooms.

Tahini An oily paste made from ground sesame seeds, tahini has a strong nutty flavour and is popular in the Middle East.

Tamari is a fermented Japanese soy sauce, similar to shoyu. It has a more mellow flavour than regular soy sauce.

Tamarind The tropical tamarind tree bears fruit in pods like large, brown beans. The fruit is tart-tasting and has fibrous flesh and a flat stone at the centre. An essential flavour in many Asian dishes, tamarind is available in bottles as tamarind concentrate (also known as tamarind purée), a rich brown, ready-to-use liquid, and as blocks of compressed pulp that has to be soaked, kneaded and seeded. Tamarind purée is widely available in Asian food shops.

Tatsoi, also called spoon mustard, is an Asian green with small, dark green spoon-shaped leaves and crunchy pale green stalks that form a thick rosette. It has a soft creamy texture and mild, almost sweet mustard flavour. It can be eaten raw but is usually added to stir-fries at the last minute.

Tempeh To make tempeh, soya beans are cooked, split and sometimes blended with other grains such as rice or millet. They are then inoculated with a beneficial bacteria and left to ferment for about 24 hours. Fermentation delivers many benefits to the soya bean—it helps break down complex sugars and makes the protein easier to digest. Because it is made from whole soya beans, it contains more protein, fibre and vitamins than tofu. It has a deep, nutty flavour and also freezes well.

Thai basil has slightly serrated green leaves on purple stems. It has a sweet anise flavour and is used in stir-fries and curries. If unavailable, substitute sweet basil or coriander (cilantro) in cooked dishes and fresh mint in salads.

Tofu Also called bean curd, tofu is a processed extract of soya beans. It is an excellent source of protein, and although it is quite bland in taste, it takes on the flavour of the other ingredients it is cooked with. The best-quality tofu is made from organically grown soya beans, which are coagulated with nigari (calcium and magnesium salts derived from sea water). Fresh tofu comes in two forms: a soft, white variety, also known as silken tofu, and a firm variety. Both are available in blocks sealed in plastic packaging; once opened, store tofu in the refrigerator in water that is changed daily, and use it within a few days. You can also buy smoked tofu, as well as tofu puffs, which are cubes of tofu that have been deep-fried until puffed and golden. Tofu is sold in the refrigerated section of supermarkets and Asian grocery stores.

Tomato passata (puréed tomatoes) This is a bottled tomato sauce commonly used in Italian cooking. The sauce is made with fresh, ripe tomatoes which are peeled, seeded and slowly cooked down with basil, onion and garlic. The thickened sauce is then passed through a sieve before bottling.

Turmeric This bitter-tasting spice comes from the root of a plant related to ginger. It is used for its intense, bright yellow-orange colour; dried and ground, it is the main ingredient in many curry powders. The fresh root is used in the same way as fresh ginger root—peel away the skin, then finely slice, chop or grate the flesh (it is a good idea to wear gloves while doing this, to stop your hands staining). Store in a plastic bag in the refrigerator.

Udon noodles are white, wheat flour noodles used in Japanese cooking. They may be round or flat. Cook them in boiling water or miso soup before using in soups or simmered dishes.

Vegetarian oyster sauce is made from mushrooms rather than oysters, but has a traditional Asian flavour that vegetarians can enjoy. Soy sauce can be substituted. It is sold in Asian grocery stores.

Vietnamese mint Also called laksa leaf and Cambodian mint, this trailing herb with narrow, pointed, pungent-tasting leaves doesn't belong to the mint family at all, despite its common name. It has a flavour that resembles coriander (cilantro) but is slightly sharper, and is eaten raw in salads, or as an accompaniment to many Vietnamese dishes.

Vine leaves are the young, large green leaves of the grape vine, sold in tins, jars, plastic packs or in brine. They are used in Greece and the Middle East to wrap foods for cooking. Vine leaves in brine should be rinsed before using to remove some of the salty flavour. Fresh vine leaves should be simmered in water for 10 minutes to soften them before using.

Wasabi Also known as Japanese horseradish, this is a pungent paste made from the knobbly dark-green root of the wasabi, an aquatic plant native to Japan. It is also sold in a powdered dried form that can be mixed to a paste with a little water. Wasabi is used to flavour sushi, sashimi and some sauces. It is extremely hot, so use sparingly.

Water chestnuts These white-fleshed roots of an aquatic grass are prized for their semi-sweet taste and crisp, crunchy texture. They are used throughout China and South-East Asia in both savoury and sweet dishes. Tinned whole or sliced water chestnuts are sold in supermarkets. Fresh water chestnuts can be found in Chinese food stores. If using fresh water chestnuts, cut off the woody base, peel away the papery skin and cover them in water to stop them discolouring before cooking.

Wild rice is not actually a rice at all, but an aquatic grass seed. Wild rice has more B vitamins and protein than other rice, and a stronger flavour. It is best used

in combination with brown rice, to soften the taste. Wild rice generally takes 1 hour to cook. After cooking, let it sit and steam with the lid on for 10 minutes.

Witlof (chicory/Belgian endive) This salad leaf has a bitter flavour and a crisp, crunchy texture when raw. Gentle braising or sautéeing softens the flavour. It is available in both pale yellow and purple varieties, although the flavour is identical.

Won ton wrappers are thin squares of a dough made from wheat flour and egg. They are used in Asian cooking to wrap savoury fillings for steaming or deep-frying, and to enclose dumplings that are cooked in a soup. They are sold in packets in the refrigerator cabinet of Asian grocery stores and larger supermarkets.

Yellow split peas are not as sweet as dried green split peas, but have an earthier flavour and soft texture that is quite similar to lentils. These versatile legumes break apart during cooking and are excellent for thick soups, stews, dips and dal.

Zucchini (courgette) flowers Available from good greengrocers in spring and summer, these large, exquisite bright yellow flowers are widely enjoyed in Italy either stuffed, steamed, roasted or fried. The male flower is more delicate than the female flower and has a thin stem, while the female is generally bigger and with a sweeter stem. They are highly perishable so buy them on the day you plan to use them.

We all know breakfast is the most important meal of the day. After a long night's slumber, morning is the time when we need to refuel our bodies so we can pick ourselves up and power through the day—or until lunchtime at least. Without breakfast we start the day running on empty, reducing our concentration and energy and making us more likely to overeat later on. Here are some wonderful breakfast ideas that are worth getting up for—some quick ones for when you're dashing out the door and need breakfast in a shake, and some more elegant offerings for lazy days and weekends when you have the luxury of lingering over a leisurely breakfast or brunch. Rise and shine!

BREAKFAST
& BRUNCH

ENERGY FRUIT SMOOTHIE

Serves 4

½ rockmelon or any orange-fleshed melon
1 mango
2 tablespoons toasted muesli
1 tablespoon honey
1 tablespoon malted milk powder
100 g (3½ oz/⅓ cup) Greek-style apricot
   yoghurt
125 ml (4 fl oz/½ cup) orange juice
250 ml (9 fl oz/1 cup) skim milk

1 Peel the melon and scoop out the seeds. Roughly chop the flesh and place in a blender.
2 Slice the cheeks off the mango using a sharp knife. Using a large spoon, scoop the flesh out of the skin. Cut the flesh into chunks and place in the blender.
3 Add the muesli and blend for 20 seconds, or until smooth. Add the honey, malted milk powder and yoghurt and blend for a further 10 seconds.
4 Pour in the orange juice and milk and blend for a final 30 seconds, or until foaming. Pour into four glasses to serve.
Note For a colder drink, refrigerate the fruit beforehand and serve in chilled glasses.

MIXED BERRY COUSCOUS

Serves 4

185 g (6½ oz/1 cup) instant couscous
500 ml (17 fl oz/2 cups) apple and
    cranberry juice
1 cinnamon stick
2 teaspoons orange zest
250 g (9 oz/2 cups) raspberries
250 g (9 oz/1⅔ cups) blueberries
250 g (9 oz/1⅔ cups) strawberries, halved
200 g (7 oz) Greek-style yoghurt
golden syrup or maple syrup, for drizzling
4 mint leaves

1 Put the couscous in a bowl. Pour the apple and cranberry juice into a saucepan and add the cinnamon stick. Cover and bring to the boil, then remove from the heat and pour over the couscous. Cover with plastic wrap and leave for 5 minutes, or until all the liquid has been absorbed. Remove the cinnamon stick.
2 Separate the couscous grains with a fork, then gently fold the orange zest and most of the berries through. Spoon the mixture into four serving bowls and sprinkle with the remaining berries.
3 Top each bowl with a dollop of yoghurt, then drizzle with golden or maple syrup. Garnish with a mint leaf and serve.

PORRIDGE

Makes 960 g (2 lb 2 oz/8 cups) dry weight

400 g (14 oz/4 cups) rolled (porridge) oats
100 g (3½ oz/1 cup) rice flakes
130 g (4½ oz/1 cup) barley flakes
130 g (4½ oz/1 cup) rye flakes
200 g (7 oz/1 cup) millet

1 Put all the ingredients in a large bowl and stir together thoroughly. Store the dry porridge mixture in an airtight container until ready to use.
2 To prepare porridge for four people, put 280 g (10 oz/2 cups) of the dry porridge mix in a saucepan with a pinch of sea salt and 500 ml (17 fl oz/2 cups) water. Stir well and leave to stand for 5 minutes (this creates a smoother, creamier porridge).
3 Stir the porridge a few times, then pour in another 500 ml (17 fl oz/2 cups) water. Bring to the boil over medium heat, stirring occasionally. Reduce the heat to low and simmer, stirring often, for 12–15 minutes, or until the porridge is soft and creamy and the grains are cooked.
Note This porridge is delicious served with your choice of milk (or milk substitute), a dollop of yoghurt, a drizzle of honey, golden syrup or maple syrup, or a sprinkling of dark brown sugar.

SPANISH HOT CHOCOLATE

Serves 4

500 ml (17 fl oz/2 cups) milk
a 4 x 3 cm (1½ x 1¼ inch) strip of orange zest
250 g (9 oz/1⅔ cups) finely chopped
good-quality dark chocolate

1 Put the milk in a heavy-based saucepan. Remove any white pith remaining on the orange zest and lightly score the skin using a small sharp knife. Add to the saucepan and bring to the boil over medium heat, stirring constantly. As soon as the milk comes to the boil, remove the pan from the heat and set aside to infuse for 5 minutes.

2 Discard the orange zest and return the saucepan to the stovetop over low heat. Add the chocolate and stir until the chocolate has melted, making sure it doesn't stick to the bottom of the pan.

3 Using an immersion blender fitted with a blending or general-purpose blade, blend the milk for 40 seconds, or until thick and frothy. Pour into four mugs or heatproof glasses and serve.

FRUIT SALAD IN LEMON GRASS SYRUP

Serves 4

500 g (1 lb 2 oz) watermelon, diced
250 g (9 oz) honeydew melon, diced
½ small pineapple, chopped
1 mango, diced
250 g (9 oz/1⅔ cups) strawberries, halved
3 tablespoons small mint sprigs

Lemon grass syrup
125 ml (4 fl oz/½ cup) lime juice
45 g (1½ oz/¼ cup) soft brown sugar
1 lemon grass stem, white part only, finely sliced
2 tablespoons grated fresh ginger
1 vanilla bean, split

1 Place the fruit and mint in a bowl and mix gently.
2 To make the syrup, put the lime juice, sugar and 125 ml (4 fl oz/½ cup) water in a small saucepan and stir over low heat until the sugar dissolves. Add the lemon grass, ginger and vanilla bean. Bring to the boil, reduce the heat and simmer for 10 minutes, or until the syrup is reduced and slightly thickened.
3 Remove the vanilla bean, pour the syrup over the fruit and refrigerate until cold.
Note If you prefer your syrup without the lemon grass slices but like their flavour, don't slice the lemon grass. Leave it intact, bruise it with a rolling pin, cook it in the syrup, then remove with the vanilla bean.

SUMMER FRUIT SOY SMOOTHIE

Serves 4

1 banana
4 peaches, pitted and chopped,
　plus extra peach slices, to serve
175 g (6 oz/¾ cup) apricot and mango
　soy yoghurt or vanilla soy yoghurt
1 tablespoon lecithin meal
1 teaspoon natural vanilla extract
625 ml (21½ fl oz/2½ cups) soy milk
1 tablespoon maple syrup (optional)
ice cubes, to serve

1 Put the banana and peach in a blender and add the yoghurt, lecithin meal, vanilla and 250 ml (9 fl oz/1 cup) of the soy milk. Blend for 30 seconds, or until smooth.
2 Add the remaining soy milk and blend for a further 30 seconds, or until combined. Taste for sweetness and add the maple syrup, if desired.
3 Put the ice and extra peach slices in four glasses, pour in the smoothie and serve.

MIXED MUSHROOMS IN BRIOCHE

Serves 6

750 g (1 lb 10 oz) mixed mushrooms, such as Swiss brown, shiitake, button, field, oyster
75 g (2½ oz) butter
4 spring onions (scallions), chopped
2 garlic cloves, crushed
125 ml (4 fl oz/½ cup) dry white wine
300 ml (10½ fl oz) pouring (whipping) cream
2 tablespoons chopped thyme
6 small brioche (see Note)

1 Preheat the oven to 180°C (350°F/Gas 4). Wipe the mushrooms with a clean damp cloth to remove any dirt. Cut the larger mushrooms into thick slices but leave the smaller ones whole.

2 Melt the butter in a large frying pan over medium heat. Add the spring onion and garlic and cook for 2 minutes. Increase the heat, add the mushrooms and sauté for 5 minutes, or until the mushrooms are soft and all the liquid has evaporated. Pour in the wine and boil for 2 minutes to reduce slightly.

3 Stir in the cream and boil for a further 5 minutes to reduce and slightly thicken the sauce. Season to taste with sea salt and freshly cracked black pepper. Stir in the thyme and set aside for 5 minutes.

4 Slice the top off each brioche. Using your fingers, pull out some of the bread. Place the brioche and their tops on a baking tray and warm in the oven for 5 minutes.

5 Place each brioche on an individual serving plate. Spoon the mushroom sauce into each brioche, allowing it to spill over one side. Replace the top and serve warm.

Note If you can't find brioche, use good-quality sourdough rolls instead.

POACHED EGGS WITH GARLIC YOGHURT DRESSING AND SPINACH

Serves 4

Garlic yoghurt dressing
125 g (4½ oz/½ cup) sheep's milk yoghurt
1 small garlic clove, crushed
1 tablespoon snipped chives

300 g (10½ oz) baby English spinach leaves
30 g (1 oz) butter, chopped
herbed salt, to taste
4 tomatoes, halved
1 tablespoon white vinegar
8 eggs
1 round loaf of light rye bread, cut into
    8 thick slices

1 Mix together the garlic yoghurt dressing ingredients and set aside.

2 Wash the spinach and place in a large saucepan with just a little water left clinging to the leaves. Cover and cook over low heat for 3–4 minutes, or until the spinach has wilted. Add the butter and season with herbed salt. Set aside and keep warm.

3 Meanwhile, cook the tomatoes under a hot grill (broiler) for 3–5 minutes.

4 Fill a frying pan three-quarters full of cold water and add the vinegar and some salt to stop the egg whites spreading. Bring to a gentle simmer. Gently break the eggs one by one into a small bowl, then carefully slide each one into the water. Reduce the heat so that the water barely moves. Cook for 1–2 minutes, or until the eggs are just set. Remove with a slotted spatula and allow to drain.

5 Meanwhile, toast the bread. Top each slice with the spinach, an egg and some dressing. Serve with the tomato halves.

RICOTTA PANCAKES WITH PEARS AND GOAT'S MILK YOGHURT

Serves 4

185 g (6½ oz/1½ cups) plain (all-purpose) flour
2 teaspoons baking powder
2 teaspoons ground ginger
2 tablespoons caster (superfine) sugar
4 eggs, separated
350 g (12 oz) low-fat ricotta cheese
1 pear, peeled, cored and grated
310 ml (10¾ fl oz/1¼ cups) milk
80 g (2¾ oz) butter
3 beurre bosc pears, unpeeled
1 tablespoon soft brown sugar
1 teaspoon ground cinnamon
200 g (7 oz) goat's milk yoghurt

1 Sift the flour, baking powder, ground ginger and sugar into a bowl and make a well in the centre. Combine the egg yolks, ricotta, grated pear and milk, then pour into the well and mix until smooth.

2 Beat the egg whites until soft peaks form, then fold into the mixture.

3 Melt some of the butter in a frying pan over medium heat. Pour 60 ml (2 fl oz/ ¼ cup) of the batter into the pan and swirl gently to create an even pancake. Cook for 1–1½ minutes, or until bubbles form on the surface, then turn and cook the other side for 1 minute, or until golden. Repeat using some more butter and the remaining batter to make 12 pancakes. Keep warm.

4 Cut the pears into thick slices lengthways. Melt the remaining butter in a frying pan. Add the sugar and cinnamon, then stir until the sugar has dissolved. Add the pears and cook in batches, turning once, until tender.

5 Serve the pancakes in stacks, topped with the pear slices and drizzled with yoghurt.

CORN MUFFINS
Makes 12

310 g (11 oz/2½ cups) self-raising flour
75 g (2½ oz/½ cup) fine polenta
250 ml (9 fl oz/1 cup) milk
125 g (4½ oz) butter, melted
2 eggs, lightly beaten
130 g (4½ oz) tin corn kernels, drained
2 spring onions (scallions), finely chopped
60 g (2¼ oz/½ cup) grated cheddar cheese
cream cheese or butter, to serve

1 Preheat the oven to 210°C (415°F/
Gas 6–7). Grease two six-hole muffin tins.
2 Sift the flour and polenta into a large
bowl and make a well in the centre.
3 In a separate bowl, whisk together the
remaining ingredients and season with
sea salt and freshly ground black pepper.
Pour into the well in the flour mixture and
gently fold using a metal spoon until just
combined. Do not overmix—the batter
should still be very lumpy.
4 Spoon the batter into the muffin holes
and bake for 20–25 minutes, or until lightly
golden. Remove from the oven and leave
in the tins for 5 minutes before turning
out. Serve the muffins hot or at room
temperature, split in half and spread with
cream cheese or butter.
Variation Muffins are so versatile. Try
adding 2 tablespoons chopped chives,
40 g (1½ oz/¼ cup) chopped, drained
sun-dried tomatoes, 2 finely chopped red
chillies or ½ finely chopped red or green
capsicum (pepper) to the milk mixture.
Storage The muffins will keep in an
airtight container for up to 2 days.

WARM ASPARAGUS AND EGG SALAD WITH HOLLANDAISE

Serves 4

Hollandaise sauce
175 g (6 oz) butter
4 egg yolks
1 tablespoon lemon juice

4 eggs, at room temperature
20 asparagus spears, trimmed
shaved parmesan cheese, to serve
lemon wedges, to serve

1 To make the hollandaise sauce, melt the butter in a small saucepan and skim off any froth. Remove from the heat and cool. Mix the egg yolks and 2 tablespoons water in another small saucepan for 30 seconds, or until pale and foamy. Place the pan over very low heat and whisk for 2–3 minutes, or until thick and foamy—don't overheat or the eggs will scramble. Remove from the heat. Whisking well, gradually add the melted butter (avoid using the whey at the bottom). Stir in the lemon juice and season to taste. If the sauce is runny, return to the heat and whisk until thick, but do not scramble.

2 Place the eggs in a saucepan half filled with water. Bring to the boil and cook for 6–7 minutes, stirring occasionally to centre the yolks. Drain and cover with cold water until cooled a little, then peel off the shells.

3 Plunge the asparagus into a large pot of boiling water and cook for 3 minutes, or until just tender. Drain and pat dry, then divide among four plates and spoon the hollandaise over. Cut the eggs in half and arrange on each plate. Scatter the parmesan over and serve with lemon wedges.

FRIED TOMATOES WITH MARINATED HALOUMI

Serves 4

400 g (14 oz) haloumi cheese, cut into eight
  1 cm (½ inch) slices
250 g (9 oz) cherry tomatoes, halved
250 g (9 oz) teardrop tomatoes, halved
1 garlic clove, crushed
2 tablespoons lemon juice
1 tablespoon balsamic vinegar
2 teaspoons lemon thyme
60 ml (2 fl oz/¼ cup) extra virgin olive oil
2 tablespoons olive oil
1 small loaf of wholegrain bread, cut into
  8 thick slices

1 Place the haloumi and tomatoes in a non-metallic dish. Whisk together the garlic, lemon juice, vinegar, thyme and extra virgin olive oil and pour over the haloumi mixture. Cover and marinate for 3 hours or overnight. Drain well, reserving the marinade.

2 Heat the olive oil in a large frying pan. Add the haloumi and cook in batches over medium heat for 1 minute on each side, or until golden brown. Transfer to a plate and keep warm. Add the tomatoes to the pan and cook over medium heat for 5 minutes, or until their skins begin to burst. Transfer to a plate and keep warm.

3 Meanwhile, toast the bread until golden. Top with the haloumi, then the tomatoes, drizzle with the reserved marinade and serve.

SCRAMBLED EGGS

Serves 2

6 eggs
1 tablespoon milk or pouring (whipping) cream
50 g (1¾ oz) butter
2 slices of bread, toasted

1 Crack the eggs into a bowl, add the milk or cream and season with sea salt. Whisk gently with a fork until well combined.
2 Melt half the butter in a small saucepan or frying pan over low heat. Add the egg mixture and stir constantly using a wooden spoon. Do not turn up the heat—scrambling must be done slowly and gently. When most of the egg has set, add the remaining butter and remove the pan from the heat. There should be enough heat left in the pan to finish cooking the eggs and melt the butter. Scrambled eggs should be creamy, not dry or rubbery. Serve immediately on toast—they will not sit even for a minute.

Note It is very important to use fresh eggs when scrambling. To check whether an egg is fresh, put it in a bowl of cold water. If it sinks on its side it is fresh; if it floats on its end it is stale. If it is somewhere between the two it is not perfectly fresh but still good enough to scramble.

Variation Scrambled eggs are delicious with a cheese such as gruyère stirred through, or a handful of chopped fresh herbs. You can also add roasted vegetables such as capsicum (pepper), tomato, onion and a few basil leaves to make a version of the French dish pipérade.

HASH BROWNS

Serves 4

800 g (1 lb 12 oz) all-purpose potatoes,
  such as desiree or pontiac, peeled
125 g (4½ oz) butter

1 Boil, steam or microwave the potatoes until just tender. Drain, leave to cool, then chop coarsely and season to taste.
2 Heat half the butter in a large heavy-based frying pan and place four lightly greased egg rings in the pan. Spoon the chopped potato into the egg rings, filling the rings to the top and pressing the potato down lightly to form flat cakes. Cook over low–medium heat for 5–7 minutes, or until a crust forms underneath. Keep an eye on them so they don't burn, shaking the pan gently now and then to prevent sticking.
3 Flip the hash browns using a spatula. Gently loosen the egg rings and remove with tongs. Cook for a further 4–5 minutes, or until browned and crisp, then remove and drain on paper towels. Add a little more butter to the pan, if necessary, and cook the remaining potato in the same way. Serve immediately.
Note If you don't have egg rings, you can cook the potato as one large cake.

MINI FRITTATAS

Makes 12

1 kg (2 lb 4 oz) orange sweet potato,
   peeled and finely diced
1 tablespoon olive oil
30 g (1 oz) butter
4 leeks, white part only, finely sliced
2 garlic cloves, crushed
250 g (9 oz) feta cheese, crumbled
8 eggs
125 ml (4 fl oz/½ cup) pouring
   (whipping) cream

1 Preheat the oven to 180°C (350°F/Gas 4). Grease or brush twelve 250 ml (9 fl oz/ 1 cup) muffin holes with oil or melted butter. Cut small rounds of baking paper and line the base of each muffin hole.

2 Boil, steam or microwave the sweet potato until just tender. Drain well and set aside.

3 Heat the olive oil and butter in a frying pan and sauté the leek for 10 minutes, or until very soft and lightly golden. Add the garlic and cook for a further 1 minute. Remove from the heat and set aside to cool slightly, then stir in the feta and sweet potato. Divide among the muffin holes.

4 Whisk the eggs and cream together and season with sea salt and freshly cracked black pepper. Pour the mixture into each muffin hole until three-quarters filled, then press the vegetables down gently. Bake for 25–30 minutes, or until golden and set. Leave in the tins for 5 minutes, then ease out with a knife. Serve hot or at room temperature.

BUBBLE AND SQUEAK

Serves 4

750 g (1 lb 10 oz) roasting potatoes, scrubbed
125 ml (4 fl oz/½ cup) milk
90 g (3¼ oz) butter
450 g (1 lb) mixed green vegetables, such as cabbage, leek, brussels sprouts or spinach, finely sliced

1 Cut the potatoes into even-sized pieces and boil, steam or microwave until just tender. Drain thoroughly.

2 Heat the milk in a saucepan. Add the potatoes and half the butter, then mash until smooth and creamy.

3 Heat the grill (broiler) to high. Melt half the remaining butter in a large cast-iron frying pan (if you don't have one, simply cover your frying pan handle with foil so it doesn't melt under the grill). Add the green vegetables to the pan and sauté over medium heat until tender and cooked through. Add them to the mashed potato and mix together well. Season to taste.

4 Melt the remaining butter in the frying pan and spoon in the potato mixture to make four patties, smoothing off the top. Cook until browned and crispy underneath.

5 Remove the pan from the heat and place it under the grill until the top of the patties are browned and golden. Bubble and squeak is delicious by itself, or served with poached eggs (see page 47).

Note If you prefer, you can turn the bubble and squeak over and cook the other side in the frying pan, but grilling the top is easier as the patties can be quite fragile.

CORN AND POLENTA PANCAKES WITH TOMATO SALSA

Serves 4

Tomato salsa
2 ripe tomatoes
150 g (5½ oz/1 cup) frozen broad (fava) beans
2 tablespoons chopped basil
1 small Lebanese (short) cucumber, diced
2 small garlic cloves, crushed
1½ tablespoons balsamic vinegar
1 tablespoon extra virgin olive oil

Corn and polenta pancakes
90 g (3¼ oz/¾ cup) self-raising flour
110 g (3¾ oz/¾ cup) fine polenta
250 ml (9 fl oz/1 cup) milk
310 g (11 oz) tin corn kernels, drained
olive oil, for pan-frying

1 To make the salsa, score a cross in the base of each tomato, then place in a bowl of boiling water for 30 seconds. Plunge into cold water and peel the skin away from the cross. Dice and place in a bowl.
2 Pour boiling water over the broad beans and leave for 2–3 minutes. Drain and rinse under cold water, then remove the skins. Add the beans to the tomato and stir in the remaining salsa ingredients.
3 To make the pancakes, sift the flour into a bowl and stir in the polenta. Add the milk and corn and stir until just combined, adding more milk if the batter is too dry. Season.
4 Heat some olive oil in a large frying pan. Spoon in half the batter, to make four 9 cm (3½ inch) pancakes. Cook for 2 minutes on each side, or until golden and cooked through. Repeat with the remaining batter, adding more oil if necessary. Drain on paper towels and serve with the salsa.

INDIVIDUAL OVEN-BAKED ROSTI

Makes 12

30 g (1 oz) butter, melted
500 g (1 lb 2 oz) all-purpose potatoes,
    such as desiree or pontiac, peeled
1 onion

1 Preheat the oven to 220°C (425°F/Gas 7). Using some of the melted butter, grease a 12-hole standard muffin tin.
2 Cook the potatoes in a saucepan of boiling salted water for 7 minutes, or until just tender. Drain thoroughly.

3 Grate the potatoes and onion into a bowl and pour the melted butter over. Season with sea salt and mix together well. Using two forks, divide the mixture among the muffin holes, gently pressing it in. Bake for 45 minutes, or until golden.
4 Run a small palette knife around each rösti to loosen them. Serve hot.

When you're in special need of nurture and nourishment, a bowl of steaming hot soup is often just what the doctor ordered: the restorative powers of the humble soup are legendary indeed! Soups make a fabulous warming lunch on a crisp day or a marvellous light supper with a good chunk of crusty bread. Spicy, soothing, elegant or hearty, soups are a wonderful way to use up the season's bounty and those odds and ends lurking in the fridge or cupboard. Nutrition wise, these bowls of hearty goodness pack a powerful punch—and yet another bonus is that many freeze well and taste even better the next day, so leftovers are never a problem. Having a pot of soup bubbling away inspires comfort like little else, warming the very cockles of your soul. Ladle up with love.

SOUPS

ZUCCHINI PESTO SOUP

Serves 4

1 tablespoon olive oil
1 large onion, finely chopped
2 garlic cloves, crushed
750 g (1 lb 10 oz) zucchini (courgettes),
   thinly sliced
750 ml (26 fl oz/3 cups) vegetable stock
60 ml (2 fl oz/¼ cup) pouring (whipping) cream
toasted ciabatta bread, to serve

Pesto

2 very large handfuls of basil
25 g (1 oz/¼ cup) finely grated parmesan cheese
2 tablespoons pine nuts, toasted
2 tablespoons extra virgin olive oil

1 Heat the olive oil in a large heavy-based saucepan. Sauté the onion and garlic over medium heat for 5 minutes, or until the onion has softened.

2 Add the zucchini and stock, bring to the boil, then reduce the heat, cover and simmer for 10 minutes, or until the zucchini is very soft.

3 To make the pesto, put the basil, parmesan and pine nuts in a food processor and blend for 20 seconds, or until finely chopped. Gradually add the olive oil and process until smooth. Spoon into a small bowl.

4 Process the soup in batches in a food processor until smooth. Return to the saucepan, stir in the cream and 2 tablespoons of the pesto and gently reheat. Season to taste and serve with toasted ciabatta bread, with the remaining pesto on the side.

Note You can cover any left-over pesto with a layer of olive oil and refrigerate it for up to 1 week.

POTATO AND SWEET CORN CHOWDER

Serves 6

6 cobs of sweet corn
2 tablespoons vegetable oil
1 onion, finely diced
3 garlic cloves, crushed
1 celery stalk, diced
1 carrot, diced
2 large boiling potatoes, peeled and diced
1 litre (35 fl oz/4 cups) vegetable stock
2 tablespoons finely chopped flat-leaf
   (Italian) parsley

1 Cook the corn cobs in a large saucepan of boiling salted water for 5 minutes. Remove the corn cobs and reserve 250 ml (9 fl oz/1 cup) of the cooking water. Cut the kernels from the cobs, place half in a blender with the reserved cooking water, then blend until smooth.

2 Heat the oil in a large saucepan. Add the onion, garlic, celery and a pinch of sea salt and sauté over medium heat for 5 minutes.

3 Add the carrot and potatoes, cook for 5 minutes, then add the stock, remaining corn kernels and blended corn mixture. Reduce the heat and simmer for 20 minutes, or until the vegetables are tender. Season well, stir in the parsley and serve.

MISO SOUP WITH UDON AND TOFU

Serves 2–4

3 tablespoons red (genmai) miso
2 tablespoons soy sauce
400 g (14 oz) fresh udon noodles, separated
400 g (14 oz) silken firm tofu, diced
100 g (3½ oz) fresh shiitake mushrooms, sliced
500 g (1 lb 2 oz/1 bunch) baby bok choy
  (pak choy), leaves separated

1 Put the miso and soy sauce in a large heavy-based saucepan with 1.25 litres (44 fl oz/5 cups) water and bring to the boil. Reduce the heat and simmer for 10 minutes.

2 Add the noodles and cook for 5 minutes, or until soft. Stir in the tofu, mushrooms and bok choy and cook for a further 3 minutes, or until the bok choy wilts. Serve immediately.

LAKSA

Serves 4

200 g (7 oz) dried rice vermicelli
2 tablespoons peanut oil
2–3 tablespoons laksa paste
1 litre (35 fl oz/4 cups) vegetable stock
750 ml (26 fl oz/3 cups) coconut milk
250 g (9 oz) snowpeas (mangetout),
  halved diagonally
5 spring onions (scallions), cut into 3 cm
  (1¼ inch) lengths
2 tablespoons lime juice
125 g (4½ oz/1⅓ cups) bean sprouts
200 g (7 oz) fried tofu puffs, halved
3 tablespoons chopped Vietnamese mint
a good handful of coriander (cilantro) leaves

1 Place the vermicelli in a large bowl, cover with boiling water and leave to soak for 5 minutes.

2 Meanwhile, heat the peanut oil in a large heavy-based saucepan, add the laksa paste and cook, stirring, over medium heat for 1 minute, or until fragrant.

3 Add the stock, coconut milk, snowpeas and spring onion and bring to the boil, then reduce the heat and simmer for 5 minutes. Add the lime juice and season to taste with sea salt and freshly ground black pepper.

4 Drain the vermicelli and divide among four bowls. Top with the bean sprouts and tofu. Ladle the soup into the bowls, sprinkle with the herbs and serve.

GREEN SOUP WITH PISTOU

Serves 4

1 zucchini (courgette)
1 head of broccoli, trimmed
150 g (5½ oz) green beans, trimmed
155 g (5½ oz/1 bunch) asparagus, trimmed
60 ml (2 fl oz/¼ cup) olive oil
1 onion, finely chopped
2 garlic cloves, crushed
1 celery stalk, chopped
1.5 litres (52 fl oz/6 cups) vegetable stock
150 g (5½ oz/1 cup) green peas
80 g (2¾ oz/2 cups) shredded silverbeet
   (Swiss chard) leaves

Pistou
3 garlic cloves, peeled
a large handful of basil
80 ml (2½ fl oz/⅓ cup) olive oil
50 g (1¾ oz/½ cup) grated parmesan cheese

1 Chop the zucchini, broccoli, green beans and asparagus into 1 cm (½ inch) pieces and set aside.
2 Heat the olive oil in a large heavy-based saucepan. Sauté the onion, garlic and celery over medium heat for 5 minutes, or until golden. Add the zucchini and broccoli and sauté for a further 5 minutes.
3 Add the stock and bring to the boil. Simmer for 5 minutes, then add the beans, asparagus, peas and silverbeet. Simmer for 5 minutes, or until the vegetables are tender. Season well with sea salt and freshly ground black pepper.
4 To make the pistou, put the garlic and basil in a mortar and pestle or small food processor and crush together. Slowly add the olive oil, and blend to a smooth paste. Stir in the parmesan and season to taste.
5 Ladle the soup into bowls and serve with a dollop of pistou.

CHILLI, CORN AND
RED CAPSICUM SOUP

Serves 4

1 whole coriander (cilantro) root,
    with leaves and stems attached
4 cobs of sweet corn
30 g (1 oz) butter
2 red capsicums (peppers), diced
1 small onion, finely chopped
1 small red chilli, finely chopped
1 tablespoon plain (all-purpose) flour
500 ml (17 fl oz/2 cups) vegetable stock
125 ml (4 fl oz/½ cup) pouring
    (whipping) cream

1 Pick the leaves off the coriander and
reserve; finely chop the stems and root.
Cut the kernels off the corn cobs.
2 Melt the butter in a large heavy-based
saucepan over medium heat. Add the corn
kernels, capsicum, onion and chilli and stir
to coat in the butter. Reduce the heat to
low, then cover and cook for 10 minutes,
or until soft, stirring occasionally.
3 Increase the heat to medium, add the
coriander root and stem and stir for
30 seconds, or until fragrant. Sprinkle
with the flour and stir for 1 minute.
4 Remove from the heat and gradually stir
in the stock. Add 500 ml (17 fl oz/2 cups)
water and return to the heat. Bring to
the boil, reduce the heat to low and
simmer, covered, for 30 minutes. Allow
to cool slightly.
5 Ladle 500 ml (17 fl oz/2 cups) of the
soup into a blender and purée until smooth.
Stir the purée back into the soup with the
cream and gently reheat. Season to taste,
sprinkle with the reserved coriander leaves
and serve. This soup is delicious with
grilled cheese on pitta bread.

PUMPKIN AND RED LENTIL SOUP

Serves 4

1 tablespoon olive oil
1 long red chilli, seeded and chopped, plus extra, to garnish
1 onion, finely chopped
500 g (1 lb 2 oz) butternut pumpkin (squash), chopped
350 g (12 oz) orange sweet potato, chopped
1.5 litres (52 fl oz/6 cups) vegetable stock
125 g (4½ oz/½ cup) red lentils
1 tablespoon tahini

1 Heat the olive oil in a large heavy-based saucepan. Sauté the chilli and onion over medium heat for 2–3 minutes, or until the onion has softened.

2 Reduce the heat to low, add the pumpkin and sweet potato, then cover and cook for 8 minutes, stirring occasionally.

3 Add the stock and bring to the boil. Reduce the heat to low, then cover and simmer for 10 minutes. Add the lentils, put the lid back on and cook for 10 minutes, or until tender.

4 Process the soup in batches in a blender or food processor, add the tahini and blend until smooth. Return to the saucepan and gently reheat. Serve garnished with chilli.

MUSHROOM, SHALLOT AND SOUR CREAM SOUP

Serves 4

2 tablespoons butter
4 French shallots, roughly chopped
3 garlic cloves, crushed
2 large handfuls of flat-leaf (Italian) parsley
600 g (1 lb 5 oz) button mushrooms, chopped
¼ teaspoon ground nutmeg
¼ teaspoon cayenne pepper, plus extra,
   for sprinkling
310 ml (10¾ fl oz/1¼ cups) vegetable stock
310 ml (10¾ fl oz/1¼ cups) milk
150 g (5½ oz/⅔ cup) light sour cream

1 Melt the butter in a large heavy-based saucepan. Sauté the shallots, garlic and parsley over medium heat for 3 minutes, or until the shallots have softened.

2 Add the mushrooms, season with sea salt and freshly cracked black pepper, then stir in the nutmeg and cayenne pepper. Cook, stirring, for 1 minute. Add the stock and milk, bring to the boil, then reduce the heat and simmer for 5 minutes.

3 Transfer the soup to a blender or food processor and blend until smooth. Return to the saucepan, stir in the sour cream, adjust the seasoning and reheat gently. Serve sprinkled with cayenne pepper.

Tip Fry diced button mushrooms in a little butter until golden and use as a garnish.

SILVERBEET AND RISONI SOUP WITH GRUYÈRE CROUTONS

Serves 6

30 g (1 oz) butter
1 large onion, finely chopped
1 garlic clove, crushed
2 litres (70 fl oz/8 cups) hot vegetable stock
200 g (7 oz/1 cup) risoni
500 g (1 lb 2 oz) silverbeet (Swiss chard),
    central stalks removed, leaves shredded
a large handful of basil, torn

Gruyère croutons
½ baguette, cut into 6 slices
15 g (½ oz) butter, melted
1 teaspoon dijon mustard
50 g (1¾ oz/heaped ½ cup) coarsely grated
    gruyère cheese

1 Heat the butter in a large heavy-based saucepan. Sauté the onion and garlic over medium heat for 4–5 minutes, or until the onion has softened.

2 Add the stock and bring to the boil. Stir in the risoni, reduce the heat and simmer for 8 minutes, stirring occasionally.

3 Meanwhile, heat the grill (broiler) to high. To make the gruyère croutons, spread the baguette slices on a baking tray and toast under the grill until golden brown on top. Turn the slices over and brush with the combined melted butter and mustard. Top with the gruyère and grill until the cheese has melted.

4 Add the silverbeet and basil to the soup and simmer for 1 minute, or until the risoni is *al dente* and the silverbeet is cooked. Season with sea salt and freshly ground black pepper and serve with the hot gruyère croutons.

SPICY PARSNIP SOUP

Serves 6

30 g (1 oz) butter
1 onion, cut into quarters and finely sliced
1 leek, white part only, finely sliced
500 g (1 lb 2 oz) parsnips, peeled and
    finely sliced
1 tablespoon curry powder
1 teaspoon ground cumin
1.25 litres (44 fl oz/5 cups) vegetable stock
310 ml (10¾ fl oz/1¼ cups) pouring (whipping)
    cream (optional)
a large handful of coriander (cilantro) leaves

1 Melt the butter in a large heavy-based saucepan. Add the onion, leek and parsnip, then cover and cook over medium heat for 5 minutes, stirring occasionally.
2 Add the curry powder and cumin and cook for 1 minute. Stir in the stock, put the lid back on and cook for 10 minutes, or until the vegetables are tender.
3 Process the soup in batches in a blender or food processor until smooth. Return to the saucepan, stir in the cream, if using, and gently reheat. Season to taste with sea salt and freshly ground black pepper and serve scattered with coriander.

CURRIED LENTIL, CARROT AND CASHEW SOUP

Serves 6

1.5 litres (52 fl oz/6 cups) vegetable stock
750 g (1 lb 10 oz) carrots, grated
185 g (6½ oz/¾ cup) red lentils
1 tablespoon olive oil
1 large onion, chopped
80 g (2¾ oz/½ cup) unsalted cashew nuts
1 tablespoon curry paste
2 large handfuls of coriander (cilantro),
    plus extra leaves, to garnish
125 g (4½ oz/½ cup) Greek-style yoghurt

1 Bring the stock to the boil in a large heavy-based saucepan. Add the carrot and lentils, bring the mixture back to the boil, then simmer over low heat for 8 minutes, or until the carrot and lentils are soft.
2 Meanwhile, heat the olive oil in a frying pan. Add the onion and cashews and cook over medium heat for 3 minutes, or until the onion is soft and browned. Add the curry paste and coriander and cook for 1 minute, or until fragrant. Stir the paste into the soup.
3 Process the soup in batches in a blender or food processor until smooth. Return to the saucepan and gently reheat. Season to taste and serve with a dollop of yoghurt and a sprinkling of coriander.
Variation For extra kick, sprinkle some chilli flakes over the soup.

CAPSICUM, SPINACH AND CHICKPEA SOUP

Serves 4

1 tablespoon olive oil
8 spring onions (scallions), finely sliced
1 red capsicum (pepper), finely diced
1 garlic clove, crushed
1 teaspoon cumin seeds
375 ml (13 fl oz/1½ cups) tomato passata
    (puréed tomatoes)
750 ml (26 fl oz/3 cups) vegetable stock
300 g (10½ oz) tin chickpeas, rinsed and
    drained
2 teaspoons red wine vinegar
1–2 teaspoons sugar
100 g (3½ oz/2¼ cups) baby English
    spinach leaves

1 Heat the olive oil in a large heavy-based saucepan. Add the spring onion, cover and cook over medium heat for 2–3 minutes, or until softened. Add the capsicum, garlic and cumin seeds and cook for 1 minute.
2 Add the passata and stock and bring to the boil, then reduce the heat and simmer for 10 minutes. Add the chickpeas, vinegar and sugar and simmer for 5 minutes.
3 Stir in the baby spinach and season to taste with sea salt and freshly ground black pepper. Cook just until the spinach begins to wilt, then serve.

ZUPPA DI FAGGIOLI

Serves 4

2 x 400 g (14 oz) tins cannellini beans
1 tablespoon olive oil
1 leek, white part only, finely chopped
2 garlic cloves, crushed
1 teaspoon thyme
2 celery stalks, diced
1 carrot, diced
1 kg (2 lb 4 oz) silverbeet (Swiss chard),
   trimmed and roughly chopped
1 ripe tomato, diced
1 litre (35 fl oz/4 cups) vegetable stock
2 small crusty rolls, each cut into 4 slices
2 teaspoons balsamic vinegar
shaved parmesan cheese, to serve

1 Put one tin of beans and its liquid in a blender and blend until smooth. Drain the other tin and rinse the beans.

2 Heat the olive oil in a large heavy-based saucepan. Sauté the leek, garlic and thyme over medium heat for 3 minutes, or until the leek has softened. Add the celery, carrot, silverbeet and tomato and cook until the silverbeet wilts.

3 Stir the puréed cannellini beans and stock into the vegetable mixture. Bring to the boil, then reduce the heat and simmer for 5–10 minutes, or until the vegetables are tender. Add the drained beans and stir until heated through. Season to taste with sea salt and freshly cracked black pepper.

4 Place 2 slices of bread in each soup bowl. Stir the vinegar into the soup and ladle it over the bread. Scatter with parmesan and serve.

Variation This recipe is the authentic bean soup from Florence. If you like you can spice it up by adding chopped fresh chilli.

SPLIT PEA AND VEGETABLE SOUP

Serves 4

1 tablespoon peanut or vegetable oil
1 onion, chopped
2 garlic cloves, chopped
1½ teaspoons chopped fresh ginger
1½ tablespoons curry paste
100 g (3½ oz/½ cup) yellow split peas
1 large zucchini (courgette), chopped
1 large carrot, chopped
170 g (6 oz/2 cups) roughly chopped
   button mushrooms
1 celery stalk, chopped
1 litre (35 fl oz/4 cups) vegetable stock
125 ml (4 fl oz/½ cup) pouring (whipping) cream

1 Heat the oil in a large heavy-based saucepan. Sauté the onion over low heat for 5 minutes, or until softened.
2 Add the garlic, ginger and curry paste and cook over medium heat for 2 minutes. Stir in the split peas until well coated with the paste, then add the zucchini, carrot, mushroom and celery and cook for a further 2 minutes.
3 Add the stock, bring to the boil, then reduce the heat and simmer, partly covered, for 1 hour. Remove from the heat and allow to cool slightly.
4 Process the soup in batches in a blender or food processor until smooth. Return to the saucepan, stir in the cream and gently reheat. Delicious served with naan bread.

CARROT AND GINGER SOUP

Serves 4

1 tablespoon olive oil
1 onion, chopped
1 tablespoon grated fresh ginger
750 ml (26 fl oz/3 cups) vegetable stock
1 kg (2 lb 4 oz) carrots, chopped
2 tablespoons chopped coriander
   (cilantro) leaves

1 Heat the olive oil in a large heavy-based saucepan. Sauté the onion and ginger over medium heat for 5 minutes, or until the onion has softened.
2 Add the stock and carrot. Bring to the boil, then reduce the heat and simmer for 10–15 minutes, or until the carrot is tender.
3 Process the soup in batches in a blender or food processor until smooth. Return to the saucepan and add a little more stock or water to thin the soup to your preferred consistency.
4 Gently reheat, then season to taste with sea salt and freshly ground black pepper. Stir in the coriander and serve.

ASIAN NOODLE SOUP

Serves 4

8 dried Chinese mushrooms
100 g (3½ oz) dried rice vermicelli
800 g (1 lb 12 oz) Chinese broccoli,
    cut into 5 cm (2 inch) lengths
8 fried tofu puffs, cut into strips
125 g (4½ oz/1⅓ cups) bean sprouts
1 litre (35 fl oz/4 cups) vegetable stock
2 tablespoons light soy sauce
1½ tablespoons Chinese rice wine
3 spring onions (scallions), finely chopped
coriander (cilantro) leaves, to serve

1 Place the mushrooms in a bowl, cover with boiling water and soak for 15 minutes. Drain, reserving 125 ml (4 fl oz/½ cup) of the liquid. Discard the mushroom stems, thinly slice the caps and set aside.

2 Soak the vermicelli in boiling water for 5 minutes. Drain the vermicelli and divide among four serving bowls, then top with the broccoli, tofu and bean sprouts.

3 Meanwhile, place the reserved mushroom liquid, stock, soy sauce, rice wine, spring onion and mushrooms in a saucepan and bring to the boil. Cover and cook for 10 minutes. Ladle into the serving bowls, garnish with coriander and serve.

SAFFRON AND JERUSALEM ARTICHOKE SOUP

Serves 4

a pinch of saffron threads
2½ tablespoons lemon juice
250 g (9 oz) Jerusalem artichokes
1 tablespoon olive oil
1 large onion, finely chopped
3 teaspoons ground cumin
500 g (1 lb 2 oz) all-purpose potatoes, such as desiree, peeled and grated
1 litre (35 fl oz/4 cups) vegetable stock

1 Put the saffron in a bowl with 2 tablespoons boiling water and set aside to infuse.
2 Add 2 tablespoons of the lemon juice to a bowl of water. Peel and thinly slice the artichokes, dropping them into the bowl as you go so they don't discolour.
3 Heat the olive oil in a large heavy-based saucepan. Sauté the onion over medium heat for 5 minutes, or until softened. Add the cumin and cook for a further 30 seconds, or until fragrant.
4 Add the drained artichokes, potato, saffron mixture, stock and remaining lemon juice. Bring to the boil, then reduce the heat and simmer for 15–18 minutes, or until the artichokes are very soft.
5 Transfer the soup to a blender or food processor and blend until smooth. Return to the saucepan and season to taste. Gently reheat and serve.

MINESTRONE

Serves 4

80 g (2¾ oz/½ cup) dried macaroni
1 tablespoon olive oil
1 leek, white part only, sliced
2 garlic cloves, crushed
1 carrot, sliced
1 boiling potato, chopped
1 zucchini (courgette), sliced
2 celery stalks, sliced
100 g (3½ oz) green beans, chopped
400 g (14 oz) tin chopped tomatoes
2 litres (70 fl oz/8 cups) vegetable stock
2 tablespoons tomato paste (concentrated purée)
400 g (14 oz) tin cannellini beans, rinsed and drained
2 tablespoons chopped flat-leaf (Italian) parsley
shaved parmesan cheese, to serve

1 Cook the macaroni in a large saucepan of rapidly boiling salted water until *al dente*. Drain and set aside.
2 Meanwhile, heat the olive oil in a large heavy-based saucepan. Add the leek and garlic and sauté over medium heat for 3–4 minutes.
3 Add the carrot, potato, zucchini, celery, green beans, tomato, stock and tomato paste. Bring to the boil, then reduce the heat and simmer for 10 minutes, or until the vegetables are tender.
4 Stir in the macaroni and cannellini beans and heat through. Ladle into bowls and garnish with the parsley and parmesan.
Note Just about any vegetable can be added to minestrone, so this is a great recipe for using up odds and ends left in the larder or crisper.

ASPARAGUS SOUP

Serves 4

750 g (1 lb 10 oz) asparagus spears
1 litre (35 fl oz/4 cups) vegetable stock
30 g (1 oz) butter
1 tablespoon plain (all-purpose) flour
½ teaspoon finely grated lemon zest,
    plus extra, to garnish

1 Trim off any woody ends from the asparagus and cut the spears into 2 cm (¾ inch) lengths. Place in a large saucepan and pour in 500 ml (17 fl oz/2 cups) of the stock. Cover and bring to the boil, then reduce the heat and simmer for 10 minutes, or until the asparagus is tender.

2 Working in batches, transfer the asparagus and the hot stock to a blender or food processor and purée until smooth. Set aside.
3 Wipe out the saucepan, then add the butter and melt over low heat. Add the flour and stir for 1 minute, or until pale and foaming. Remove from the heat and gradually add all the remaining stock, stirring constantly until smooth.
4 Return the saucepan to the heat, bring to the boil, then simmer for 2 minutes.
5 Stir in the asparagus purée and gently reheat. Stir in the lemon zest and season to taste with sea salt and freshly ground black pepper. Serve garnished with a little extra lemon zest.

SWEET POTATO AND PEAR SOUP

Serves 4

25 g (1 oz) butter
1 small white onion, finely chopped
750 g (1 lb 10 oz) orange sweet potato,
    peeled and cut into 2 cm (¾ inch) dice
2 firm pears (about 500 g/1 lb 2 oz), peeled,
    cored and cut into 2 cm (¾ inch) dice
750 ml (26 fl oz/3 cups) vegetable stock
250 ml (9 fl oz/1 cup) pouring (whipping) cream
mint leaves, to garnish

1 Melt the butter in a saucepan. Sauté the onion over medium heat for 2–3 minutes, or until softened but not browned.
2 Add the sweet potato and pear and cook, stirring, for 1–2 minutes. Pour in the stock, bring to the boil, then reduce the heat and simmer for 20 minutes, or until the sweet potato and pear are soft.
3 Working in batches, transfer the soup to a blender or food processor and blend until smooth. Return to the saucepan, stir in the cream and gently reheat. Season to taste with sea salt and freshly ground black pepper and serve garnished with the mint.

VEGETABLE LENTIL SOUP WITH SPICED YOGHURT

Serves 6

2 tablespoons olive oil
1 small leek, white part only, chopped
2 garlic cloves, crushed
2 teaspoons curry powder
1 teaspoon ground cumin
1 teaspoon garam masala
1 litre (35 fl oz/4 cups) vegetable stock
1 bay leaf
185 g (6½ oz/1 cup) brown lentils
450 g (1 lb) butternut pumpkin (squash),
　 peeled and cut into 1 cm (½ inch) dice
2 zucchini (courgettes), cut in half lengthways
　 and sliced
400 g (14 oz) tin chopped tomatoes
200 g (7 oz) broccoli, cut into small florets
1 small carrot, diced
80 g (2¾ oz/½ cup) fresh or frozen peas
1 tablespoon shredded mint

Spiced yoghurt
250 g (9 oz/1 cup) Greek-style yoghurt
1 tablespoon chopped coriander (cilantro) leaves
1 garlic clove, crushed
3 dashes of Tabasco sauce

1 Heat the olive oil in a large heavy-based saucepan. Sauté the leek and garlic over medium heat for 5 minutes, or until lightly golden. Add the spices and cook for 1 minute, or until fragrant.
2 Add the stock, bay leaf, lentils and pumpkin. Bring to the boil, then reduce the heat to low and simmer for 10–15 minutes, or until the lentils are tender. Season well.
3 Add the zucchini, tomato, broccoli, carrot and 500 ml (17 fl oz/2 cups) water and simmer for 10 minutes, or until the vegetables are tender. Add the peas and simmer for 2–3 minutes.
4 Meanwhile, put the spiced yoghurt ingredients in a small bowl and mix well.
5 Ladle the soup into bowls. Dollop with the yoghurt and serve sprinkled with mint.

CREAM OF FENNEL AND LEEK SOUP

Serves 6

3 leeks, white part only
30 g (1 oz) butter
2 large fennel bulbs, thinly sliced
1 litre (35 fl oz/4 cups) vegetable stock
2 rosemary sprigs
a pinch of ground nutmeg
80 g (2¾ oz/⅓ cup) sour cream
25 g (1 oz/¼ cup) finely grated parmesan
   cheese, plus extra, to serve
1 tablespoon olive oil

1 Slice one of the leeks in half lengthways, then finely cut into 4 cm (1½ inch) lengths and set aside for the garnish. Thinly slice the other two leeks.

2 Melt the butter in a large heavy-based pan. Add the thinly sliced leeks and fennel, then cover and cook over medium heat for 2–3 minutes, stirring occasionally. Set aside.
3 Put the stock, rosemary sprigs and nutmeg in a large pan and bring to the boil. Simmer over low heat for 15 minutes. Remove the rosemary and add the fennel mixture.
4 Process the soup in batches in a blender or food processor until smooth. Return to the saucepan, stir in the sour cream and parmesan and gently reheat. Season to taste and keep warm.
5 Heat the olive oil in a frying pan and gently fry the reserved chopped leek for 2–3 minutes, or until soft but not browned.
6 Ladle the soup into bowls and top with the fried leek. Sprinkle with a little extra parmesan and serve.

At the end of the day, nothing whets the appetite like a little plate of savoury morsels to nibble on before the dinner bell rings—but be warned: so yummy are the starters in this chapter you might forget about dinner altogether! Whether you're entertaining friends, family or just yourself, first impressions count, but in the world of vegetarian cooking this needn't mean slaving over a stove for hours on end—a superb beginning to a memorable meal can be as simple and effortless as a colourful antipasti platter to feast the eyes and palate upon. Here follows a tempting selection to get you started, although more mouthwatering ideas can be found in other chapters. Be creative and follow your nose: a wonderful world of grazing awaits!

STARTERS

MUSHROOM PATE ON MELBA TOAST

Makes 24

50 g (1¾ oz) butter
1 small onion, chopped
3 garlic cloves, crushed
375 g (13 oz) button mushrooms, quartered
125 g (4½ oz/1 cup) slivered almonds, toasted
2 tablespoons pouring (whipping) cream
2 tablespoons finely chopped thyme
3 tablespoons finely chopped flat-leaf
    (Italian) parsley
6 thick slices of wholegrain or wholemeal
    (whole-wheat) bread

1 Melt the butter in a large frying pan. Sauté the onion and garlic over medium heat for 2 minutes, or until softened. Increase the heat, add the mushrooms and cook for 5 minutes, or until the mushrooms are soft and most of the liquid has evaporated. Leave to cool for 10 minutes.
2 Put the almonds in a food processor or blender and chop roughly. Add the mushroom mixture and blend until smooth. With the motor running, gradually pour in the cream. Stir in the herbs and season with sea salt and cracked black pepper.
3 Spoon into two 250 ml (9 fl oz/1 cup) ramekins and smooth the surface. Cover and refrigerate for 4–5 hours to allow the flavours to develop.
4 Preheat the oven to 180°C (350°F/Gas 4). To make the melba toast, toast one side of each slice of bread under a hot grill (broiler) until golden. Remove the crusts and cut each slice into four triangles.
5 Place on a large baking tray in a single layer, toasted side down, and bake for 5–10 minutes, or until crisp. Spread with the pâté and serve immediately.

STUFFED ZUCCHINI FLOWERS

Makes 20

75 g (2½ oz/scant ⅔ cup) plain
   (all-purpose) flour
100 g (3½ oz) mozzarella cheese
10 basil leaves, torn
20 zucchini (courgette) blossoms,
   stems and pistils removed
olive oil, for pan-frying
lemon wedges, to serve

1 Put the flour in a bowl with a pinch of sea salt. Mix in about 250 ml (9 fl oz/1 cup) water, or enough to obtain a creamy consistency.
2 Cut the mozzarella into 20 matchsticks. Insert a sliver of mozzarella and some basil into each zucchini blossom. Gently press the petals closed.
3 Pour oil into a heavy-based frying pan to a depth of 2.5 cm (1 inch). Heat until a drop of batter sizzles when dropped in the oil.
4 Dip one flower at a time in the batter, shaking off the excess. Cook in batches for 3 minutes, or until crisp and golden. Drain on paper towels. Season and serve immediately with lemon wedges.

BETEL AND TOFU BITES

Makes 24

2 tablespoons sugar
24 betel leaves or large basil leaves
1 tablespoon vegetable oil
2 garlic cloves, crushed
1 tablespoon grated fresh ginger
2 small red chillies, seeded and finely chopped
3 tablespoons lime juice
2 tablespoons shaved palm sugar (jaggery)
    or soft brown sugar
200 g (7 oz) fried tofu puffs, shredded
2 makrut (kaffir lime) leaves, finely shredded
3 tablespoons coriander (cilantro) leaves
25 g (1 oz/¼ cup) desiccated coconut, toasted

1 In a bowl, combine the sugar and 500 ml (17 fl oz/2 cups) water. Stir in the betel leaves, soak for 10 minutes, then drain.
2 Heat the oil in a frying pan and cook the garlic, ginger and chilli over medium heat for 1 minute. Mix together the lime juice and palm sugar and add to the pan with the tofu, lime leaves and coriander. Stir until the tofu is heated through.
3 Put 1 tablespoon of the tofu mixture onto each betel leaf and lightly sprinkle with coconut. Serve as open leaves, or serve the leaves tightly rolled into little parcels.

RED CAPSICUM AND WALNUT DIP WITH TOASTED PITTA WEDGES

Serves 6–8

4 large red capsicums (peppers), cut into large flat pieces, seeds and membranes removed
1 small red chilli
4 garlic cloves, unpeeled
100 g (3½ oz/1 cup) walnuts, lightly toasted
50 g (1¾ oz) sourdough bread, crusts removed
2 tablespoons lemon juice
1 tablespoon pomegranate molasses
1 teaspoon ground cumin
pitta bread, to serve
olive oil, for drizzling
sea salt, for sprinkling

1 Put the capsicum pieces on a baking tray, skin side up, with the chilli and whole garlic cloves. Cook under a hot grill (broiler) until the capsicum skin blackens and blisters. Leave to cool in a plastic bag. Gently peel away the capsicum and chilli skins, and remove the garlic skins.

2 Grind the walnuts in a food processor. Add the capsicum and chilli flesh, garlic, bread, lemon juice, pomegranate molasses and cumin, then blend until smooth. Mix in 2 tablespoons warm water. Season with sea salt, then cover and refrigerate overnight to allow the flavours to develop.

3 Preheat the oven to 200°C (400°F/Gas 6). Cut the pitta bread into wedges, brush with olive oil and lightly sprinkle with sea salt. Bake for 5 minutes, or until golden brown. Allow to cool and become crisp.

4 Drizzle a little olive oil over the dip and serve with the toasted pitta wedges.

MINI THAI SPRING ROLLS

Makes 40

Filling

80 g (2¾ oz) dried rice vermicelli
2 garlic cloves, crushed
1 carrot, grated
4 spring onions (scallions), finely chopped
1 tablespoon sweet chilli sauce, plus extra,
   to serve
2 teaspoons grated fresh ginger
2 coriander (cilantro) roots, finely chopped
1½ tablespoons lime juice
1 teaspoon shaved palm sugar (jaggery)
   or soft brown sugar
2 tablespoons chopped coriander
   (cilantro) leaves
3 teaspoons sesame oil
1 tablespoon kecap manis

40 square (13 cm/5 inch) spring roll wrappers
vegetable oil, for deep-frying

1 To make the filling, put the vermicelli noodles in a bowl, cover with boiling water and leave to soak for 5 minutes. Drain well, then cut into short lengths and place in a large bowl. Add the remaining filling ingredients and mix together well.
2 Working with one wrapper at a time, spoon 1 tablespoon of the filling onto one corner, on the diagonal. Brush the edges with water and roll up diagonally, tucking in the edges as you go. Repeat with the remaining filling and wrappers.
3 Fill a wok or deep heavy-based saucepan one-third full of oil and heat to 180°C (350°F), or until a cube of bread dropped into the oil browns in 15 seconds. Cook in batches for 2–3 minutes, or until golden brown. Drain on paper towels. Serve hot, with sweet chilli sauce.

UDON NOODLE SUSHI ROLLS

Makes 36 pieces

300 g (10½ oz) flat udon or soba noodles
6 roasted nori sheets
50 g (1¾ oz) pickled daikon, cut into thin strips
3 tablespoons drained pickled ginger, sliced
light soy sauce, to serve

1 Cook the noodles according to the packet instructions until *al dente*. Rinse under cold water and pat dry.

2 Working on a flat surface, lie one sheet of nori on a sushi mat. Arrange one-sixth of the noodles along the bottom half of the nori sheet, then arrange one-sixth of the daikon and pickled ginger along the centre of the noodles. Roll the nori up firmly to enclose the filling. Cut the roll in half across the middle, then cut each half into three equal pieces. Repeat with the remaining ingredients.

3 Serve with a little bowl of light soy sauce for dipping into.

VEGETABLE DUMPLINGS

Makes 25

1 tablespoon vegetable oil
3 spring onions (scallions), sliced
2 garlic cloves, chopped
2 teaspoons grated fresh ginger
3 tablespoons chopped garlic chives
425 g (15 oz/1 bunch) choy sum, shredded
2 tablespoons sweet chilli sauce
3 tablespoons chopped coriander
  (cilantro) leaves
40 g (1½ oz/¼ cup) water chestnuts,
  drained and chopped
25 gow gee wrappers

Dipping sauce

½ teaspoon sesame oil
½ teaspoon peanut oil
1 tablespoon soy sauce
1 tablespoon lime juice
1 small red chilli, finely chopped

1 Heat the oil in a frying pan over medium heat. Sauté the spring onion, garlic, ginger and chives for 1–2 minutes, or until soft. Increase the heat to high, add the choy sum and cook for 4–5 minutes, or until wilted. Stir in the sweet chilli sauce, coriander and water chestnuts. Remove from the heat and allow to cool, then squeeze out any excess moisture.

2 Lay a gow gee wrapper on a work surface. Place a heaped teaspoon of the filling in the centre. Moisten the edge of the wrapper with water and pinch together to seal, forming a ball. Trim. Repeat with the remaining wrappers and filling.

3 Half-fill a wok with water and bring to the boil. Line a bamboo steamer with baking paper. Steam the dumplings, seam side up, for 5–6 minutes.

4 Mix all the dipping sauce ingredients together in a small bowl and serve with the hot dumplings.

POTS OF BAKED RICOTTA AND MUSHROOMS

Serves 4

20 g (¾ oz) butter
1 teaspoon olive oil
125 g (4½ oz/1⅓ cups) sliced button
   mushrooms
1 garlic clove, crushed
1 teaspoon chopped marjoram, plus
   4 marjoram sprigs
a pinch of ground nutmeg
extra virgin olive oil, for drizzling
400 g (14 oz) block of ricotta cheese (see Note)

1 Preheat the oven to 180°C (350°F/Gas 4). Heat the butter and olive oil in a small frying pan. Add the mushrooms and garlic and briefly fry over high heat until lightly golden. Remove from the heat, then stir in the marjoram, nutmeg, and some sea salt and freshly cracked black pepper to taste.

2 Brush four 125 ml (4 fl oz/½ cup) ramekins with a little extra virgin olive oil and line the bases with a circle of baking paper. Put the tip of a marjoram sprig in the base of each ramekin.

3 Gently mix together the mushroom mixture and ricotta cheese. Divide among the ramekins and press down firmly.

4 Bake for 20–25 minutes, or until the tops are crusty and the mixture has started to shrink from the side of the ramekins. Remove from the oven and leave to cool for 5 minutes before turning out. Serve hot, warm or cold, drizzled with a little extra virgin olive oil.

Note Buy the ricotta for this recipe from a bulk block; it is much drier and has a better texture than that sold in pre-weighed tubs. You'll find blocks of ricotta in the delicatessen section of larger supermarkets.

ARTICHOKES IN AROMATIC VINAIGRETTE

Serves 4

2 tablespoons lemon juice
4 large globe artichokes
1 teaspoon sea salt
2 garlic cloves, crushed
1 teaspoon finely chopped oregano
½ teaspoon ground cumin
½ teaspoon ground coriander
a pinch of chilli flakes
3 teaspoons sherry vinegar
60 ml (2 fl oz/¼ cup) olive oil

1 Add the lemon juice to a large bowl of cold water. Working one at a time, trim the artichokes, cutting off the stalks to within 5 cm (2 inches) of the base and removing the tough outer leaves. Cut off the top quarter of the leaves, then slice each artichoke in half from top to base, or into quarters if large. Remove the small, furry choke with a teaspoon, then put each artichoke in the bowl of lemon water as you work to stop them discolouring.

2 Bring a large, non-aluminium saucepan of water to the boil. Add the artichokes and salt and simmer for 20 minutes, or until tender. The cooking time will depend on the artichoke size. Test by pressing a skewer into the base: if cooked, the artichoke will be soft and give little resistance. Strain, then place the artichokes on their cut side to drain.

3 Put the garlic, oregano, cumin, coriander and chilli flakes in a bowl. Season well, then mix in the vinegar. Whisking constantly, slowly pour in the olive oil to form an emulsion. (This can also be done in a small food processor.)

4 Arrange the artichokes in rows on a platter. Pour the vinaigrette over the top and leave to cool completely.

BRUSCHETTA

Serves 8

Classic Tuscan topping
6 ripe roma (plum) tomatoes
a handful of basil, shredded
1 garlic clove, finely chopped
2 tablespoons extra virgin olive oil

Mushroom and parsley topping
2 tablespoons olive oil
200 g (7 oz) small button mushrooms, quartered
1 tablespoon lemon juice
50 g (1¾ oz/⅓ cup) crumbled goat's cheese
1 tablespoon finely chopped flat-leaf (Italian)
   parsley
1 teaspoon chopped thyme

16 slices of crusty white Italian-style bread,
   cut into 1 cm (½ inch) slices
4 garlic cloves, halved
60 ml (2 fl oz/¼ cup) olive oil

1 To make the classic Tuscan topping, score a cross in the base of each tomato, place in a heatproof bowl and cover with boiling water. Leave for 30 seconds, then plunge into cold water and peel the skin away from the cross. Cut in half and scoop out the seeds with a teaspoon. Finely dice the flesh, then place in a bowl with the basil, garlic and olive oil. Mix well and set aside.
2 To make the mushroom and parsley topping, heat the olive oil in a frying pan and sauté the mushrooms over medium heat for 5 minutes, or until softened. Place in a small bowl and stir in the lemon juice, goat's cheese, parsley and thyme.
3 Toast the bread and, while still hot, rub each slice with the cut side of a garlic clove. Drizzle olive oil over each slice of bread and sprinkle with sea salt and freshly ground black pepper. Divide the toppings among the bread slices (each topping will cover eight slices of toast). Serve immediately.

ASPARAGUS GREMOLATA

Serves 4

50 g (1¾ oz) butter
80 g (2¾ oz/1 cup) coarse fresh white
  breadcrumbs
3 tablespoons chopped flat-leaf (Italian) parsley
2 garlic cloves, very finely chopped
3 teaspoons very finely chopped lemon zest
400 g (14 oz) asparagus, trimmed
1½ tablespoons extra virgin olive oil

1 Melt the butter in a heavy-based frying pan over high heat. Add the breadcrumbs and stir with a wooden spoon until the crumbs are golden and crisp. Remove to a plate to cool slightly.

2 In a bowl, mix together the parsley, garlic and lemon zest. Add the breadcrumbs and season to taste with freshly ground black pepper.

3 Bring a large, wide saucepan of water to the boil. Add the asparagus and cook for 2–3 minutes, or until just tender when pierced with a fine skewer. Drain well and arrange on a warmed serving plate. Drizzle with the olive oil, sprinkle the gremolata over the top and serve immediately.

CARAMELISED ONION TARTLETS WITH FETA AND THYME

Makes 24

1½ sheets of ready-rolled shortcrust pastry
30 g (1 oz) unsalted butter
750 g (1 lb 10 oz) red onions, thinly sliced
1½ tablespoons soft brown sugar
1½ tablespoons balsamic vinegar
1 teaspoon chopped thyme
100 g (3½ oz) feta cheese
thyme sprigs, to garnish

1 Preheat the oven to 180°C (350°F/Gas 4). Using a 5 cm (2 inch) round cutter, cut out 24 circles from the pastry. Place in lightly greased patty pan or mini muffin tins and bake for 15 minutes, or until golden.
2 Meanwhile, melt the butter in a large heavy-based frying pan. Sauté the onion over low heat for 35–40 minutes, or until very soft and golden. Stir in the sugar, vinegar and thyme, season to taste and cook for a further 10 minutes.
3 Spoon the mixture into the pastry shells and crumble the feta over the top. Cook under a hot grill (broiler) for 30 seconds, or until the feta melts slightly. Garnish with thyme sprigs and serve.

ROASTED MUSHROOMS WITH TARRAGON AND LEMON CREME FRAICHE

Serves 4

80 ml (2½ fl oz/⅓ cup) olive oil
2 tablespoons lemon juice
4 garlic cloves, crushed
12 large flat field mushrooms
2 tablespoons finely chopped flat-leaf
(Italian) parsley
toasted bread, to serve

Tarragon and lemon crème fraîche
60 g (2¼ oz/¼ cup) crème fraîche
2 teaspoons lemon juice
1 garlic clove, crushed
2 teaspoons chopped tarragon

1 Preheat the oven to 200°C (400°F/Gas 6). Put the olive oil, lemon juice and garlic in a large roasting tin.

2 Wipe the mushrooms with a clean damp cloth to remove any dirt. Trim the stems. Add the mushrooms to the roasting tin and gently toss until coated. Arrange in a single layer and season well with sea salt and freshly cracked black pepper. Roast for 30 minutes, turning to cook evenly.

3 Meanwhile, in a small bowl, mix together all the ingredients for the tarragon and lemon crème fraîche.

4 Sprinkle the hot mushrooms and their cooking juices with the parsley. Serve with the crème fraîche and toasted bread.

CARROT TIMBALES WITH SAFFRON AND LEEK SAUCE
Serves 6

60 g (2¼ oz) butter
2 leeks, white part only, sliced
2 garlic cloves, crushed
1 kg (2 lb 4 oz) carrots, sliced
375 ml (13 fl oz/1½ cups) vegetable stock
1½ tablespoons finely chopped sage
60 ml (2 fl oz/¼ cup) pouring
   (whipping) cream
4 eggs, lightly beaten

Saffron and leek sauce
40 g (1½ oz) butter
1 small leek, white part only, finely sliced
1 large garlic clove, crushed
60 ml (2 fl oz/¼ cup) white wine
a pinch of saffron threads
90 g (3¼ oz/⅓ cup) crème fraîche

1 Preheat the oven to 170°C (325°F/Gas 3). Lightly grease six 185 ml (6 fl oz/¾ cup) timbale moulds or ramekins.

2 Melt the butter in a saucepan and sauté the leek over medium heat for 3–4 minutes. Add the garlic and carrot and cook for 2–3 minutes. Pour in the stock and 500 ml (17 fl oz/2 cups) water. Bring to the boil, then reduce the heat, cover and simmer for 5 minutes, or until the carrot is tender. Strain, reserving 185 ml (6 fl oz/¾ cup) of the liquid.

3 Blend the carrot, sage and 125 ml (4 fl oz/ ½ cup) of the reserved liquid until smooth. Cool slightly. Stir in the cream and egg, season and pour into the moulds. Place the moulds in a roasting tin and pour in enough hot water to come halfway up the side. Bake for 30–40 minutes, or until just set.

4 To make the sauce, melt the butter in a saucepan and sauté the leek over medium heat for 3–4 minutes without browning. Add the garlic and cook for 30 seconds. Add the wine, remaining reserved liquid and saffron, then simmer for 5 minutes, or until reduced. Stir in the crème fraîche.

5 Invert the timbales onto serving plates and serve with the sauce.

CAPSICUM ROLLED WITH GOAT'S CHEESE, BASIL AND CAPERS

Serves 4

4 large red capsicums (peppers)
3 tablespoons chopped flat-leaf (Italian) parsley
2 tablespoons chives, snipped
2 tablespoons baby capers, rinsed and
  finely chopped
1 tablespoon balsamic vinegar
150 g (5½ oz/1¼ cups) crumbled goat's cheese
16 basil leaves
olive oil, for covering
crusty Italian bread, to serve

1 Cut the capsicums into large flat pieces and remove the seeds and membranes. Cook, skin side up, under a hot grill (broiler) until the skins blister and blacken. Leave to cool in a plastic bag, then peel away the skin and cut the flesh into strips 3 cm (1¼ inches) wide.

2 Put the parsley, chives, capers, vinegar and goat's cheese in a small bowl. Season with plenty of black pepper and mix well.

3 Place a basil leaf on the inside of each capsicum piece, then top with a teaspoon of the goat's cheese mixture. Roll the capsicum over the goat's cheese and secure with a toothpick.

4 Place in an airtight container, cover with olive oil and refrigerate until required. Serve at room temperature with crusty Italian bread.

EGGPLANT, TOMATO AND GOAT'S CHEESE STACK

Serves 4

4 vine-ripened tomatoes
4 garlic cloves, chopped
1 tablespoon shredded basil, plus 8 whole
basil leaves
2 tablespoons finely chopped flat-leaf (Italian)
parsley
60 ml (2 fl oz/¼ cup) olive oil
1 large eggplant (aubergine), cut into 5 mm
(¼ inch) slices
80 g (2¾ oz/⅔ cup) crumbled goat's cheese

1 Preheat the oven to 180°C (350°F/Gas 4). Cut the tomatoes in half and scoop out the pulp. Divide the garlic among the tomato halves, then the shredded basil and parsley. Arrange the tomato halves on a baking tray, drizzle with 1 tablespoon of the olive oil, season to taste and bake for 40 minutes, or until soft.
2 Spread the eggplant slices on an oiled baking tray and brush with the remaining oil. Cook under a hot grill (broiler) for 5 minutes, or until crisp and golden.
3 Lightly oil four 185 ml (6 fl oz/¾ cup) ramekins or dariole moulds. Line each with some eggplant, then two basil leaves, a tomato half, some goat's cheese, another tomato half, then a final slice of eggplant. Bake for 20 minutes, then leave in the ramekins for 5 minutes before turning out.

VEGETABLE PAKORAS WITH CORIANDER YOGHURT

Serves 4

650 g (1 lb 7 oz) selection of vegetables such
   as zucchini (courgette), red capsicum
   (pepper), orange sweet potato and onion
125 g (4½ oz/heaped 1 cup) besan
   (chickpea flour)
1 teaspoon sea salt
2 teaspoons curry powder
1 teaspoon ground turmeric
1 tablespoon sunflower oil
1 tablespoon lemon juice
vegetable oil, for deep-frying

Coriander yoghurt
4 large handfuls of coriander (cilantro) leaves
1 large green chilli, seeded and finely chopped
1 garlic clove, crushed
250 g (9 oz/1 cup) Greek-style yoghurt
1 tablespoon lemon juice

1 Peel and cut the vegetables into thin strips.
Sift the besan into a bowl and stir in the
sea salt, curry powder and turmeric. Make a
well in the centre and gradually beat in the
oil, lemon juice and 185 ml (6 fl oz/¾ cup)
water to make a smooth batter. Set aside.
2 To make the coriander yoghurt, blend the
coriander, chilli, garlic and 2 tablespoons
cold water in a food processor until smooth.
Transfer to a bowl and stir in the yoghurt
and lemon juice. Season and set aside.
3 Heat 5 cm (2 inches) of vegetable oil
in a wok or deep heavy-based saucepan
to 180°C (350°F), or until a cube of bread
dropped into the oil browns in 15 seconds.
Lightly whisk the batter and stir in the
vegetables.
4 Carefully slip bundles of batter-coated
vegetables into the hot oil and fry in
batches for 2–3 minutes, or until golden.
Drain on paper towels and keep warm in
a low oven while cooking the remaining
pakoras. Serve hot, with the yoghurt.

STUFFED ARTICHOKES

Serves 4

40 g (1½ oz/¼ cup) raw almonds
80 ml (2½ fl oz/⅓ cup) lemon juice
4 young globe artichokes
150 g (5½ oz/⅔ cup) ricotta cheese
2 garlic cloves, crushed
80 g (2¾ oz/1 cup) coarse fresh white
   breadcrumbs
1 teaspoon finely grated lemon zest
50 g (1¾ oz/½ cup) grated parmesan cheese
3 tablespoons chopped flat-leaf (Italian) parsley
1 tablespoon olive oil
40 g (1½ oz) butter

1 Preheat the oven to 180°C (350°F/Gas 4).
Spread the almonds on a baking tray and
bake for 5–10 minutes, or until lightly
golden. Remove from the oven, leave
to cool, then roughly chop.
2 Add half the lemon juice to a bowl
of cold water. Working one at a time,

remove any tough outer leaves from the
artichokes. Cut across the artichokes, about
3 cm (1¼ inches) from the top, and trim
the stalks, leaving about 2 cm (¾ inch)
attached. Put each artichoke in the bowl
of lemon water as you work to stop them
discolouring.
3 Combine the almonds, ricotta, garlic,
breadcrumbs, lemon zest, parmesan and
parsley in a bowl and season. Gently
separate the artichoke leaves and push
the filling in between them.
4 Carefully place the artichokes in a
steamer and drizzle with the olive oil.
Steam for 25–30 minutes, or until tender
when pierced with a skewer. Remove and
cook under a hot grill (broiler) for about
5 minutes to brown the filling.
5 Melt the butter in a saucepan, then remove
from the heat and stir in the remaining
lemon juice. Arrange the artichokes on a
serving platter, drizzle with the lemon
butter, season well and serve.

From golden little savoury-filled parcels of pastry to great big plump, puffy pies and smartly turned-out tarts, who doesn't find pastries of any description enticing? They are an offering few of us can resist—and when they're filled with goodness from the mighty vegetable kingdom, who would even want to? Pies and pastries bring out in us a special joy, a certain child-like glee: they are a present in which the wrapping is every bit as delicious as the filling! This chapter brings together savoury concoctions ranging from more delicate little morsels ideal for simple entertaining to full-on affairs destined to feed a family. Many also make ideal fare for leisurely picnics or a lazy Sunday lunch. Dish them up and watch them go!

SAVOURY PIES, TARTS & PASTRIES

VEGETABLE SAMOSAS

Makes 32

500 g (1 lb 2 oz/4 cups) plain (all-purpose) flour
1 teaspoon sea salt
2 tablespoons vegetable oil

Filling
600 g (1 lb 5 oz) waxy potatoes, quartered
185 g (6½ oz/1½ cups) cauliflower florets
2 tablespoons vegetable oil
1 onion, chopped
2 garlic cloves, finely chopped
2 tablespoons grated fresh ginger
2 tablespoons mild curry powder
100 g (3½ oz/⅔ cup) frozen peas
2 tablespoons lemon juice
vegetable oil, for deep-frying

1 Put the flour and salt in a food processor and process for 5 seconds. Mix the oil with 250 ml (9 fl oz/1 cup) warm water, add to the flour and process in short bursts until the mixture just comes together. Turn out onto a lightly floured surface and gather into a ball. Cover with plastic wrap and refrigerate for 30 minutes.

2 Meanwhile, make the filling. Boil, steam or microwave the potato and cauliflower separately until tender, then drain, allow to cool and finely dice.
3 Heat the oil in a large frying pan and sauté the onion over medium heat for 5 minutes, or until softened. Add the garlic, ginger and curry powder and cook for 2 minutes. Add the potato, cauliflower, peas and lemon juice and mix well. Remove from the heat and leave to cool.
4 Divide the dough into 16 portions. On a lightly floured surface, roll each portion into a 15 cm (6 inch) round. Cut each in half to make two semi-circles, then put a tablespoon of the filling in the middle of each. Brush the edges with a little water and fold the pastry over the mixture, pressing the edges to seal.
5 Fill a deep heavy-based saucepan one-third full of oil. Heat until a cube of bread dropped into the oil browns in 15 seconds. Deep-fry the samosas in batches for 1 minute, or until golden. Drain on paper towels and serve hot. These samosas are delicious with mango chutney, sweet chilli sauce or Greek-style yoghurt.

BOREKAS

Makes 24

225 g (8 oz/1½ cups) crumbled feta cheese
200 g (7 oz) cream cheese, slightly softened
2 eggs, lightly beaten
¼ teaspoon ground nutmeg
20 sheets of filo pastry
60 g (2¼ oz) butter, melted
3 tablespoons sesame seeds
lemon wedges, to serve

1 Preheat the oven to 180°C (350°F/Gas 4). Put the feta, cream cheese, egg and nutmeg in a bowl and mix until just combined—the mixture will be lumpy.
2 Lay five sheets of filo pastry on a work surface and cover the rest with a damp cloth so they don't dry out. Brush each pastry sheet with melted butter and lay them on top of each other. Using a ruler as a guide, cut the filo into six equal strips.
3 Place 1 tablespoon of the cheese filling at one end of a strip, leaving a narrow border. Fold the pastry over to enclose the filling and form a triangle. Continue folding the triangle over until you reach the end of the pastry, tucking any excess pastry under. Repeat with the remaining ingredients to make 24 triangles, placing them on a lined baking tray.
4 Lightly brush the pastries with the remaining melted butter and sprinkle with sesame seeds. Bake for 15–20 minutes, or until puffed and golden. Serve hot, with lemon wedges.

SWEET POTATO AND LENTIL POUCHES

Makes 32

2 tablespoons olive oil
1 large leek, white part only, finely chopped
2 garlic cloves, crushed
125 g (4½ oz/1⅓ cups) chopped button
   mushrooms
2 teaspoons ground cumin
2 teaspoons ground coriander
95 g (3¼ oz/½ cup) brown or green lentils
125 g (4½ oz/½ cup) red lentils
500 ml (17 fl oz/2 cups) vegetable stock
300 g (10½ oz) sweet potato, peeled and diced
4 tablespoons chopped coriander (cilantro)
8 sheets of frozen puff pastry, thawed
1 egg, lightly beaten
200 g (7 oz) plain yoghurt
2 tablespoons grated Lebanese (short)
   cucumber
½ teaspoon soft brown sugar

1 Heat the olive oil in a saucepan. Sauté the leek over medium heat for 3 minutes. Add the garlic, mushroom and ground spices and cook for 1 minute, or until fragrant.
2 Add the lentils and stock and bring to the boil. Reduce the heat and simmer for 20–25 minutes, or until the lentils are tender, stirring occasionally. Add the sweet potato during the last 5 minutes. Stir in the coriander, season to taste and leave to cool.
3 Meanwhile, preheat the oven to 200°C (400°F/Gas 6). Cut each pastry sheet into four squares. Place 1½ tablespoons of filling into the centre of each and bring the edges together to form a pouch. Pinch together, then tie each pouch with string. Lightly brush with egg and place on lined baking trays. Bake for 20–25 minutes, or until puffed and golden. Remove the strings.
4 Put the yoghurt, cucumber and sugar in a bowl and mix to make a sauce. Serve with the hot pouches.

TOFU PASTRIES

Serves 4

150 g (5½ oz) firm tofu, drained
2 spring onions (scallions), chopped
3 teaspoons chopped coriander (cilantro)
½ teaspoon grated orange zest
2 teaspoons soy sauce
1 tablespoon sweet chilli sauce
2 teaspoons grated fresh ginger
1 teaspoon cornflour (cornstarch)
2 sheets of frozen puff pastry, thawed
1 egg, lightly beaten

Dipping sauce
3 tablespoons sugar
125 ml (4 fl oz/½ cup) rice vinegar
1 small Lebanese (short) cucumber,
   finely diced
1 small red chilli, thinly sliced
1 spring onion (scallion), thinly sliced
   on the diagonal

1 Pat the tofu dry and cut into small dice. Place in a bowl with the spring onion, coriander, orange zest, soy and sweet chilli sauces, ginger and cornflour. Mix gently, then cover and refrigerate for 3–4 hours.
2 Meanwhile, make the dipping sauce. Put the sugar and vinegar in a small saucepan and stir over low heat until the sugar dissolves. Tip into a small bowl and add the cucumber, chilli and spring onion. Allow to cool completely.
3 Preheat the oven to 220°C (425°F/Gas 7). Cut each pastry sheet into four squares. Drain the tofu filling and divide into eight portions. Place one portion in the centre of each square and brush the edges with beaten egg. Fold each one into a triangle and seal the edges with a fork.
4 Place on two lined baking trays, brush with beaten egg and bake for 15 minutes, or until the pastry is puffed and golden. Serve hot, with the dipping sauce.

SPINACH AND FETA TRIANGLES

Makes 8

1 kg (2 lb 4 oz) English spinach
60 ml (2 fl oz/¼ cup) olive oil
1 onion, chopped
10 spring onions (scallions), sliced
4 tablespoons chopped parsley
1 tablespoon chopped dill
a large pinch of ground nutmeg
35 g (1¼ oz/⅓ cup) grated parmesan cheese
150 g (5½ oz/1 cup) crumbled feta cheese
90 g (3¼ oz/⅓ cup) ricotta cheese
4 eggs, lightly beaten
40 g (1¼ oz) butter, melted and mixed with
    1 tablespoon olive oil
12 sheets of filo pastry

1 Trim any coarse stems from the spinach. Wash the leaves, roughly chop and place in a large saucepan with just a little water clinging to the leaves. Cover and cook over low heat for 5 minutes, or until wilted.

Drain well, cool slightly, then squeeze tightly to remove the excess water.
2 Heat the olive oil in a heavy-based frying pan. Sauté the onion over low heat for 10 minutes, or until soft and golden. Add the spring onion and cook for 3 minutes, then remove from the heat. Stir in the spinach, parsley, dill, nutmeg, parmesan, feta, ricotta and egg. Season well.
3 Preheat the oven to 180°C (350°F/Gas 4). Grease two baking trays. Lay three sheets of pastry on a work surface and cover the rest with a damp cloth. Brush each sheet with the melted butter, lay them on top of each other, then cut in half lengthways. Spoon 4 tablespoons of the filling on an angle at the end of each strip. Fold the pastry over to enclose the filling and form a triangle. Continue folding the triangle over until you reach the end. Repeat to make eight triangles.
4 Place on the baking trays and brush with more butter mixture. Bake for 20 minutes, or until golden brown. Serve hot.

MINI PUMPKIN AND CURRY QUICHES

Makes 8

185 g (6½ oz/1½ cups) plain (all-purpose) flour
125 g (4½ oz/½ cup) cream cheese, chopped
125 g (4½ oz) cold butter, chopped

Filling
1 tablespoon olive oil
2 onions, finely chopped
3 garlic cloves, crushed
1 teaspoon curry powder
3 eggs
125 ml (4 fl oz/½ cup) thick
  (double/heavy) cream
250 g (9 oz/1 cup) mashed,
  cooked pumpkin (winter squash)
2 teaspoons cumin seeds

1 Sift the flour into a large bowl. Using your fingertips, rub in the cream cheese and butter until the mixture is smooth and comes together in a ball. Turn out onto a lightly floured surface and knead for 10 seconds, or until smooth. Cover with plastic wrap and refrigerate for 30 minutes.

2 Preheat the oven to 210°C (415°F/Gas 6–7). Grease eight deep, 10 cm (4 inch) flan (tart) tins. Divide the pastry into eight portions and roll out on a lightly floured surface to fit the tins. Trim the edges and bake for 15 minutes, or until lightly browned. Remove from the oven and reduce the temperature to 180°C (350°F/Gas 4).

3 Meanwhile, make the filling. Heat the olive oil in a small saucepan and sauté the onion and garlic over low heat for 5 minutes, or until softened. Add the curry powder and stir for 1 minute. Allow to cool slightly, then spread the onion mixture into the pastry shells.

4 Beat the eggs, cream and pumpkin in a large bowl until combined, then pour into the pastry shells. Sprinkle with the cumin seeds and bake for 20 minutes, or until the filling has set. Serve hot or warm.

ARTICHOKE AND PROVOLONE QUICHES

Serves 6

250 g (9 oz/2 cups) plain (all-purpose) flour
125 g (4½ oz) cold butter, chopped
1 egg yolk
60 ml (2 fl oz/¼ cup) iced water

Filling
1 small eggplant (aubergine), sliced
olive oil, for brushing
6 eggs, lightly beaten
3 teaspoons wholegrain mustard
150 g (5½ oz/1½ cups) grated provolone
   cheese
200 g (7 oz) marinated artichokes, sliced
125 g (4½ oz/¾ cup) semi-dried (sun-blushed)
   tomatoes

1 Put the flour and butter in a food processor and process for 15 seconds, or until crumbly. Add the egg yolk and iced water and process in short bursts until the mixture just comes together, adding a little extra iced water if you think the dough is a bit too dry. Turn out onto a lightly floured surface and gather into a ball. Cover with plastic wrap and refrigerate for at least 30 minutes.
2 Preheat the oven to 190°C (375°F/Gas 5). Grease six 11 cm (4¼ inch) oval pie tins.
3 To make the filling, brush the eggplant slices with olive oil and cook under a hot grill (broiler) until golden. In a bowl, mix together the eggs, mustard and cheese.
4 Divide the pastry into six portions, roll out on a lightly floured surface into rounds and use them to line the tins. Trim and decorate the edges. Divide the eggplant, artichoke and tomato among the pastry shells. Pour the egg mixture over and bake for 25 minutes, or until the filling has set and the pastry is golden. Serve hot or warm.

GOAT'S CHEESE AND OLIVE TART

Serves 6

125 g (4½ oz/1 cup) plain (all-purpose) flour
60 ml (2 fl oz/¼ cup) olive oil
80 ml (2½ fl oz/⅓ cup) iced water

Filling
1 tablespoon olive oil
2 onions, thinly sliced
1 teaspoon thyme leaves
125 g (4½ oz/½ cup) ricotta cheese
100 g (3½ oz/heaped ¾ cup) crumbled
   goat's cheese
12 pitted niçoise olives
1 egg, lightly beaten
60 ml (2 fl oz/¼ cup) whipping (pouring) cream

1 Sift the flour and a pinch of sea salt into a large bowl and make a well in the centre. Add the olive oil and mix with a flat-bladed knife until crumbly. Gradually work in 60 ml (2 fl oz/¼ cup) of the iced water until the mixture comes together, adding a little more iced water if necessary. Turn out onto a lightly floured work surface and gather together into a ball. Cover with plastic wrap and refrigerate for 30 minutes.
2 Meanwhile, start making the filling. Heat the olive oil in a frying pan, add the onion, then cover and cook over low heat for 30 minutes. Season with sea salt and freshly ground black pepper and stir in half the thyme. Allow to cool slightly.
3 Preheat the oven to 180°C (350°F/Gas 4). Put a baking tray in the oven to heat.
4 Roll out the pastry on a lightly floured work surface to a 30 cm (12 inch) circle.
5 Spread the onion over the pastry, leaving a 2 cm (¾ inch) border. Sprinkle the ricotta and goat's cheese over the onion. Arrange the olives on top, then sprinkle with the remaining thyme. Fold the pastry in to the edge of the filling, gently pleating as you go.
6 Mix together the egg and cream, then carefully pour over the filling. Place the tart on the heated baking tray and bake for 45 minutes, or until the pastry is golden. Serve warm or at room temperature.

INDIVIDUAL ITALIAN SUMMER TARTS

Serves 4

2 tablespoons olive oil
2 red onions, sliced
1 tablespoon balsamic vinegar
1 teaspoon soft brown sugar
1 tablespoon chopped thyme, plus
   extra thyme sprigs, to garnish
1 sheet of frozen puff pastry, thawed
170 g (6 oz) jar marinated quartered
   artichokes, drained well
16 black olives, pitted
extra virgin olive oil, for drizzling

1 Heat the olive oil in a heavy-based saucepan. Add the onion and cook over low heat for 15 minutes, or until soft, stirring occasionally. Add the vinegar and sugar and cook for a further 15 minutes, or until lightly browned. Remove from the heat, stir in the thyme and set aside to cool.
2 Preheat the oven to 220°C (425°F/Gas 7). Place a lightly greased baking tray in the oven to heat. Cut four 10 cm (4 inch) rounds from the pastry and spread the onion over them, leaving a 1.5 cm (⅝ inch) border.
3 Place the pastry bases on the hot baking tray and bake in the top half of the oven for 12–15 minutes, or until the edges are risen and the pastry is golden brown.
4 Arrange the artichoke and olives over the pastry bases. Drizzle the tarts with a little extra virgin olive oil and garnish with thyme sprigs. Serve hot.

ROAST PUMPKIN, FETA AND PINE NUT PASTIE

Serves 4

800 g (1 lb 12 oz) jap or kent pumpkin
  (winter squash), peeled and cut into
  1 cm (½ inch) thick slices
2 tablespoons olive oil
3 garlic cloves, crushed
4 sheets of frozen butter puff pastry, thawed
  and cut into 15 cm (6 inch) squares
100 g (3½ oz) marinated feta cheese, crumbled
  (reserve the oil)
3 tablespoons roughly chopped oregano leaves
2 tablespoons pine nuts, toasted
1 egg yolk
1 tablespoon milk
1 tablespoon sesame seeds
sea salt, for sprinkling

1 Preheat the oven to 220°C (425°F/Gas 7). Put the pumpkin on a baking tray and toss with the olive oil, garlic and some sea salt and freshly ground black pepper. Roast for 40 minutes, or until the pumpkin is cooked and golden. Remove from the oven and leave to cool.

2 Divide the pumpkin among the four pastry squares, placing it in the centre. Top with the feta, oregano and pine nuts. Drizzle with a little of the feta marinating oil. Bring two diagonal corners into the middle and pinch them together over the filling. Bring the other opposite corners together, then pinch to seal along the edges—the base will be square; the top will form a pyramid. Twist the top to seal where all four corners meet.

3 Put the egg yolk and milk in a small bowl and whisk together with a fork.

4 Place the pasties on a greased baking tray and brush with the eggwash. Sprinkle with the sesame seeds and sea salt and bake for 15 minutes, or until golden. Serve hot.

ITALIAN ZUCCHINI PIE

Serves 6

600 g (1 lb 5 oz) zucchini (courgettes)
150 g (5½ oz/1½ cups) grated provolone cheese
125 g (4½ oz/½ cup) ricotta cheese
3 eggs, lightly beaten
2 garlic cloves, crushed
2 teaspoons finely chopped basil
a pinch of ground nutmeg
2 sheets of frozen shortcrust (pie) pastry,
    thawed
1 egg, extra, lightly beaten

1 Grate the zucchini into a bowl, add a generous pinch of sea salt and mix well. Transfer to a colander and leave to drain for 30 minutes.
2 Preheat the oven to 200°C (400°F/Gas 6) and place a baking tray in the oven to heat. Grease a 23 cm (9 inch) pie dish.
3 Squeeze out any excess liquid from the zucchini. Place in a bowl with the provolone, ricotta, eggs, garlic, basil and nutmeg. Season and mix well.
4 Using two-thirds of the pastry, line the base and sides of the pie dish. Spoon the cheese filling into the pastry shell and smooth the surface. Brush the exposed rim of the pastry with some of the extra beaten egg. Use two-thirds of the remaining pastry to make a lid, then place it over the filling, pressing the edges together firmly. Trim the edge, reserving the scraps. Crimp the pastry edge, prick the top all over with a skewer and brush with beaten egg.
5 From the remaining pastry, cut out a 30 x 10 cm (12 x 4 inch) strip. Cut this into nine lengths 1 cm (½ inch) wide. Press three ropes together at one end, then press onto a work surface and plait together. Make two more plaits, then trim the ends and arrange in parallel rows across the centre of the pie. Brush with egg.
6 Bake on the hot baking tray for 50 minutes, or until the pastry is golden. Serve hot.

MUSHROOM POT PIES

Serves 4

125 ml (4 fl oz/½ cup) olive oil
1 leek, white part only, sliced
1 garlic clove, crushed
1 kg (2 lb 4 oz) large field mushrooms,
   wiped clean and roughly chopped
1 teaspoon chopped thyme
300 ml (10½ fl oz) pouring (whipping) cream
1 sheet of frozen puff pastry, thawed
1 egg yolk, beaten

1 Preheat the oven to 180°C (350°F/Gas 4). Heat 1 tablespoon of the olive oil in a frying pan. Sauté the leek and garlic over medium heat for 5 minutes, or until the leek is soft and translucent. Transfer to a large saucepan.
2 Heat the remaining oil in the frying pan over high heat. Add the mushrooms in two batches and cook, stirring frequently, for 5–7 minutes per batch, or until the mushrooms have released their juices and are soft and slightly coloured. Transfer to the saucepan, then add the thyme.
3 Place the saucepan over high heat and stir in the cream. Stirring occasionally, cook for 7–8 minutes, or until the cream has reduced to a thick sauce. Remove from the heat and season well with sea salt and freshly ground black pepper. Divide among four 310 ml (10¾ fl oz/1¼ cup) ramekins or ovenproof bowls.
4 Cut the pastry into rounds slightly larger than each ramekin. Brush the rim of each ramekin with some of the beaten egg yolk, place the pastry rounds on top and press down on the rim to seal. Brush the tops with the remaining egg yolk.
5 Place the ramekins on a baking tray and bake for 20–25 minutes, or until the pastry is puffed and golden brown. Serve hot.

ASPARAGUS PIE

Serves 6

800 g (1 lb 12 oz) asparagus
20 g (¾ oz) butter
½ teaspoon chopped thyme
1 French shallot, chopped
1 large sheet of frozen shortcrust (pie)
  pastry, thawed
2 eggs
80 ml (2½ fl oz/⅓ cup) pouring
  (whipping) cream
2 tablespoons grated parmesan cheese
a pinch of ground nutmeg

1 Preheat the oven to 200°C (400°F/Gas 6) and grease a 21 cm (8¼ inch) fluted, loose-based flan (tart) tin. Trim the asparagus spears to a length of 10 cm (4 inches), then cut any thick spears in half lengthways.

2 Melt the butter in a large frying pan over medium heat. Add the asparagus, thyme, shallot, 1 tablespoon water and season well. Cook, stirring, for 3 minutes, or until the asparagus is tender.

3 Roll the pastry out to a 30 cm (12 inch) circle, about 2 mm (¹⁄₁₆ inch) thick. Line the flan tin and trim the pastry using kitchen scissors, leaving about 8 cm (3¼ inches) above the top of the tin. Arrange half the asparagus in one direction over the pastry base. Cover with the remaining asparagus, running in the opposite direction.

4 Crack one of the eggs into a small bowl; whisk in the cream, parmesan and nutmeg. Season well, then pour over the asparagus. Fold the pastry over the filling, forming loose pleats. Lightly beat the remaining egg and brush over the pastry. Bake for 25 minutes, or until golden. Serve hot.

CORN AND CAPSICUM TARTLETS

Makes about 36

3 sheets of frozen puff pastry, thawed
310 g (11 oz) tin corn kernels, drained
150 g (5½ oz/heaped 1 cup) grated red
  leicester cheese
1 small red capsicum (pepper), finely
  chopped
2 eggs, lightly beaten
60 ml (2 fl oz/¼ cup) buttermilk
170 ml (5½ fl oz/⅔ cup) thick (double/heavy)
  cream
1 teaspoon dijon mustard
a dash of Tabasco sauce
snipped chives, to garnish

1 Preheat the oven to 200°C (400°F/Gas 6).
Lightly grease three 12-hole round-based patty pan or mini muffin tins. Use a 6 cm (2½ inch) round pastry cutter to cut out circles from the pastry sheets. Press the pastry circles into the tins and prick the bases all over with a fork.

2 Put the corn, cheese and capsicum in a bowl, mix together and season to taste with sea salt and freshly ground black pepper. In a pouring jug, whisk together the eggs, buttermilk, cream, mustard and Tabasco.

3 Spoon some of the corn mixture into the pastry cases, then pour the egg mixture over the top until the cases are almost full. Bake for 20–25 minutes, or until the pastry has risen and the filling is set.

4 Remove from the oven and leave to cool. Serve cold, garnished with chives.

Note These tarts can be made a day ahead and refrigerated in an airtight container. They can also be frozen for up to 2 months.

SPINACH PIES

Makes about 20

2 teaspoons active dried yeast
1 teaspoon sugar
375 g (13 oz/3 cups) plain (all-purpose) flour
125 ml (4 fl oz/½ cup) olive oil
750 g (1 lb 10 oz) English spinach, trimmed
1 large onion, finely chopped
1 garlic clove, crushed
80 g (2¾ oz/½ cup) pine nuts, toasted
1 teaspoon finely grated lemon zest
2 tablespoons lemon juice
¼ teaspoon ground nutmeg
1 egg, beaten

1 Pour 60 ml (2 fl oz/¼ cup) warm water into a bowl. Sprinkle with the yeast and sugar and leave in a draught-free place for 10 minutes, or until foamy.
2 Sift the flour into a bowl. Add the yeast mixture, 2 tablespoons of the olive oil and 185 ml (6 fl oz/¾ cup) warm water. Mix to form a dough, then turn out onto a lightly floured surface and knead for 10 minutes, or until smooth and elastic. Place in an oiled bowl, turning to coat in the oil, and leave in a draught-free place for up to 2 hours, or until doubled in size.
3 Preheat the oven to 190°C (375°F/Gas 5). Grease two large baking trays. Wash the spinach, leaving the water on the leaves. Place in a saucepan, cover and cook over high heat until wilted. Drain well, squeeze out the excess water and roughly chop.
4 Heat 1 tablespoon of the olive oil in a frying pan. Sauté the onion and garlic until softened. Place in a bowl with the spinach, pine nuts, lemon zest and juice. Add the nutmeg, season to taste and set aside to cool.
5 Turn the dough out onto a floured surface and gently punch down. Divide into balls the size of an egg, then roll each one out to a 10 cm (4 inch) round. Place 1 tablespoon of the spinach filling in the centre of each. Brush the edges with water, then bring up the sides at three points to form a triangle, pressing together to seal.
6 Place on the baking trays, leaving space in between for spreading. Brush with beaten egg and bake for 15 minutes, or until golden. Serve hot.

BROWN RICE TART WITH TOMATO AND FETA

Serves 6

200 g (7 oz/1 cup) brown rice
60 g (2¼ oz/½ cup) grated cheddar cheese
1 egg, lightly beaten

Filling
6 roma (plum) tomatoes, halved
6 garlic cloves, unpeeled
1 tablespoon olive oil
8 lemon thyme sprigs
45 g (1½ oz/⅓ cup) crumbled feta or
   goat's cheese
3 eggs
60 ml (2 fl oz/¼ cup) milk

1 Boil the rice for 35–40 minutes, or until tender; drain and leave to cool. Meanwhile, preheat the oven to 200°C (400°F/Gas 6).

2 Put the rice, cheese and egg in a bowl and mix together well. Spread the mixture over the base and sides of a lightly greased 25 cm (10 inch) flan (tart) tin or quiche dish and bake for 15 minutes. Remove from the oven and set aside.

3 To make the filling, place the tomatoes on a non-stick baking tray, cut side up, along with the garlic. Brush with the olive oil and grind some black pepper over the top. Bake for 30 minutes, then remove from the oven and leave to cool slightly. Squeeze the garlic cloves out of their skins.

4 Reduce the oven temperature to 180°C (350°F/Gas 4). Arrange the tomato halves, garlic, lemon thyme sprigs and feta over the rice crust.

5 In a bowl, whisk together the eggs and milk, then pour over the tomatoes. Bake for 1 hour, or until the filling has set. Serve hot or cold.

POLENTA-CRUSTED CHARGRILLED VEGIE PIE

Serves 4–6

125 g (4½ oz/1 cup) plain (all-purpose) flour
75 g (2½ oz/½ cup) polenta
90 g (3¼ oz) cold butter, chopped
90 g (3¼ oz/⅓ cup) cream cheese, chopped
1 kg (2 lb 4 oz) eggplant (aubergine), sliced
    lengthways
2–3 tablespoons olive oil
1–2 garlic cloves, crushed
2 red capsicums (peppers), halved
8 cherry tomatoes, halved
a handful of small basil leaves
2 teaspoons baby capers
1 teaspoon balsamic vinegar, mixed with
    1 teaspoon olive oil

1 Put the flour, polenta, butter and cream cheese in a food processor. Process in short bursts until the mixture just comes together; add 1–2 teaspoons iced water if the mixture looks too dry. Turn out onto a floured surface and quickly bring together into a ball. Cover with plastic wrap and refrigerate for at least 30 minutes.

2 Spread the eggplant on an oiled baking tray. Mix together the olive oil and garlic, then brush over the eggplant. Cook under a hot grill (broiler) for 10–12 minutes, turning once and brushing several times. Remove and set aside.

3 Grill the capsicum, skin side up, until the skin blackens and blisters. Leave to cool in a plastic bag, then peel away the skin and slice the flesh. Set aside.

4 Grill the tomatoes, cut side up, for 2–3 minutes, then set aside.

5 Roll the pastry out on baking paper to fit a shallow 21 x 28 cm (8¼ x 11¼ inch) loose-based flan (tart) tin. Press the pastry into the sides, trim off any excess, then refrigerate for 20 minutes. Meanwhile, preheat the oven to 190°C (375°F/Gas 5).

6 Line the pastry with baking paper and fill with baking beads or rice. Bake for 15 minutes, then remove the paper and beads and bake for a further 15 minutes, or until the pastry is cooked.

7 Layer the cooked pastry shell with the capsicum, eggplant, tomato halves, some basil leaves and capers. Brush with the balsamic vinegar mixture before serving.

PUMPKIN AND FETA PIE

Serves 6

700 g (1 lb 9 oz) butternut pumpkin (squash),
  peeled and cut into 2 cm (¾ inch) pieces
4 garlic cloves, unpeeled
80 ml (2½ fl oz/⅓ cup) olive oil
2 small red onions, halved and sliced
1 tablespoon balsamic vinegar
1 tablespoon soft brown sugar
100 g (3½ oz/⅔ cup) crumbled feta cheese
1 tablespoon chopped rosemary
1 large sheet of frozen shortcrust (pie) pastry,
  thawed

1 Preheat the oven to 200°C (400°F/Gas 6).
Spread the pumpkin and garlic cloves on a
baking tray, drizzle with 2 tablespoons of
the olive oil and bake for 25–30 minutes,
or until the pumpkin is tender. Transfer the
pumpkin to a large bowl and the garlic
cloves to a plate. Leave to cool.

2 Meanwhile, heat the remaining oil in a
frying pan. Add the onion and cook over
medium heat for 10 minutes, stirring
occasionally. Add the vinegar and sugar
and cook for a further 15 minutes, or until
the onion is dark golden. Add to the
pumpkin and leave to cool completely.

3 Add the feta and rosemary to the
pumpkin mixture. Squeeze the garlic cloves
out of their skins and mix them through
the vegetables. Season to taste with sea salt
and freshly ground black pepper.

4 Roll out the pastry between two sheets
of baking paper to a 35 cm (14 inch) circle.
Remove the top sheet of paper and place
the bottom sheet with the pastry on a
baking tray. Arrange the pumpkin mixture
over the top, leaving a 4 cm (1½ inch)
border. Fold over the pastry edges, gently
pleating as you fold.

5 Bake for 30 minutes, or until the pastry
is crisp and golden. Serve hot or warm.

RUSTIC GREEK PIE

Serves 4

450 g (1 lb) packet of frozen spinach, thawed
1 large sheet of frozen shortcrust (pie) pastry,
  thawed
3 garlic cloves, finely chopped
150 g (5½ oz) haloumi cheese, grated
125 g (4½ oz/heaped ¾ cup) crumbled
  feta cheese
1 tablespoon oregano leaves
2 eggs
60 ml (2 fl oz/¼ cup) pouring (whipping) cream
lemon wedges, to serve

1 Preheat the oven to 210°C (415°F/ Gas 6–7). Squeeze out the excess liquid from the spinach.

2 Place the pastry on a baking tray and spread the spinach in the middle, leaving a 3 cm (1¼ inch) border around the edge. Sprinkle the garlic over the spinach and pile the haloumi and feta on top. Sprinkle with the oregano and season well. Cut a short slit into each corner of the pastry, then tuck each side of the pastry over to form a border around the filling.

3 Lightly beat the eggs with the cream and carefully pour the egg mixture over the filling. Bake for 30–40 minutes, or until the pastry is golden and the filling has set. Serve with the lemon wedges.

THAI THREE MUSHROOM TART

Serves 8

375 g (13 oz) block of frozen puff pastry, thawed
1 teaspoon sesame oil
2 teaspoons vegetable oil
150 g (5½ oz) shiitake mushrooms, trimmed
150 g (5½ oz) button mushrooms, halved
150 g (5½ oz) oyster mushrooms, halved
125 ml (4 fl oz/½ cup) coconut milk
1 lemon grass stem, white part only, chopped
1½ teaspoons grated fresh ginger
1 garlic clove, chopped
2 tablespoons chopped coriander (cilantro)
1 egg
1 tablespoon plain (all-purpose) flour
1 spring onion (scallion), sliced diagonally

1 Preheat the oven to 210°C (415°F/Gas 6–7). Grease a round, 25 cm (10 inch) loose-based flan (tart) tin, or a shallow 19 x 28 cm (7½ x 11¼ inch) rectangular one. Roll out the pastry to line the base and sides of the tin and trim off any excess. Prick all over with a fork, then bake for 20 minutes, or until crisp. Leave to cool (gently press down the pastry if it has puffed too high). Reduce the oven temperature to 200°C (400°F/Gas 6).

2 Heat the oils in a pan. Add the shiitake and button mushrooms and stir until lightly browned. Add the oyster mushrooms, then leave to cool. Pour away any liquid.

3 In a food processor, blend the coconut milk, lemon grass, ginger, garlic and coriander until fairly smooth. Add the egg and flour and blend in short bursts until combined. Season well.

4 Pour into the pastry case, top with the mushrooms and spring onion and bake for 30 minutes, or until the filling has set.

SWEET POTATO FILO PIE

Serves 8

750 g (1 lb 10 oz) orange sweet potato, peeled and cut into 2.5 cm (1 inch) dice
12 small French shallots, peeled
6 new potatoes, peeled and halved
125 ml (4 fl oz/½ cup) olive oil
1 teaspoon sweet paprika
1 teaspoon ground ginger
2 teaspoons ground cumin
¼ teaspoon ground cinnamon
100 g (3½ oz/2¼ cups) baby English spinach
60 g (2¼ oz/½ cup) sultanas (golden raisins)
85 g (3 oz/⅔ cup) slivered almonds, toasted
100 g (3½ oz/¾ cup) pistachio kernels, chopped
a large handful of coriander (cilantro) leaves, chopped
2½ tablespoons golden syrup or maple syrup
80 g (2¾ oz/⅓ cup) plain yoghurt
400 g (14 oz) tin chickpeas, rinsed and drained
3 garlic cloves, finely chopped
a pinch of cayenne pepper
60 ml (2 fl oz/¼ cup) lemon juice
9 sheets of filo pastry
125 g (4½ oz) butter, melted

1 Preheat the oven to 200°C (400°F/Gas 6). Put the sweet potato, shallots and potatoes in a large roasting tin. Combine the olive oil and spices, then pour over the vegetables and toss to coat. Roast for 25 minutes, then turn the vegetables and roast for 15 minutes more. Remove from the oven and reduce the temperature to 180°C (350°F/Gas 4). Put a baking tray in the oven to heat.
2 Toss the spinach and sultanas through the vegetables, then set aside for 5 minutes for the spinach to wilt. Tip into a large bowl and add the nuts and coriander.
3 In a food processor, blend 2 tablespoons of the golden syrup with the yoghurt, chickpeas, garlic, cayenne pepper and lemon juice until smooth. Season to taste, add to the vegetables and mix through.
4 Cover the filo pastry with a damp cloth. Brush a 28 x 21 cm (11¼ x 8¼ inch) loose-based flan (tart) tin with melted butter. Brush a sheet of filo with butter and loosely lay it on a point over one end of the tin, leaving a 10 cm (4 inch) overhang; don't push the pastry into the sides of the tin. Brush another sheet with butter and lay it at the opposite end of the tin. Brush a third sheet with butter and lay it in the middle. Repeat twice more with the remaining filo pastry.
5 Pile the filling mixture in the centre. Starting in the middle, bring the opposite sides of the filo together, encasing the filling tightly, but with the filo sticking up. Brush with more butter and drizzle with remaining golden syrup. Place on the hot baking tray and bake for 30 minutes, or until golden. Cool for 5 minutes before serving.

TOMATO TARTE TATIN

Serves 4

12 roma (plum) tomatoes
80 ml (2½ fl oz/⅓ cup) olive oil
3 red onions, finely sliced
2 garlic cloves, finely sliced
1 tablespoon balsamic vinegar
1 teaspoon soft brown sugar
a small handful of finely shredded basil
60 g (2¼ oz/½ cup) crumbled goat's cheese
1 sheet of frozen butter puff pastry, thawed

1 Preheat the oven to 150°C (300°F/ Gas 2). Score a cross in the base of each tomato. Place in a heatproof bowl and cover with boiling water. Leave for 30 seconds, then plunge into cold water and peel the skin away from the cross.
2 Place a rack on a baking tray. Cut the tomatoes in half lengthways, season well with sea salt and freshly ground black

pepper, then place on the rack, cut side up. Transfer to the oven and bake for 3 hours.
3 Meanwhile, heat 2 tablespoons of the olive oil in a heavy-based saucepan. Add the onion and cook over very low heat for 1 hour, or until caramelised, stirring often.
4 When the tomatoes are done, remove them from the oven and increase the temperature to 200°C (400°F/Gas 6).
5 Heat the remaining olive oil in a 20 cm (8 inch) ovenproof frying pan over medium heat. Add the garlic, vinegar, sugar and 1 tablespoon water and stir until the sugar has dissolved. Remove from the heat.
6 Arrange the tomatoes in the pan in one layer, cut side up. Top with the onion, basil and goat's cheese. Cover with the pastry sheet, then trim the edges and tuck the pastry down around the side of the pan.
7 Bake for 25–30 minutes, or until the pastry is golden. Invert the tart onto a plate, cool to room temperature and serve.

A deeply adored comfort food, pasta comes in myriad shapes and sizes, from the skinniest spaghettini and delicate angel hair to great wide sheets of lasagne, plump little parcels of ravishable ravioli and springy globs of gnocchi, to hollow tubes and chunky spirals designed to soak up a sumptuous, slurpy sauce. The sauces too are just as diverse, so the humble pasta can rise to nearly any culinary challenge. Whether you're scratching around for a throw-together meal ransacked from the depths of the pantry to more refined dinner-party fare, the pasta world is replete with possibilities. The following recipes are just a starting point from which to launch into creations of your own invention—truly, pasta dishes are endlessly variable.

PASTA

ARTICHOKE RISONI

Serves 4

30 g (1 oz) butter
1 tablespoon olive oil
2 fennel bulbs, sliced
350 g (12 oz) marinated artichoke hearts,
    drained and chopped
300 ml (10½ fl oz) pouring (whipping) cream
1 tablespoon dijon mustard
60 ml (2 fl oz/¼ cup) dry white wine
50 g (1¾ oz/½ cup) grated parmesan cheese
375 g (13 oz) risoni
125 g (4½ oz/2 cups) shredded English spinach
toasted Italian bread, to serve

1 Heat the butter and olive oil in a frying pan. Sauté the fennel over medium heat for 20 minutes, or until soft and caramelised.
2 Add the artichoke and cook for a further 5–10 minutes. Stir in the cream, mustard, wine and parmesan and bring to the boil, then reduce the heat and simmer for 5 minutes.
3 Meanwhile, cook the risoni in a large saucepan of rapidly boiling salted water until *al dente*, then drain well.
4 Add the risoni and spinach to the sauce and cook until the spinach has just wilted. Serve with toasted Italian bread.

PAPPARDELLE WITH ZUCCHINI FLOWERS AND GOAT'S CHEESE

Serves 4

175 g (6 oz/¾ cup) ricotta cheese
125 ml (4 fl oz/½ cup) thick (double/heavy) cream
2 teaspoons thyme
¼ teaspoon ground nutmeg
ground white pepper, to taste
300 g (10½ oz) dried pappardelle, or 400 g (14 oz) fresh pappardelle or other ribbon pasta
60 ml (2 fl oz/¼ cup) olive oil
4 small zucchini (courgettes), cut into thin batons
16 zucchini (courgette) flowers (see Note)
plain (all-purpose) flour, for dusting
100 g (3½ oz) soft goat's cheese

1 Put the ricotta, cream, thyme and nutmeg in a bowl. Season liberally with sea salt and white pepper and mix well. Cover and set aside in a cool place for 1 hour, but do not refrigerate.

2 Cook the pasta in a large saucepan of rapidly boiling salted water until *al dente*.

3 Meanwhile, heat the olive oil in a large frying pan. Sauté the zucchini over medium–high heat for 4 minutes, or until lightly golden. Remove with a slotted spoon and drain on paper towels.

4 Dust the zucchini flowers with flour, shake off the excess and fry for 1 minute, or until lightly golden.

5 Drain the pasta and place in a large bowl. Add the zucchini, zucchini flowers and ricotta mixture and toss lightly. Crumble the goat's cheese over the top and serve.

Note Before using zucchini flowers, discard any attached baby zucchini, remove and discard the stamen from inside the flower, then wash the flower and make sure it does not harbour any insects.

BEETROOT RAVIOLI WITH SAGE BURNT BUTTER SAUCE

Serves 4

340 g (12 oz) jar of baby beetroot (beets) in
   sweet vinegar
40 g (1½ oz/⅓ cup) grated parmesan cheese,
   plus extra shaved parmesan, to serve
250 g (9 oz/1 cup) ricotta cheese
fine polenta, for sprinkling
750 g (1 lb 10 oz) fresh lasagne sheets
   (or 4 fresh lasagne sheets)
200 g (7 oz) butter, chopped
3 tablespoons torn sage leaves
2 garlic cloves, crushed

1 Drain the beetroot, then grate into a
bowl. Mix in the parmesan and ricotta.
2 Line a tray with baking paper and
sprinkle with polenta.
3 Lay a sheet of pasta on a work surface.
Place evenly spaced tablespoons of the
beetroot mixture on the pasta to give
12 mounds (four across and three down).
Flatten the mounds slightly. Lightly brush
the edges of the pasta sheet and around
each pile of filling with water. Place a
second pasta sheet over the top and gently
press around each mound to seal and
enclose the filling. Using a pasta wheel or
sharp knife, cut the pasta into 12 ravioli,
and set them on the prepared tray. Repeat
with the remaining filling and pasta to
make 24 ravioli. Gently remove any
air bubbles after cutting so they are
completely sealed.
4 Cook the ravioli in a large saucepan of
rapidly boiling salted water until *al dente*.
Drain well, divide among shallow serving
bowls and keep warm.
5 Cook the butter in a pan for 3 minutes, or
until golden brown. Remove from the heat,
stir in the sage and garlic and spoon over the
ravioli. Top with shaved parmesan and serve.

CONCHIGLIE RIGATE WITH SPRING VEGETABLES

Serves 4

310 g (11 oz/2 cups) frozen peas
310 g (11 oz/2 cups) frozen broad (fava) beans
80 ml (2½ fl oz/⅓ cup) olive oil
6 spring onions (scallions), cut into 3 cm
    (1¼ inch) lengths
2 garlic cloves, finely chopped
250 ml (9 fl oz/1 cup) vegetable stock
12 thin asparagus spears, cut into 5 cm
    (2 inch) lengths
500 g (1 lb 2 oz) conchiglie rigate or other
    shell pasta
½ teaspoon finely grated lemon zest
60 ml (2 fl oz/¼ cup) lemon juice
shaved parmesan cheese, to serve

1 Bring a saucepan of water to the boil. Add the peas and cook for 1–2 minutes, or until tender. Remove with a slotted spoon and plunge into cold water. Add the broad beans to the same saucepan and cook for 1–2 minutes, then drain and plunge into cold water. Drain the peas and broad beans, then slip the skins off the beans. Set aside.

2 Heat 2 tablespoons of the olive oil in a frying pan. Sauté the spring onion and garlic over medium heat for 2 minutes, or until softened. Pour in the stock and cook for 5 minutes, or until slightly reduced.

3 Add the asparagus and cook for a further 3–4 minutes, or until bright green and just tender. Stir in the peas and broad beans and cook for 2–3 minutes, or until heated through.

4 Meanwhile, cook the pasta in a large saucepan of rapidly boiling salted water until al dente. Drain, then return to the pan.

5 Toss the remaining olive oil through the pasta, then add the vegetables, lemon zest and lemon juice. Season and toss together well. Serve topped with shaved parmesan.

FETTUCINE WITH CREAMY SPINACH AND ROAST TOMATO

Serves 4–6

6 roma (plum) tomatoes
40 g (1½ oz) butter
1 onion, chopped
2 garlic cloves, crushed
500 g (1 lb 2 oz) English spinach, trimmed
250 ml (9 fl oz/1 cup) vegetable stock
125 ml (4 fl oz/½ cup) thick (double/heavy) cream
500 g (1 lb 2 oz) fresh spinach fettucine
50 g (1¾ oz/½ cup) shaved parmesan cheese

1 Preheat the oven to 220°C (425°F/Gas 7). Cut the tomatoes in half lengthways, then cut each half into three wedges. Place on a lightly greased baking tray and roast for 30–35 minutes, or until softened.

2 Meanwhile, melt the butter in a large frying pan. Sauté the onion and garlic over medium heat for 5 minutes, or until the onion is soft. Add the spinach, stock and cream, increase the heat to high and bring to the boil. Simmer rapidly for 5 minutes.

3 Meanwhile, cook the pasta in a large saucepan of rapidly boiling salted water until *al dente*. Drain well and return to the pan.

4 Remove the spinach mixture from the heat and season well. Cool slightly, then blend in a food processor until smooth. Toss through the pasta until well coated. Divide among serving bowls, top with the roasted tomatoes and parmesan and serve.

FREEFORM PUMPKIN, SPINACH AND RICOTTA LASAGNE

Serves 4

60 ml (2 fl oz/¼ cup) olive oil
1.5 kg (3 lb 5 oz) butternut pumpkin (squash), cut into 1.5 cm (⅝ inch) dice
500 g (1 lb 2 oz) English spinach, trimmed
4 fresh lasagne sheets (12 x 20 cm/4½ x 8 inches)
500 g (1 lb 2 oz/2 cups) ricotta cheese
2 tablespoons thick (double/heavy) cream
25 g (1 oz/¼ cup) grated parmesan cheese
a pinch of ground nutmeg

1 Heat the olive oil in a non-stick frying pan. Add the pumpkin and toss over medium heat. Cook, stirring occasionally, for 15 minutes, or until tender (don't worry if the pumpkin is slightly mashed). Season with sea salt and freshly ground black pepper and keep warm.

2 Blanch the spinach in a large saucepan of boiling water for 30 seconds, or until wilted. Using a slotted spoon, transfer to a bowl of cold water. Drain well, squeeze out as much excess water as possible, then finely chop.
3 Add the lasagne to the pan of boiling water and cook, stirring occasionally, until *al dente*. Drain and lay the sheets side by side on a clean tea towel (dish towel). Cut each sheet widthways into thirds.
4 Put the ricotta, cream, parmesan, spinach and nutmeg in a small saucepan. Stir over low heat for 2–3 minutes, or until warmed through.
5 Working quickly to assemble, place a lasagne strip on each serving plate. Top with half the pumpkin, then another lasagne strip. Top with half the ricotta mixture, then a final lasagne strip. Arrange the remaining pumpkin and ricotta mixture over the top. Sprinkle with sea salt and freshly ground black pepper and serve.

SPICED CARROT AND FETA GNOCCHI
Serves 6–8

1 kg (2 lb 4 oz) carrots
200 g (7 oz/1⅓ cups) crumbled feta cheese
280 g (10 oz/2¼ cups) plain (all-purpose) flour
¼ teaspoon ground nutmeg
¼ teaspoon garam masala
1 egg, lightly beaten

Minted cream sauce
30 g (1 oz) butter
2 spring onions (scallions), sliced
2 garlic cloves, crushed
250 ml (9 fl oz/1 cup) pouring (whipping) cream
2 tablespoons shredded mint

1 Cut the carrots into large pieces and steam, boil or microwave until tender. Drain and allow to cool slightly.
2 Put the carrot in a food processor, add the feta and blend until smooth. Transfer to a large bowl and sift the flour and spices over the top. Add the egg and mix to form a soft dough. Lightly coat your fingertips with flour and shape teaspoons of the mixture into flat circles. Place on a lightly floured surface and set aside.
3 To make the minted cream sauce, melt the butter in a frying pan and sauté the spring onion and garlic over medium heat for 3 minutes, or until the garlic is soft and golden. Stir in the cream, bring to the boil, then reduce the heat and simmer for 3 minutes, or until thickened slightly. Remove from the heat and keep warm.
4 Meanwhile, cook the gnocchi, in batches, in a large saucepan of boiling salted water for 2 minutes, or until they float to the surface. Transfer to warmed serving plates using a slotted spoon. Stir the mint through the sauce, drizzle over the gnocchi and serve.
Note This mixture is not as firm as some other gnocchi recipes.

SPAGHETTI WITH CHILLI, LEMON AND ROCKET

Serves 4

375 g (13 oz) spaghetti
100 g (3½ oz) rocket (arugula), finely shredded
1 tablespoon finely chopped lemon zest
1 garlic clove, finely chopped
1 small red chilli, seeded and finely chopped
1 teaspoon chilli oil
125 ml (4 fl oz/½ cup) extra virgin olive oil
55 g (2 oz/½ cup) finely grated parmesan
  cheese

1 Cook the pasta in a large saucepan of rapidly boiling salted water until *al dente.*
2 Meanwhile, put the rocket, lemon zest, garlic, chilli, chilli oil, olive oil and two-thirds of the parmesan in a large bowl and mix together gently.
3 Drain the pasta well, then add to the rocket mixture and toss together. Season well with sea salt and freshly ground black pepper and serve sprinkled with the remaining parmesan.
Variation You can substitute basil leaves for the rocket if you prefer.

BALSAMIC CAPSICUM ON ANGEL HAIR

Serves 4

2 red capsicums (peppers)
2 yellow capsicums (peppers)
2 green capsicums (peppers)
4 garlic cloves, crushed
2 tablespoons orange juice
80 ml (2½ fl oz/⅓ cup) balsamic vinegar
300 g (10½ oz) angel hair pasta
100 g (3½ oz/heaped ¾ cup) crumbled
   goat's cheese
a large handful of basil

1 Cut the capsicums into large flat pieces and remove the seeds and membranes. Cook, skin side up, under a hot grill (broiler) until the skins blister and blacken. Leave to cool in a plastic bag, then peel away the skin and cut the flesh into thin strips. Place in a bowl with the garlic, orange juice and vinegar. Mix gently and set aside.

2 Cook the pasta in a large saucepan of rapidly boiling salted water until *al dente*. Drain well and return to the pan. Add the capsicum mixture and gently toss.

3 Serve topped with goat's cheese and basil and a sprinkling of freshly cracked black pepper.

FUSILLI WITH BROCCOLINI, CHILLI AND OLIVES

Serves 4

60 ml (2 fl oz/¼ cup) olive oil
1 onion, finely chopped
3 garlic cloves, crushed
1 teaspoon chilli flakes
700 g (1 lb 9 oz) broccolini, cut into 1 cm
   (½ inch) pieces
125 ml (4 fl oz/½ cup) vegetable stock
400 g (14 oz) fusilli pasta
90 g (3¼ oz/¾ cup) pitted black olives, chopped
3 tablespoons finely chopped parsley
25 g (1 oz/¼ cup) grated pecorino cheese
2 tablespoons shredded basil

1 Heat the olive oil in a large non-stick frying pan. Sauté the onion, garlic and chilli over medium heat for 5 minutes, or until the onion has softened. Add the broccolini and sauté for a further 5 minutes. Pour in the stock, then cover and cook for 5 minutes.

2 Meanwhile, cook the pasta in a large saucepan of rapidly boiling salted water until *al dente*. Drain well and keep warm.

3 When the broccolini is tender, remove the mixture from the heat. Add to the pasta with the olives, parsley, pecorino and basil. Season well with sea salt and freshly ground black pepper, gently toss together and serve.

TAGLIATELLE WITH GREEN OLIVES AND EGGPLANT

Serves 4

500 g (1 lb 2 oz) tagliatelle
2 tablespoons olive oil
2 garlic cloves, crushed
1 large eggplant (aubergine), cut into small dice
175 g (6 oz/1 cup) green olives, chopped
  and pitted
125 ml (4 fl oz/½ cup) lemon juice
2 tablespoons chopped flat-leaf (Italian) parsley
50 g (1¾ oz/½ cup) grated parmesan cheese

1 Cook the pasta in a large saucepan of rapidly boiling salted water until *al dente*. Drain and return to the pan.

2 Meanwhile, heat the olive oil in a frying pan. Add the garlic and stir for 30 seconds, then add the eggplant and cook over medium heat for 6 minutes, or until tender, stirring frequently. Stir in the olives and lemon juice and season to taste with sea salt and freshly ground black pepper.
3 Add the sauce to the pasta and toss together well. Serve in warmed bowls, sprinkled with the parsley and parmesan.
Note If you prefer, the eggplant can be salted to draw out any bitter juices. Sprinkle the cut eggplant liberally with salt and leave to stand for 30 minutes. Rinse well before using.

HERB-FILLED RAVIOLI WITH SAGE BUTTER

Serves 4

300 g (10½ oz) plain (all-purpose) flour
3 eggs, beaten
60 ml (2 fl oz/¼ cup) olive oil
250 g (9 oz/1 cup) ricotta cheese
2 tablespoons grated parmesan cheese, plus
    extra shaved parmesan, to serve
2 teaspoons snipped chives
1 tablespoon chopped flat-leaf (Italian) parsley
2 teaspoons chopped basil
1 teaspoon chopped thyme
200 g (7 oz) butter
12 sage leaves

1 Sift the flour into a bowl and make a well in the centre. Gradually mix in the eggs and olive oil. Turn out onto a floured surface and knead for 6 minutes, or until smooth. Cover with plastic wrap and leave for 30 minutes.
2 Lightly flour a large work surface. Cut the dough into four even portions. Using a floured long rolling pin, roll out one piece from the centre to the edge, always rolling outwards and rotating the dough often. Fold the dough in half and roll it out again. Continue seven times to make a smooth circle of pasta about 5 mm (¼ inch) thick. Roll this sheet out quickly and smoothly to a thickness of 2.5 mm (⅛ inch). Repeat to make four sheets of pasta, two slightly larger than the others. Cover with a cloth.
3 Combine the ricotta, parmesan and herbs and season to taste. Spread out a small pasta sheet and place heaped teaspoons of the filling in rows at 5 cm (2 inch) intervals. Brush a little water between the mounds. Place a large sheet on top and firmly press together around the mounds. Cut the ravioli using a pasta wheel or sharp knife and place on a lightly floured baking tray. Repeat with the remaining dough and filling.
4 Melt the butter over low heat in a small saucepan, without stirring. Carefully pour the clear butter into a container and discard the white sediment. Return the butter to a clean pan and heat gently. Add the sage and cook over medium heat until crisp but not brown. Remove and drain on paper towels, reserving the warm butter.
5 Cook the ravioli in batches in a large pan of salted simmering water for 5–6 minutes, or until tender (make sure the water isn't rapidly boiling or the ravioli will split).
6 Serve topped with the warm sage butter, the sage leaves and shaved parmesan.

CREAMY TAGLIATELLE OF ROOT VEGETABLES

Serves 4

4 large carrots, peeled
2 large parsnips, peeled
185 ml (6 fl oz/¾ cup) whipping (pouring) cream
1 garlic clove, crushed
35 g (1¼ oz/⅓ cup) grated parmesan cheese
2 tablespoons snipped chives

1 Bring a large saucepan of salted water to the boil. Using a vegetable peeler, peel the carrots and parsnips into long thin strips, until you reach the hard core. Blanch the carrot and parsnip strips in the boiling water for 1 minute. Drain, then refresh in a bowl of iced water.

2 Pour the cream into a saucepan. Add the garlic and stir over medium heat until the cream has reduced to about 100 ml (3½ fl oz). Stir in half the parmesan and half the chives, then season well with sea salt and freshly ground black pepper.

3 Drain the vegetable strips thoroughly, then add to the cream mixture and stir gently over medium heat for 2 minutes, or until warmed through.

4 Serve garnished with the remaining parmesan and chives.

BAKED SWEET POTATO AND WATERCRESS GNOCCHI

Serves 6

700 g (1 lb 9 oz) orange sweet potato
300 g (10½ oz) all-purpose potatoes,
 such as desiree
350 g (12 oz/2¾ cups) plain (all-purpose) flour
35 g (1¼ oz/⅓ cup) grated parmesan cheese,
 plus extra, to serve
30 g (1 oz/1 cup) watercress leaves,
 finely chopped
1 garlic clove, crushed
60 g (2¼ oz) butter
2 tablespoons chopped parsley

1 Wash the sweet potato and potatoes. Boil, steam or microwave them in their skins until tender, then drain. When cool enough to handle, peel them and then press through a potato ricer or mouli into a bowl. Add the flour, parmesan, watercress and garlic and season well.

2 Gently bring the mixture together with your hands until a soft dough forms—don't overwork the dough or the gnocchi will be tough. Portion into walnut-sized pieces and press into a traditional 'gnocchi' shape using the back of a fork.

3 Melt the butter in a large shallow roasting tin. Preheat the grill (broiler) to medium–high.

4 Cook the gnocchi in a large saucepan of boiling salted water for 2 minutes, or until they float to the surface. Scoop out with a slotted spoon, draining the water off well.

5 Place the gnocchi in the roasting tin and toss gently in the butter. Grill for 5 minutes, or until lightly golden. Serve sprinkled with the parsley and some extra parmesan.

FETTUCCINE WITH PRIMAVERA SAUCE

Serves 4–6

500 g (1 lb 2 oz) fettuccine
15 green beans, trimmed and cut into
  shorter lengths
155 g (5½ oz/1 cup) frozen broad (fava) beans
40 g (1½ oz) butter
1 celery stalk, finely sliced
155 g (5½ oz/1 cup) frozen peas
310 ml (10¾ fl oz/1¼ cups) pouring
  (whipping) cream
50 g (1¾ oz/½ cup) grated parmesan cheese

1 Cook the pasta in a large saucepan of rapidly boiling salted water until *al dente*. Drain well and return to the pan.
2 Meanwhile, bring another saucepan of water to the boil. Add the green beans and cook for 2 minutes, or until tender. Remove with a slotted spoon and plunge into cold water. Add the broad beans to the same saucepan and cook for 1–2 minutes, then drain and plunge into cold water. Drain the green beans and broad beans, then slip the skins off the beans. Set aside.
3 Melt the butter in a frying pan. Sauté the celery for 2 minutes, then add the peas and cream and cook for 3 minutes. Stir in the green beans and broad beans and cook for a further 2–3 minutes, or until heated through. Add the parmesan and season with sea salt and freshly ground black pepper. Bring to the boil and cook for 1 minute.
4 Add the sauce to the pasta and toss to combine. Serve immediately in warmed pasta bowls.
Variation Try using other vegetables in this dish, such as leek, zucchini (courgettes), asparagus and sugar snap peas, and add some chopped dill or basil if you like.

ROASTED CHUNKY RATATOUILLE CANNELLONI

Serves 6–8

1 eggplant (aubergine)
2 zucchini (courgettes)
1 large red capsicum (pepper)
1 large green capsicum (pepper)
3–4 ripe roma (plum) tomatoes
12 unpeeled garlic cloves
60 ml (2 fl oz/¼ cup) olive oil
300 ml (10½ fl oz) tomato passata
  (puréed tomatoes)
350 g (12 oz) cannelloni tubes
3 tablespoons shredded basil
300 g (10½ oz/1¼ cups) ricotta cheese
100 g (3½ oz/⅔ cup) crumbled feta
  cheese
1 egg, lightly beaten
50 g (1¾ oz/½ cup) grated pecorino
  pepato cheese

1 Preheat the oven to 200°C (400°F/Gas 6). Cut the eggplant, zucchini, capsicums and tomatoes into 2 cm (¾ inch) dice. Place in a baking dish with the garlic cloves, drizzle with the olive oil and toss to coat. Bake for 1½ hours, or until the vegetables are tender and the tomatoes slightly mushy. Peel and lightly mash the garlic cloves.

2 Pour the passata over the base of a large baking dish. Spoon the roasted vegetable mixture into the cannelloni tubes and arrange in the baking dish.

3 In a bowl, mix together the basil, ricotta, feta and egg. Season well with sea salt and freshly ground black pepper and spoon the mixture over the cannelloni. Sprinkle with the pecorino and bake for 30 minutes, or until the cannelloni is soft. Serve hot.

PENNE WITH OLIVES AND TOMATO AND ONION JAM

Serves 4

60 ml (2 fl oz/¼ cup) olive oil
4 red onions, sliced
1 tablespoon soft brown sugar
2 tablespoons balsamic vinegar
2 x 400 g (14 oz) tins chopped tomatoes
500 g (1 lb 2 oz) penne rigate
150 g (5½ oz/1 cup) small pitted black olives,
   or pitted and halved kalamata olives
75 g (2½ oz/¾ cup) grated parmesan cheese

1 Heat the olive oil in a frying pan. Add the onion and sugar and cook over medium heat for 25–30 minutes, or until the onion has caramelised, stirring often.

2 Stir in the vinegar, then bring to the boil and cook for 5 minutes. Add the tomato, return to the boil, then reduce the heat to low–medium and simmer for 25 minutes, or until the tomato has reduced and become jam-like.

3 Meanwhile, cook the pasta in a large saucepan of rapidly boiling salted water until *al dente*. Drain well and return to the pan.

4 Add the tomato mixture and olives to the pasta and toss until well combined. Season with sea salt and freshly ground black pepper and serve sprinkled with the parmesan.

Note Caramelised onions will keep for a few days if covered with oil and refrigerated. The onions can be combined with goat's cheese to make a quick puff pastry tart or used as a pizza topping.

GIANT CONCHIGLIE WITH RICOTTA AND ROCKET

Serves 6

40 giant conchiglie (shell pasta)
600 ml (21 fl oz) bottled pasta sauce
2 tablespoons oregano, chopped
2 tablespoons basil

Filling
500 g (1 lb 2 oz/2 cups) ricotta cheese
100 g (3½ oz/1 cup) grated parmesan cheese
150 g (5½ oz) rocket (arugula), finely shredded
1 egg, lightly beaten
4 marinated artichokes, finely chopped
80 g (2¾ oz/½ cup) sun-dried tomatoes, finely chopped
95 g (3¼ oz/½ cup) sun-dried capsicum (pepper), finely chopped

Cheese sauce
60 g (2¼ oz) butter
30 g (1 oz/¼ cup) plain (all-purpose) flour
750 ml (26 fl oz/3 cups) milk
100 g (3½ oz/¾ cup) grated gruyère cheese
2 tablespoons chopped basil

1 Preheat the oven to 180°C (350°F/Gas 4). Cook the pasta in a large saucepan of rapidly boiling salted water until *al dente*. Drain and spread on two non-stick baking trays to stop them sticking together. Cover lightly with plastic wrap.

2 Put all the filling ingredients in a large bowl and mix together well. Spoon into the pasta shells, taking care not to overfill them or they will split.

3 To make the cheese sauce, melt the butter in a small saucepan over low heat. Add the flour and stir for 1 minute, or until golden and smooth. Remove from the heat and gradually stir in the milk. Return to the heat and stir constantly until the sauce boils and begins to thicken. Simmer for a further minute, then remove from the heat and stir in the gruyère and basil. Season to taste.

4 Spread 250 ml (9 fl oz/1 cup) of the cheese sauce over the base of a 3 litre (105 fl oz/12 cup) ovenproof dish. Arrange the pasta shells over the sauce, top with the remaining cheese sauce and bake for 30 minutes, or until the sauce is golden.

5 Pour the bottled pasta sauce into a saucepan and add the oregano. Cook over medium heat for 5 minutes, or until heated through. Divide the sauce among warmed serving plates, top with the pasta shells, sprinkle with the basil and serve.

This chapter is devoted to things that go flash in the pan, from darling little savoury pikelets (griddle cakes) and nibble-able fritters to pancakes big and small, with some ever-versatile omelettes and frittatas thrown in for good measure. All you need are some fresh organic eggs, a good hot frying pan and a few other basics and you're on your way. When the cupboards are a bit bare or you're too tired to dally long in the kitchen, an omelette or frittata makes a wonderfully nourishing meal with a simple salad or a chunk of rustic bread. And once you get into the swing of it you can always cut loose and jazz things up by adding or substituting your favourite herbs, spices and gourmet flourishes.

PANCAKES, FRITTERS & OMELETTES

CRISPY ASIAN NOODLE PANCAKES

Makes about 25

150 g (5½ oz) dried rice vermicelli noodles
a handful of chopped coriander (cilantro)
3 spring onions (scallions), finely sliced
1 small red chilli, finely chopped
1 lemon grass stem, white part only,
 finely chopped
1 garlic clove, crushed
vegetable oil, for pan-frying

1 Put the noodles in a bowl and cover with boiling water. Stand for 5 minutes, or until soft. Rinse under cold water, then drain and dry with paper towels.
2 Place the noodles in a bowl with the coriander, spring onion, chilli, lemon grass and garlic. Season to taste with sea salt and mix together well.
3 Heat about 2 m (¾ inch) oil in a heavy-based frying pan. Working in batches, add 2 tablespoons of the mixture, flatten with a spatula and fry over medium heat until crisp and golden on both sides. Drain on paper towels and keep warm while cooking the remaining pancakes. Serve warm, sprinkled with sea salt.

BROAD BEAN ROTOLLO WITH SALAD GREENS

Serves 4

750 g (1 lb 10 oz) fresh broad (fava) beans
4 eggs
4 egg yolks
2 teaspoons finely chopped mint
2 teaspoons finely chopped basil
20 g (¾ oz) butter
80 g (2¾ oz/1 cup) grated pecorino cheese

Salad
1 tablespoon chopped basil
80 ml (2½ fl oz/⅓ cup) olive oil
2 tablespoons lemon juice
1½ tablespoons pine nuts, toasted
2 baby cos (romaine) lettuces, trimmed
2 witlof (chicory/Belgian endive), trimmed

1 Shell the broad beans, add to a saucepan of salted boiling water and simmer for 2 minutes. Drain and plunge into iced water. Drain again, then peel off the skins.
2 Preheat the oven to 160°C (315°F/ Gas 2–3). In a bowl, beat the eggs, egg yolks, mint and basil together. Season with sea salt and freshly ground black pepper.

3 Melt half the butter in a 20 cm (8 inch) non-stick frying pan. Pour in half the egg mixture and cook over medium–high heat until the base has set but the top is still a little runny.
4 Slide the omelette onto a sheet of baking paper. Scatter half the pecorino and half the broad beans over the top. Using the baking paper as a guide, gently roll the omelette into a tight sausage. Roll the baking paper around the omelette and tie both ends with string to stop it unrolling. Place on a baking tray. Make another roll with the remaining ingredients and set on the baking tray. Bake for 8 minutes. Remove from the oven, set aside for 2–3 minutes, then unwrap and set aside to cool.
5 Meanwhile, make the salad. Put the basil, olive oil, lemon juice and 1 tablespoon of the pine nuts in a small food processor or blender and process to a smooth dressing. Season to taste. Put the lettuce and witlof leaves in a bowl, drizzle with 2 tablespoons of the dressing and toss together.
6 Slice the rotollo into rounds and place over the salad. Sprinkle with the remaining pine nuts. Drizzle the remaining dressing over the top and serve.

SPINACH AND LEEK FRITTERS

Makes 8

40 g (1½ oz) butter
40 g (1½ oz/¼ cup) pine nuts
1 leek, white part only, thinly sliced
100 g (3½ oz/2¼ cups) baby English spinach
  leaves, chopped
3 eggs
1 egg yolk
1 tablespoon pouring (whipping) cream
75 g (2½ oz/¾ cup) grated parmesan cheese
1 tablespoon chopped parsley
1 tablespoon olive oil
snipped chives, to garnish

1 Melt half the butter in a frying pan. Sauté the pine nuts and leek over medium heat for 3 minutes, or until the pine nuts are golden. Add the spinach and cook for 1 minute, then remove the mixture from the pan and allow to cool a little. Wipe the pan clean.

2 In a large bowl, whisk together the eggs, egg yolk and cream. Stir in the parmesan, parsley and spinach mixture. Season well.

3 Melt half the remaining butter and half the oil in the frying pan. Place four 5–7 cm (2–2¾ inch) egg rings in the pan, then pour 60 ml (2 fl oz/¼ cup) of the spinach mixture into each. Cook over low heat for 2–3 minutes, or until the base is set. Gently flip and cook the other side for 2–3 minutes, or until firm. Transfer to a plate, slide out of the egg rings and keep warm. Repeat to make another four fritters. Serve hot, garnished with chives.

CAULIFLOWER FRITTERS

Serves 4–6

55 g (2 oz/½ cup) besan (chickpea flour)
½ teaspoon sea salt, plus extra, for sprinkling
2 teaspoons ground cumin
1 teaspoon ground coriander
1 teaspoon ground turmeric
a pinch of cayenne pepper, plus extra,
   for sprinkling
1 egg, lightly beaten
1 egg yolk
vegetable oil, for deep-frying
600 g (1 lb 5 oz) cauliflower, cut into
   bite-sized florets

1 Sift the besan, sea salt and spices into a bowl and make a well in the centre.
2 In a bowl, lightly whisk together the egg, egg yolk and 60 ml (2 fl oz/¼ cup) water. Pour into the flour mixture and whisk until smooth. Cover with plastic wrap and leave to stand for 30 minutes.
3 Fill a deep heavy-based saucepan one-third full of oil and heat to 180°C (350°F), or until a cube of bread dropped into the oil browns in 15 seconds.
4 Working in batches, dip the cauliflower florets into the batter, allowing the excess to drain off. Deep-fry for 3–4 minutes per batch, or until puffed and browned. Drain on paper towels and keep warm while making the remaining fritters. Serve hot, sprinkled with sea salt and cayenne pepper.

PARSNIP AND PECAN FRITTERS

Serves 4

Dipping sauce
200 g (7 oz/heaped ¾ cup) sour cream
1 tablespoon finely snipped chives
1 teaspoon lemon juice
2 tablespoons sweet chilli sauce
3–4 drops of Tabasco sauce

375 g (13 oz) parsnips
1 egg
30 g (1 oz/¼ cup) plain (all-purpose) flour
1 tablespoon chopped parsley
50 g (1¾ oz) butter, melted
60 ml (2 fl oz/¼ cup) milk
60 g (2¼ oz/½ cup) roughly chopped pecans
a large pinch of cayenne pepper
250 ml (9 fl oz/1 cup) vegetable oil

1 Put the dipping sauce ingredients in a small serving bowl and mix together well. Cover with plastic wrap and refrigerate until required.

2 Peel the parsnips, cut into chunks and immediately place in a saucepan of salted water. Bring to the boil, then reduce the heat and simmer for 15–20 minutes, or until tender. Drain the parsnip, then purée using a potato ricer or mouli, discarding any tough bits. Transfer to a bowl and add the egg, flour, parsley, butter, milk, pecans and cayenne pepper. Season with sea salt and mix until combined.

3 Heat the oil in a heavy-based non-stick frying pan over medium heat. Drop in 1½ tablespoons of mixture at a time and flatten slightly with the back of a spoon. Cook, turning once, for 15–20 seconds, or until golden. Remove with a slotted spoon, drain on paper towels and keep warm while cooking the remaining fritters. Serve hot, with the dipping sauce.

CHINESE OMELETTES WITH MUSHROOM SAUCE

Serves 2–4

6 dried Chinese mushrooms
vegetable oil, for pan-frying
2 garlic cloves, crushed
250 ml (9 fl oz/1 cup) vegetable stock
1 tablespoon vegetarian oyster sauce
2 teaspoons soy sauce
1 teaspoon sugar
2 spring onions (scallions), sliced diagonally
2 teaspoons cornflour (cornstarch), mixed
   with 1 tablespoon water

Omelettes
6 eggs, lightly beaten
4 spring onions (scallions), thinly sliced
1 small red capsicum (pepper), thinly sliced
90 g (3¼ oz/1 cup) bean sprouts, tails trimmed
2 teaspoons sesame oil
1 teaspoon soy sauce

1 Soak the dried Chinese mushrooms in boiling water for 15 minutes. Drain, cut off the stems and thinly slice the caps. Set aside.
2 Meanwhile, make the omelettes. Crack the eggs into a bowl and lightly beat. Stir in the spring onion, capsicum, bean sprouts, sesame oil and soy sauce. Season well.
3 Heat a wok to very hot. Add 2 teaspoons vegetable oil and swirl to coat the side. Add a quarter of the egg mixture, swirl to coat evenly and cook over high heat for 1–2 minutes, or until almost set. Turn and cook for 1 minute, or until browned underneath, then remove and keep warm. Repeat to make four omelettes, adding more oil if necessary.
4 Reheat the wok over high heat, add another 1½ tablespoons oil and swirl. Add the mushrooms and garlic and sauté for 1 minute. Add the stock, vegetarian oyster sauce, soy sauce, sugar and spring onion. Bring to the boil, then reduce the heat and simmer for 1 minute. Stir in the cornflour mixture and simmer for 2 minutes, or until thickened slightly.
5 Divide the omelettes among warmed serving plates, drizzle with the mushroom sauce and serve.

HERBED PIKELETS WITH PEAR AND BLUE CHEESE TOPPING

Makes 36

125 g (4½ oz/1 cup) self-raising flour
2 eggs, lightly beaten
125 ml (4 fl oz/½ cup) milk
2 tablespoons finely chopped parsley
2 teaspoons finely chopped sage
melted butter, for brushing

Pear and blue cheese topping
100 g (3½ oz) mild creamy blue cheese
75 g (2½ oz/heaped ¼ cup) cream cheese
2 teaspoons brandy
1 large ripe green-skinned pear
30 g (1 oz/¼ cup) toasted walnuts, finely
    chopped
½ lemon
30 g (1 oz/1 bunch) chives, cut into 3–4 cm
    (1¼–1½ inch) lengths

1 Sift the flour into a bowl and make a well in the centre. Whisk together the eggs and milk and gradually add to the well in the flour, mixing in slowly. Add the parsley and sage and season well. Whisk until a smooth batter forms.

2 Heat a large non-stick frying pan over medium heat and brush with melted butter. Working in batches, drop heaped teaspoons of the batter into the pan and flatten with a spatula to give 5 cm (2 inch) circles. Cook until bubbles appear on the surface, then turn and brown the other side. Transfer to a wire rack to cool.

3 To make the pear and blue cheese topping, beat the cheeses and brandy together until smooth. Season with black pepper. Cut the pear in half and peel and core one half, then dice it into 5 mm (¼ inch) pieces, leaving the other half intact. Stir the diced pear and walnuts into the cheese mixture. Core the other pear half but do not peel it. Thinly slice the pear lengthways, then cut each slice into 2 cm (¾ inch) triangles, with the green skin on one side. Squeeze some lemon juice over the cut surfaces to stop them turning brown.

4 Spread 1 teaspoon of the topping on each pikelet. Arrange three pear triangles on top, garnish with chives and serve.

CORN FRITTERS

Serves 4–6

155 g (5½ oz/1¼ cups) plain (all-purpose) flour
1½ teaspoons baking powder
½ teaspoon ground coriander
¼ teaspoon ground cumin
125 g (4½ oz/⅔ cup) tinned corn kernels,
   drained well
125 g (4½ oz/½ cup) tinned creamed corn
125 ml (4 fl oz/½ cup) milk
2 eggs, lightly beaten
2 tablespoons snipped chives
125 ml (4 fl oz/½ cup) olive oil

Dipping sauce
1 tablespoon dark brown vinegar
3 teaspoons soft brown sugar
1 teaspoon sambal oelek or chilli sauce
1 tablespoon snipped chives
½ teaspoon soy sauce

1 Sift the flour, baking powder, ground coriander and cumin into a bowl, then make a well in the centre. Add the corn kernels, creamed corn, milk, eggs and chives. Season with sea salt and freshly ground pepper and stir until combined.
2 Put the dipping sauce ingredients in a small saucepan and stir over low heat for 1–2 minutes, or until the sugar has dissolved. Pour into a small serving bowl and set aside.
3 Heat the olive oil in a large non-stick frying pan. Drop heaped tablespoons of the batter into the pan, about 2 cm (¾ inch) apart, and flatten slightly. Cook over medium–high heat for 2 minutes, or until golden underneath. Turn and cook the other side. Drain on paper towels and keep warm while cooking the remaining fritters. Serve with the dipping sauce.

SESAME SHAPES
Makes about 30

185 g (6½ oz/1½ cups) self-raising flour
50 g (1¾ oz/⅓ cup) sesame seeds, toasted
2 teaspoons finely grated orange zest
2 eggs
2 teaspoons sesame oil
250 ml (9 fl oz/1 cup) milk
80 ml (2½ fl oz/⅓ cup) orange juice
butter or oil, for greasing
200 g (7 oz/heaped ¾ cup) cream cheese
2 tablespoons chopped coriander (cilantro) leaves
125 g (4½ oz/¾ cup) finely chopped sun-dried
 tomatoes

1 Sift the flour and a pinch of sea salt into
a bowl. Stir in the sesame seeds and orange
zest and make a well in the centre. Whisk
together the eggs, sesame oil, milk and
orange juice, then gradually whisk into the
well in the flour, using a fork. Mix to form

a smooth batter, then cover and leave to
stand for 15 minutes.
2 Heat a frying pan and brush lightly with
melted butter or oil. Pour 80 ml (2½ fl oz/
⅓ cup) batter into the pan and cook over
medium heat for 3–4 minutes, or until
bubbles appear on the surface. Turn and
cook the other side. Transfer to a plate and
cover with a tea towel (dish towel) while
cooking the remaining batter.
3 Working in multiples of three, use biscuit
(cookie) cutters to cut out various shapes
from the pancakes (you will be sandwiching
three of each shape together, so make sure
you have the right number of each).
4 Mix together the cream cheese and
coriander and use the mixture to sandwich
together three pancake shapes. Garnish
with the sun-dried tomato.
Note The pancakes can be cut into shapes
and joined a day ahead. Store in an airtight
container in the refrigerator.

INDONESIAN PEANUT FRITTERS

Makes 25

Dipping sauce
1 tablespoon rice vinegar
1 tablespoon mirin
2 tablespoons kecap manis
¼ teaspoon finely grated fresh ginger

175 g (6 oz/1 cup) rice flour
1 garlic clove, crushed
1 teaspoon ground turmeric
½ teaspoon ground cumin
1½ teaspoons ground coriander
3 teaspoons sambal oelek or chilli sauce
1 tablespoon finely chopped coriander
   (cilantro) leaves
200 ml (7 fl oz) coconut milk
200 g (7 oz/1¼ cups) roasted unsalted
   peanuts
vegetable oil, for deep-frying

1 Put the dipping sauce ingredients in a small serving bowl and mix together well. Cover and set aside until required.
2 Put the rice flour in a bowl with the garlic, ground spices, sambal oelek and coriander leaves. Season with sea salt and mix well. Gradually add the coconut milk and whisk until smooth. Stir in the peanuts and 50 ml (1¾ fl oz) hot water.
3 Fill a wok or deep heavy-based saucepan one-third full of oil and heat to 180°C (350°F), or until a cube of bread dropped into the oil browns in 15 seconds. Working in batches, cook level tablespoons of the batter for 1–2 minutes, or until golden. Drain on paper towels and keep warm while cooking the remaining fritters. Season well and serve hot, with the dipping sauce.

POTATO TORTILLA

Serves 6–8

500 g (1 lb 2 oz) potatoes, scrubbed and left
  unpeeled, then cut into 1 cm (½ inch) slices
60 ml (2 fl oz/¼ cup) olive oil
1 brown onion, thinly sliced
4 garlic cloves, thinly sliced
2 tablespoons finely chopped flat-leaf (Italian)
  parsley
6 eggs
1 teaspoon sea salt
1 teaspoon freshly ground black pepper

1 Put the potato slices in a large saucepan, cover with cold water and bring to the boil over high heat. Boil for 5 minutes, then drain and set aside.

2 Heat the olive oil in a deep-sided non-stick frying pan. Sauté the onion and garlic over medium heat for 5 minutes, or until the onion has softened.

3 Add the potato and parsley and stir to combine, then cook for 5 minutes, gently pressing the mixture down into the pan.

4 Crack the eggs into a bowl, add the salt and pepper and whisk together. Pour the mixture evenly over the potato. Cover and cook over low–medium heat for 20 minutes, or until the egg has just set.

5 Slide the tortilla onto a serving plate or serve directly from the pan. Serve hot.

VEGETABLE FRITTATA WITH HUMMUS AND BLACK OLIVES

Makes 30 pieces

2 large red capsicums (peppers)
600 g (1 lb 5 oz) orange sweet potato, peeled and cut into 1 cm (½ inch) slices
60 ml (2 fl oz/¼ cup) olive oil
2 leeks, white part only, finely sliced
2 garlic cloves, crushed
250 g (9 oz) zucchini (courgettes), thinly sliced
500 g (1 lb 2 oz) eggplant (aubergines), cut into 1 cm (½ inch) slices
8 eggs
2 tablespoons finely chopped basil
125 g (4½ oz/1¼ cups) grated parmesan cheese
200 g (7 oz/scant 1 cup) ready-made hummus
15 black olives, pitted and halved

1 Cut the capsicums into large flat pieces and remove the seeds and membranes. Cook, skin side up, under a hot grill (broiler) until the skins blister and blacken. Leave to cool in a plastic bag, then peel away the skin.

2 Cook the sweet potato in a saucepan of boiling water for 4–5 minutes, or until just tender. Drain and set aside.

3 Heat 1 tablespoon of the olive oil in a deep, round 23 cm (9 inch) frying pan with a flameproof handle. Sauté the leek and garlic over medium heat for 1 minute, or until softened. Add the zucchini and cook for 2 minutes, then remove from the pan.

4 Heat the remaining oil and cook the eggplant in batches for 2 minutes on each side, or until golden. Line the base of the pan with half the eggplant, then the leek. Cover with the capsicum, remaining eggplant and sweet potato.

5 Whisk together the eggs, basil, parmesan and some freshly ground black pepper. Pour the mixture over the vegetables and cook over low heat for 15 minutes, or until the egg has almost set.

6 Put the pan under a hot grill (broiler) for 2–3 minutes, or until the top is golden and cooked. Allow to cool, then invert onto a board. Cut into 30 squares and serve each one topped with hummus and half an olive.

POTATO AND HERB FRITTERS
Serves 4–6

620 g (1 lb 6 oz/4 cups) finely grated potato
185 g (6½ oz/1½ cups) finely grated
  sweet potato
3 tablespoons finely snipped chives
1 tablespoon finely chopped oregano
2 tablespoons finely chopped flat-leaf
  (Italian) parsley
2 eggs, lightly beaten
30 g (1 oz/¼ cup) plain (all-purpose) flour
1 tablespoon olive oil
250 g (9 oz/1 cup) light sour cream
dill sprigs, to garnish

1 Put the potato and sweet potato in a
bowl with the chives, oregano, parsley
and eggs. Sift the flour over the top and
stir with a wooden spoon until all the
ingredients are just combined.
2 Heat the olive oil in a heavy-based frying
pan over medium–high heat. Working in
batches, spoon heaped tablespoons of the
batter into the pan and cook for 4 minutes
on each side, or until golden. Drain on
paper towels and keep warm while
cooking the remaining fritters.
3 Serve topped with sour cream,
garnished with dill sprigs.

GRATIN OF CREPES WITH PUMPKIN, GOAT'S CHEESE AND SAGE

Serves 4

310 ml (10¾ fl oz/1¼ cups) milk
50 g (1¾ oz) butter
155 g (5½ oz/1¼ cups) plain (all-purpose) flour
3 eggs, lightly beaten
melted butter, for pan-frying
400 g (14 oz) butternut pumpkin (squash), peeled
    and cut into 24 slices about 1 cm (½ inch) thick
2 tablespoons olive oil
125 ml (4 fl oz/½ cup) vegetable oil
30 g (1 oz/1 bunch) sage, leaves plucked
250 g (9 oz) soft goat's cheese, diced
300 ml (10½ fl oz) pouring (whipping) cream
150 g (5½ oz/1¼ cups) grated fontina cheese

1 Gently heat the milk and butter in a small pan. Put the flour and a good pinch of sea salt in a large bowl and make a well in the centre. Add the eggs and slowly whisk in the warm milk mixture until completely smooth. Cover and stand for 15 minutes.
2 Put a non-stick frying pan over medium heat. When hot, drizzle some melted butter over the base. Add 60 ml (2 fl oz/¼ cup) of the batter and swirl to cover the base. Cook for 30 seconds, or until bubbles start to appear. Carefully turn and cook for 30 seconds, then remove to a plate. Continue to make 12 perfect crepes. (It may take a little practice to get the first few right, but there will be plenty of batter to spare.)
3 Heat a chargrill pan to medium. Toss the pumpkin in a large bowl with the olive oil. Chargrill in batches for 1–2 minutes, or until cooked, turning once. Set aside to cool.
4 Heat the oil in a small frying pan until it starts to haze. Quickly fry the sage leaves in batches until crisp. Drain on paper towels.
5 Heat the grill (broiler) to very high. Put two pumpkin slices, some goat's cheese and a few sage leaves in one quarter of each crepe, saving some sage to garnish. Fold up into neat triangles and divide among four ovenproof oval gratin dishes.
6 Gently heat the cream, then stir in the fontina and pour over the crepes. Set the dishes on a large baking tray, put the tray under the grill and cook for 3–5 minutes, or until the cheese is bubbling. Scatter with the reserved sage leaves and serve.

CAVOLO NERO AND RICOTTA FRITTATA

Serves 4

150 g (5½ oz) cavolo nero (Italian kale)
1 tablespoon olive oil
1 small onion, finely chopped
2 garlic cloves, crushed
200 g (7 oz/heaped ¾ cup) ricotta cheese
6 eggs
½ teaspoon ground mace or nutmeg
2 tablespoons finely grated parmesan cheese
crusty bread or thick toast, to serve

1 Cut the stems off the kale. Wash the leaves and dry thoroughly, then roughly chop.
2 Heat the olive oil in a 26 cm (10½ inch) non-stick frying pan. Sauté the onion over medium heat for 5 minutes, or until soft. Add the garlic and cook for a further minute, then add half the kale and toss until softened slightly. Add the remaining leaves and cook, stirring regularly, until soft and glossy dark green.
3 Put the ricotta in a large bowl and beat using electric beaters until smooth. Add the eggs and mace and beat on low until combined—don't worry if there are still a few little lumps of ricotta. Stir in the kale mixture and parmesan and season well.
4 Place the mixture back in the frying pan and cook over low–medium heat for 8 minutes, or until set underneath.
5 Cook the top of the frittata under a hot grill (broiler) for 3–4 minutes, or until set (test by pressing with a fork). Invert onto a plate and cut into eight wedges. Serve with crusty bread or thick toast.

CREAMY ZUCCHINI OMELETTE

Serves 2

2 zucchini (courgettes)
2 tablespoons olive oil
60 g (2¼ oz) butter
1 garlic clove, finely chopped
5 eggs
2 tablespoons pouring (whipping) cream
2 tablespoons grated parmesan cheese

1 Trim the zucchini and cut lengthways into very thin slices.
2 Heat half the olive oil and half the butter in a frying pan until the butter melts. Add the zucchini and sauté over medium heat for 2–3 minutes, or until golden. Stir in the garlic and cook for a further 30 seconds.

Using a slotted spoon, transfer the mixture to a plate. Wipe the pan clean.
3 Crack the eggs into a bowl. Add the cream, season with sea salt and freshly ground black pepper and whisk to combine.
4 Reheat the pan and add the remaining oil and butter. When the pan is very hot, pour in the eggs and stir with the back of a fork. Cook for 1 minute, tilting the pan and lifting the omelette edges occasionally to allow the uncooked egg to run underneath.
5 When the egg is partly set, spread the zucchini mixture over the top. Reduce the heat and cook for 5 minutes, or until set around the edges. Remove from the heat and sprinkle with the parmesan. Cover with a lid and leave to rest in the pan for 2 minutes. Slide onto a plate, fold into a semi-circle, cut in half and serve.

Here we come to the hearty staples that should form the basis of the vegetarian diet. Grains and pulses are rich in complex carbohydrates that are so crucial for health and vitality, as well as essential vitamins, minerals and fibre. Here are just a few ideas for ways to incorporate them into your daily menu, although you will also notice that grains and pulses play a large role in many other recipes in this book. Remember that combining grains such as rice, wheat, corn, couscous or quinoa with pulses such as beans (including soya products), peas, lentils and chickpeas will ensure your daily protein requirements are met, and the ways in which you can combine them is seemingly endless. These are dishes to really make a meal of!

RICE, GRAINS & PULSES

COUSCOUS PATTIES

Makes 4

185 g (6½ oz/1 cup) couscous
vegetable oil, for pan-frying
1 eggplant (aubergine), finely diced
1 onion, finely chopped
1 garlic clove, crushed
2 teaspoons ground cumin
2 teaspoons ground coriander
1 red capsicum (pepper), finely diced
2 tablespoons chopped coriander
   (cilantro) leaves
2 teaspoons grated lemon zest
2 teaspoons lemon juice
125 g (4½ oz/½ cup) plain yoghurt
1 egg, lightly beaten

1 Put the couscous in a bowl. Add 1 cup
(250 ml/9 fl oz) boiling water and leave for
10 minutes, or until all the water has been
absorbed. Fluff up the grains with a fork.

2 Heat 2 tablespoons of oil in a large
frying pan. Sauté the eggplant over
medium heat until soft and golden, then
transfer to a large bowl.
3 Heat another tablespoon of oil in the pan.
Add the onion, garlic and ground spices and
sauté over medium heat for 3–4 minutes, or
until the onion is soft. Remove from the
pan and add to the eggplant.
4 Heat another tablespoon of oil and sauté
the capsicum for 5 minutes, or until soft.
Add to the eggplant mixture. Add the
couscous and remaining ingredients,
season liberally and mix well.
5 Using damp hands, divide the mixture
into four portions and form into large
patties about 2 cm (¾ inch) thick. Cover
and refrigerate for 15 minutes.
6 Heat some more oil in a large frying pan.
Cook the patties over medium heat for
5 minutes on each side, or until golden.
Drain well and serve.

CAULIFLOWER PILAFF

Serves 6

200 g (7 oz/1 cup) basmati rice
2 tablespoons olive oil
1 large onion, thinly sliced
¼ teaspoon cardamom seeds
½ teaspoon ground turmeric
1 cinnamon stick
1 teaspoon cumin seeds
¼ teaspoon cayenne pepper
500 ml (17 fl oz/2 cups) vegetable stock
800 g (1 lb 12 oz) head of cauliflower,
    trimmed and cut into florets
4 tablespoons chopped coriander
    (cilantro) leaves

1 Put the rice in a sieve and rinse under cold running water. Set aside to drain.
2 Heat the olive oil in a saucepan with a tightly fitting lid. Sauté the onion over medium heat for 5 minutes, or until soft and lightly golden. Add the spices and cook, stirring, for 1 minute.
3 Add the rice and stir to coat in the spices. Add the stock and cauliflower and stir until combined.
4 Cover the pan and bring to the boil, then reduce the heat to very low and cook for 15 minutes, or until the rice and cauliflower are tender and all the stock has been absorbed. Stir in the coriander and serve.

PEARL BARLEY AND MUSHROOM PILAFF

Serves 4

330 g (11½ oz/1½ cups) pearl barley
3 dried shiitake mushrooms
625 ml (21½ fl oz/2½ cups) vegetable stock
125 ml (4 fl oz/½ cup) dry sherry
2 tablespoons olive oil
1 large onion, finely chopped
3 garlic cloves, crushed
2 tablespoons grated fresh ginger
1 teaspoon sichuan peppercorns, crushed
500 g (1 lb 2 oz) mixed fresh mushrooms, such
   as oyster, Swiss brown and enoki, sliced
375 g (13 oz/1 bunch) choy sum, trimmed
3 teaspoons kecap manis
1 teaspoon sesame oil

1 Soak the pearl barley in enough cold water to cover for at least 6 hours, or preferably overnight. Drain.

2 Soak the dried mushrooms in boiling water for 15 minutes. Strain, reserving 125 ml (4 fl oz/½ cup) of the soaking liquid. Discard the stalks and finely slice the caps.

3 Heat the stock and sherry in a small saucepan. Cover and keep at a low simmer.

4 Heat the olive oil in a large saucepan. Sauté the onion over medium heat for 5 minutes, or until softened. Add the garlic, ginger and peppercorns and cook for 1 minute.

5 Increase the heat and add the fresh mushrooms, reserving any enoki for later. Cook for 5 minutes, or until softened.

6 Add the barley, soaked dried mushrooms, reserved soaking liquid and hot stock, stirring well. Bring to the boil, then reduce the heat, cover and simmer for 35 minutes, or until all the liquid has evaporated.

7 Chop the choy sum and steam until just wilted, then add to the pilaff with the enoki mushrooms. Stir in the kecap manis and sesame oil and serve.

TOFU BURGERS

Serves 6

olive oil, for pan-frying
1 red onion, finely chopped
200 g (7 oz) Swiss brown mushrooms,
    finely chopped
350 g (12 oz) hard tofu
2 large garlic cloves, peeled
3 tablespoons chopped basil
200 g (7 oz/2 cups) dry wholemeal
    (whole-wheat) breadcrumbs, plus
    150 g (5½ oz/1½ cups), for coating
1 egg, lightly beaten
2 tablespoons balsamic vinegar
2 tablespoons sweet chilli sauce,
    plus extra, to serve
6 bread rolls
ready-made mayonnaise, to serve
100 g (3½ oz/⅔ cup) semi-dried
    (sun-blushed) tomatoes
a large handful of rocket (arugula) leaves

1 Heat 1 tablespoon of olive oil in a frying pan. Sauté the onion over medium heat for 5 minutes, or until soft. Add the mushrooms and cook for a further 2 minutes, then leave to cool slightly.
2 Put 250 g (9 oz) of the tofu in a food processor with the garlic and basil and blend until smooth. Tip into a large bowl and stir in the onion mixture, breadcrumbs, egg, vinegar and sweet chilli sauce. Grate the remaining tofu and fold it through the mixture, then refrigerate for 30 minutes.
3 Divide the tofu mixture into six even portions and form into patties, pressing together well. Coat them in the extra breadcrumbs.
4 Heat 1 cm (½ inch) oil in a deep frying pan. Cook the patties in two batches for 4–5 minutes on each side, or until golden (turn them carefully so they don't break up). Drain on paper towels and season with sea salt.
5 Cut the bread rolls in half and toast under a hot grill (broiler). Spread with mayonnaise, then layer with the tomatoes, a tofu patty and rocket. Drizzle with sweet chilli sauce, top with the burger lid and serve.

RICE AND RED LENTIL PILAFF

Serves 4–6

Garam masala

1 tablespoon coriander seeds
1 tablespoon cardamom pods
1 tablespoon cumin seeds
1 teaspoon whole black peppercorns
1 teaspoon whole cloves
1 small cinnamon stick, crushed

750 ml (26 fl oz/3 cups) vegetable stock
60 ml (2 fl oz/¼ cup) vegetable oil
1 onion, chopped
3 garlic cloves, chopped
200 g (7 oz/1 cup) basmati rice
250 g (9 oz/1 cup) red lentils
spring onions (scallions), sliced on the
　　diagonal, to garnish

1 To make the garam masala, put all the spices in a dry frying pan and shake over medium heat for 1 minute, or until fragrant. Transfer to a spice grinder or blender and blend to a fine powder. Set aside.
2 Heat the stock in a small saucepan. Cover and keep at a low simmer.
3 Heat the oil in a saucepan. Add the onion, garlic and 3 teaspoons of the garam masala. Sauté over medium heat for 3 minutes, or until the onion has softened.
4 Stir in the rice and lentils and cook for 2 minutes. Stir in the stock, slowly bring to the boil, then reduce the heat, cover and simmer for 15–20 minutes, or until the rice is cooked and all the stock has been absorbed. Gently fluff the rice with a fork. Serve garnished with spring onion.
Note Leftover garam masala will keep in a small airtight jar for several months.

FALAFEL WITH TAHINI YOGHURT DRESSING

Serves 4

Falafel

250 g (9 oz/scant 1¼ cups) dried chickpeas
1 onion, finely chopped
2 garlic cloves, crushed
5 large handfuls of parsley
4 large handfuls of coriander (cilantro) leaves
2 teaspoons ground coriander
1 teaspoon ground cumin
½ teaspoon baking powder

Tahini yoghurt dressing

60 g (2 oz/¼ cup) Greek-style yoghurt
1 tablespoon tahini
1 garlic clove, crushed
1 tablespoon lemon juice
3 tablespoons extra virgin olive oil

vegetable oil, for deep-frying

1 Soak the chickpeas in plenty of cold water overnight.

2 Drain the chickpeas well, place in a food processor and blend until coarsely ground. Add the remaining falafel ingredients and process until the mixture is smooth and a vibrant green colour. Set aside for 30 minutes for the flavours to infuse.

3 Put all the tahini yoghurt dressing ingredients in a bowl and whisk until smooth. Season to taste with sea salt and freshly ground black pepper and refrigerate until required.

4 Using slightly wet hands, shape the falafel mixture into 24 ovals, each about the size of an egg. Heat 5 cm (2 inches) of oil in a wok or deep heavy-based saucepan and fry the falafel in batches for 2–3 minutes, or until dark brown. Drain on paper towels and keep warm while cooking the remaining falafel. Serve with the tahini yoghurt dressing.

CRISPY LENTIL BALLS

Makes about 30

250 g (9 oz/1 cup) red lentils
4 spring onions (scallions), chopped
2 garlic cloves, crushed
1 teaspoon ground cumin
80 g (2¾ oz/1 cup) fresh breadcrumbs
125 g (4½ oz/1 cup) grated cheddar cheese
1 large zucchini (courgette), grated
150 g (5½ oz/1 cup) polenta
vegetable oil, for deep-frying
chutney or plain yoghurt, to serve

1 Put the lentils in a saucepan and cover with water. Bring to the boil, then reduce the heat to low. Cover and simmer for 10 minutes, or until the lentils are tender. Drain and rinse well under cold water.

2 Put half the lentils in a food processor or blender with the spring onion and garlic. Process for 10 seconds, or until the mixture is pulpy. Transfer to a large bowl and add the remaining lentils, cumin, breadcrumbs, cheese and zucchini. Stir until combined.

3 Spread the polenta on a plate. Using your hands, roll level tablespoons of the lentil mixture into balls and toss lightly in the polenta.

4 Heat about 5 cm (2 inches) of oil in a heavy-based frying pan. Gently lower the balls into the oil and cook in batches over medium–high heat for 1 minute, or until golden brown and crisp. Remove with tongs or a slotted spoon and drain on paper towels. Keep warm while cooking the remaining lentil balls. Serve hot, with chutney or yoghurt.

RICE AND CASHEW PATTIES

Serves 8

1 tablespoon olive oil, plus extra, for pan-frying
1 onion, finely chopped
2 x 425 g (15 oz) tins chickpeas, drained
    and rinsed
125 g (4½ oz/½ cup) roasted cashew paste
1 egg
65 g (2¼ oz/¼ cup) tahini
1 teaspoon ground cumin
1 teaspoon ground turmeric
1 tablespoon lemon juice
1 vegetable stock (bouillon) cube
125 ml (4 fl oz/½ cup) tamari
600 g (1 lb 5 oz/3 cups) brown rice, cooked
1 small carrot, grated
40 g (1½ oz/½ cup) fresh wholemeal
    (whole-wheat) breadcrumbs
300 g (10½ oz) bok choy (pak choy), trimmed

Coriander and coconut sambal

3 large handfuls of coriander (cilantro) leaves
1 garlic clove, chopped
1 small green chilli, seeded and finely chopped
1 teaspoon garam masala
2 tablespoons lime juice
15 g (½ oz/¼ cup) shredded coconut

1 Heat the olive oil in a frying pan. Sauté the onion for 2–3 minutes, or until golden. Set aside.

2 Put the chickpeas in a food processor with the cashew paste, egg, tahini, spices, lemon juice, stock cube, 2 tablespoons of the tamari and 2 tablespoons water. Blend until smooth. Transfer to a large bowl and add the rice, onion, carrot and breadcrumbs and mix well. Divide into 16 portions and form into patties about 1.5 cm (⅝ inch) thick. Refrigerate for 30 minutes.

3 Finely chop all the sambal ingredients in a food processor. Chill until ready to use.

4 Heat some olive oil in a large deep frying pan. Add the patties in batches and cook over medium heat for 3–4 minutes on each side, or until golden and cooked through. Remove and keep warm.

5 Wipe the pan clean and heat a little more oil. Add the bok choy and toss for 1 minute, or until wilted. Add the remaining tamari and toss. Divide among serving plates and top with two patties. Dollop with the sambal and serve.

GRILLED POLENTA WITH SHAVED FENNEL SALAD

Serves 6

500 ml (17 fl oz/2 cups) milk
175 g (6 oz/scant 1¼ cups) polenta
35 g (1¼ oz/⅓ cup) grated parmesan cheese,
    plus 2 tablespoons shaved parmesan,
    to serve
20 g (¾ oz) butter
olive oil, for brushing
1 fennel bulb, fronds attached
60 g (2¼ oz/2 cups) watercress sprigs
1 tablespoon lemon juice
2 tablespoons extra virgin olive oil

1 Pour the milk and 500 ml (17 fl oz/2 cups) water into a heavy-based saucepan and bring to the boil. Whisk in the polenta until thoroughly mixed. Reduce the heat to as low as possible and simmer for 40 minutes, stirring occasionally to stop the polenta sticking. Remove from the heat, stir in the parmesan and butter and season well.

2 Pour the polenta into a greased tray to set—it should be about 2 cm (¾ inch) thick. When cold, cut into six wedges, brush with a little olive oil and cook on a hot chargrill pan or barbecue hotplate until crisp brown grill marks appear.

3 Slice the fennel as thinly as possible and chop the fronds. Toss in a bowl with the watercress, lemon juice, extra virgin olive oil and half the shaved parmesan. Season with sea salt and freshly ground black pepper.

4 Serve the polenta with the fennel salad piled to one side, with the remaining shaved parmesan scattered over the top.

ASPARAGUS AND PISTACHIO RISOTTO

Serves 4–6

1 litre (35 fl oz/4 cups) vegetable stock
250 ml (9 fl oz/1 cup) white wine
80 ml (2½ fl oz/⅓ cup) extra virgin olive oil
1 red onion, finely chopped
440 g (15½ oz/2 cups) risotto rice
350 g (12 oz/2 bunches) asparagus, trimmed
    and cut into 3 cm (1¼ inch) lengths
125 ml (4 fl oz/½ cup) pouring (whipping) cream
100 g (3½ oz/1 cup) grated parmesan cheese
40 g (1½ oz/⅓ cup) shelled pistachio nuts,
    toasted and roughly chopped

1 Pour the stock and wine into a saucepan. Bring to the boil, then reduce the heat, cover and keep at a gentle simmer.

2 Heat the olive oil in a large heavy-based saucepan. Sauté the onion over medium heat for 3 minutes, or until soft. Add the rice and stir until translucent.

3 Add 125 ml (4 fl oz/½ cup) hot stock, stirring constantly over medium heat until the liquid is absorbed. Continue adding more stock, 125 ml (4 fl oz/½ cup) at a time, stirring constantly for 20–25 minutes, or until all the stock has been absorbed and the rice is tender and creamy. Add the asparagus during the last 5 minutes of cooking.

4 Remove from the heat and leave to stand for 2 minutes, then stir in the cream and parmesan. Season to taste with sea salt and freshly ground black pepper. Serve sprinkled with the pistachios.

CHILLI BEAN TORTILLA WRAPS

Serves 4

Chilli beans

2 tablespoons olive oil

1 onion, finely chopped

2 garlic cloves, crushed

1 green capsicum (pepper), chopped

2 small red chillies, seeded and finely chopped

½ teaspoon cayenne pepper

1 teaspoon paprika

1 teaspoon ground cumin

¼ teaspoon sugar

400 g (14 oz) tin chopped tomatoes

440 g (15½ oz) tin red kidney beans, drained and rinsed

1 tablespoon tomato paste (concentrated purée)

12 soft flour tortillas, each 20 cm (8 inches) round

225 g (8 oz/1¾ cups) grated cheddar cheese

250 g (9 oz/1 cup) sour cream

coriander (cilantro) sprigs, to garnish

lime wedges, to serve

1 To make the chilli beans, heat the olive oil in a saucepan over low heat and sauté the onion, garlic and capsicum for 8–10 minutes, or until softened. Add the remaining ingredients and 125 ml (4 fl oz/ ½ cup) water. Bring to the boil, then reduce the heat and simmer for 15–20 minutes, or until the mixture has reduced. Season to taste.

2 Heat a chargrill pan or barbecue flat plate to low–medium. Lay the tortillas on a work surface. Put some chilli beans along the middle of each tortilla, sprinkle with 2 tablespoons of the cheese and roll up. Put three rolls, seam side down, on a double layer of foil, then seal the foil to form a parcel. Grill the parcels for 6–8 minutes on each side, or until heated through.

3 Unwrap the foil parcels and slide the tortillas onto serving plates. Top with the sour cream, scatter with coriander and serve with lime wedges.

Note The tortilla wraps are also delicious served with some home-made guacamole and a good ready-made tomato salsa.

THAI TEMPEH

Serves 4

Marinade

2 lemon grass stems, white part only,
 finely chopped
2 makrut (kaffir lime) leaves, shredded
2 small red chillies, seeded and finely chopped
3 garlic cloves, crushed
2 teaspoons sesame oil
125 ml (4 fl oz/½ cup) lime juice
2 teaspoons shaved palm sugar (jaggery)
125 ml (4 fl oz/½ cup) soy sauce

600 g (1 lb 5 oz) tempeh, cut into twelve
 5 mm (¼ inch) slices
60 ml (2 fl oz/¼ cup) peanut oil
1 tablespoon shaved palm sugar (jaggery)
100 g (3½ oz) snow pea (mangetout) sprouts
 or watercress
shredded makrut (kaffir lime) leaves, to garnish

1 Put the marinade ingredients in a bowl and stir until the sugar has dissolved. Add the tempeh, then cover and marinate in the refrigerator overnight, turning occasionally.
2 Drain the tempeh, reserving the marinade. Heat half the peanut oil in a heavy-based frying pan over high heat. Cook the tempeh in batches, turning once, for 5 minutes, or until crispy, adding more oil as needed. Drain on paper towels and keep warm while cooking the remaining tempeh.
3 Put the reserved marinade in a saucepan, stir in the palm sugar and heat until syrupy.
4 Place a slice of tempeh on each serving plate and top with some snow pea sprouts. Continue layering in this way, finishing with the tempeh on top. Drizzle with the marinade syrup, garnish with shredded lime leaves and serve.

MOROCCAN EGGPLANT WITH COUSCOUS

Serves 4

185 g (6½ oz/1 cup) instant couscous
200 ml (7 fl oz) olive oil
1 onion, halved and sliced
1 eggplant (aubergine)
3 teaspoons ground cumin
1½ teaspoons garlic salt
¼ teaspoon ground cinnamon
1 teaspoon paprika
¼ teaspoon ground cloves
½ teaspoon sea salt
50 g (1¾ oz) butter
a handful of roughly chopped parsley

1 Put the couscous in a large bowl. Add 375 ml (13 fl oz/1½ cups) boiling water and leave for 10 minutes, or until all the water is absorbed. Fluff up the grains with a fork.
2 Heat 2 tablespoons olive oil in a large frying pan. Sauté the onion for 8–10 minutes, or until browned. Remove from the pan using a slotted spoon and set aside.
3 Cut the eggplant into 1 cm (½ inch) slices, then into quarters, and place in a large bowl. In a small bowl, mix the spices together, then sprinkle over the eggplant, tossing until well coated.
4 Add the remaining olive oil to the pan and reheat over medium heat. Cook the eggplant, turning once, for 20–25 minutes, or until browned. Remove from the pan.
5 Melt the butter in the same pan, then add the couscous and gently cook for 2–3 minutes. Stir in the onion, eggplant and parsley. Serve at room temperature.

GREEN PILAFF WITH CASHEWS

Serves 6

100 g (3½ oz/⅔ cup) cashew nuts, chopped
2 tablespoons olive oil
6 spring onions (scallions), chopped
300 g (10½ oz/1½ cups) long-grain brown rice
2 garlic cloves, finely chopped
1 teaspoon fennel seeds
2 tablespoons lemon juice
625 ml (21½ fl oz/2½ cups) vegetable stock
3 tablespoons chopped mint
3 tablespoons chopped flat-leaf (Italian) parsley
200 g (7 oz/4½ cups) baby English spinach
leaves

1 Preheat the oven to 180°C (350°F/Gas 4). Spread the cashews on a baking tray and roast for 5–10 minutes, or until golden brown—watch carefully so they don't burn.
2 Heat the olive oil in a large frying pan and sauté the spring onion over medium heat for 2 minutes, or until soft. Add the rice, garlic and fennel seeds and stir for 1–2 minutes, or until the rice is coated.
3 Increase the heat to high and stir in the lemon juice, stock and sea salt to taste. Bring to the boil, then reduce the heat to low. Cover and simmer for 45 minutes without lifting the lid.
4 Remove the pan from the heat. Sprinkle the herbs over the rice and shred the spinach over the top. Cover and leave to stand for 8 minutes, then stir the spinach and herbs through the rice. Season with sea salt and freshly ground black pepper and serve sprinkled with the cashews.

PEA AND ASPARAGUS SAFFRON RISOTTO

Serves 4

450 g (1 lb) fresh peas in the pod, or
    235 g (8½ oz/1½ cups) frozen peas
175 g (6 oz/1 bunch) asparagus, trimmed
    and cut into 3 cm (1¼ inch) lengths
a pinch of saffron threads
1.5 litres (52 fl oz/6 cups) vegetable stock
2 tablespoons olive oil
1 onion, finely chopped
440 g (15½ oz/2 cups) risotto rice
30 g (1 oz/heaped ¼ cup) finely grated
    parmesan cheese

1 Shell the peas into a heatproof bowl and add the asparagus. Cover with boiling water and leave to stand for 3 minutes. Drain and set aside until needed.
2 Pour 60 ml (2 fl oz/¼ cup) boiling water into a small bowl. Add the saffron and leave to infuse.

3 Pour the stock into a saucepan. Bring to the boil, then reduce the heat, cover and keep at a gentle simmer.
4 Heat the olive oil in a large, heavy-based saucepan. Sauté the onion over medium heat for 5 minutes, until soft. Add the rice and stir until translucent.
5 Add 125 ml (4 fl oz/½ cup) hot stock, stirring constantly over medium heat until the liquid is absorbed. Continue adding more stock, 125 ml (4 fl oz/½ cup) at a time, stirring constantly for 20–25 minutes, or until all the stock is absorbed and the rice is tender and creamy. Add the saffron water about halfway through, and stir in the peas and asparagus about 5 minutes before the rice is ready.
6 When the rice is tender, remove from the heat and stir in the parmesan. Serve sprinkled with freshly ground black pepper.

LENTIL AND CHICKPEA BURGERS WITH CORIANDER GARLIC CREAM

Makes 10 burgers

1 tablespoon olive oil, plus extra, for pan-frying
2 onions, sliced
1 tablespoon tandoori mix powder
425 g (15 oz) tin chickpeas, drained and rinsed
1 tablespoon grated fresh ginger
1 egg
250 g (9 oz/1 cup) red lentils, cooked
3 tablespoons chopped parsley
2 tablespoons chopped coriander (cilantro)
180 g (6 oz/2 cups) dry breadcrumbs
flour, for dusting

Coriander garlic cream
125 g (4½ oz/½ cup) sour cream
125 ml (4 fl oz/½ cup) pouring (whipping) cream
1 garlic clove, crushed
2 tablespoons chopped coriander (cilantro)
2 tablespoons chopped parsley

1 Heat the olive oil in a frying pan. Sauté the onion over medium heat for 5 minutes, or until softened. Add the tandoori mix and stir until fragrant, then leave to cool slightly.
2 Put the onion in a food processor with the chickpeas, ginger, egg and half the lentils. Blend for 20 seconds, or until smooth. Transfer to a bowl, add the remaining lentils, parsley, coriander and breadcrumbs and mix well.
3 Divide into 10 portions and shape into patties. (If the mixture is too soft, refrigerate for 15 minutes; the mixture can be made up to 2 days ahead.) Toss the patties in flour and shake off the excess.
4 Heat a frying pan and brush lightly with oil. Add the patties in batches and cook over medium heat for 3–4 minutes on each side, or until browned. Keep warm.
5 Put all the coriander garlic cream ingredients in a bowl and mix well. Serve with the hot patties.

COUSCOUS VEGETABLE LOAF

Serves 6

1 litre (35 fl oz/4 cups) vegetable stock
500 g (1 lb 2 oz/2⅔ cups) instant couscous
30 g (1 oz) butter, softened
60 ml (2 fl oz/¼ cup) olive oil
1 onion, finely chopped
2 garlic cloves, crushed
1 tablespoon ground coriander
1 teaspoon ground cinnamon
1 teaspoon garam masala
250 g (9 oz) cherry tomatoes, quartered
1 zucchini (courgette), diced
130 g (4½ oz) tin corn kernels, drained
a large handful of basil leaves
150 g (5½ oz) sun-dried capsicums (peppers)
  in oil

Dressing
80 ml (2½ fl oz/⅓ cup) orange juice
1 tablespoon lemon juice
3 tablespoons chopped flat-leaf (Italian) parsley
1 teaspoon honey
1 teaspoon ground cumin

1 Bring the stock to the boil in a saucepan. Put the couscous and butter in a bowl, pour the hot stock over and leave for 10 minutes.
2 Meanwhile, heat 1 tablespoon of the olive oil in a large frying pan and sauté the onion and garlic over low heat for 5 minutes, or until the onion has softened. Add the spices and cook for 1 minute, or until fragrant. Remove from the pan.
3 Add the remaining oil to the pan and cook the tomatoes, zucchini and corn over high heat until soft. Set aside.
4 Line a 3 litre (105 fl oz/12 cup) loaf (bar) tin with plastic wrap, letting it hang over the sides. Take eight whole basil leaves and form them into two flower shapes on the base.
5 Chop the remaining basil and add to the couscous with the onion and the tomato mixtures. Drain the capsicums, reserving 2 tablespoons of the oil, then chop and add to the couscous. Mix well, leave to cool, then press the mixture into the tin and fold the plastic wrap over to cover. Weigh down with tins of food and refrigerate overnight.
6 Whisk together the reserved capsicum oil and dressing ingredients. Turn out the loaf, cut into slices and serve with the dressing.

BROWN RICE AND PUY LENTILS WITH PINE NUTS AND SPINACH

Serves 6–8

200 g (7 oz/1 cup) brown rice
100 ml (3½ fl oz) extra virgin olive oil
1 red onion, diced
2 garlic cloves, crushed
1 carrot, diced
2 celery stalks, diced
200 g (7 oz/1 cup) puy lentils or tiny blue-green lentils
2 tomatoes, seeded and diced
3 tablespoons chopped coriander (cilantro)
3 tablespoons chopped mint
2 tablespoons balsamic vinegar
1 tablespoon lemon juice
2 tablespoons toasted pine nuts
90 g (3¼ oz/2 cups) baby English spinach leaves

1 Bring a large saucepan of salted water to the boil. Add the rice and some salt and cook for 20–30 minutes, or until tender. Drain and rinse, then set aside.

2 Heat 2 tablespoons of the olive oil in a saucepan. Sauté the onion, garlic, carrot and celery over low heat for 5 minutes, or until softened, then add the lentils and 375 ml (13 fl oz/1½ cups) water. Bring to the boil, reduce the heat and simmer for 15 minutes, or until the lentils are tender. Drain well, but do not rinse.

3 Put the rice, tomato, coriander and mint in a large bowl. Add the lentil mixture and stir together.

4 Whisk the remaining oil with the vinegar and lemon juice. Season well with sea salt and freshly ground black pepper and pour over the salad. Add the pine nuts and spinach and toss well to combine. Serve at room temperature.

SPICED BASMATI AND NUT RICE

Serves 4

a small pinch of saffron threads
250 g (9 oz/1¼ cups) basmati rice
2 tablespoons vegetable oil
2 cinnamon sticks
6 cardamom pods, crushed
6 cloves
75 g (2½ oz/½ cup) blanched almonds, toasted
75 g (2½ oz/heaped ½ cup) raisins
1 teaspoon sea salt
2 tablespoons chopped coriander (cilantro) leaves

1 Pour 60 ml (2 fl oz/¼ cup) boiling water into a small bowl. Add the saffron and leave to infuse.

2 Put the rice in a sieve and wash under cold running water until the water runs clear. Set aside.

3 Heat the oil in a saucepan, add the spices and stir over medium heat for 1–2 minutes, or until fragrant. Add the rice, almonds and raisins and stir until the rice is glossy. Pour in 500 ml (17 fl oz/2 cups) cold water, add the salt and bring to the boil. Reduce the heat, cover and simmer gently over low heat for 15 minutes.

4 Remove from the heat, then drizzle the saffron water over the rice. Cover and leave to stand for a further 10 minutes. Stir the coriander through and serve.

SEMOLINA WITH THREE CHEESES

Serves 6–8

500 ml (17 fl oz/2 cups) vegetable stock
750 ml (26 fl oz/3 cups) milk
250 g (9 oz/2 cups) fine semolina
1 egg yolk
75 g (2½ oz/¾ cup) finely grated parmesan
　cheese
2–3 large handfuls of parsley, finely chopped
50 g (1¾ oz) mild gorgonzola cheese, crumbled
60 g (2¼ oz/½ cup) grated cheddar cheese
80 ml (2½ fl oz/⅓ cup) pouring (whipping) cream

1 Pour the stock and milk into a large saucepan. Stir together, bring to the boil, then remove from the heat. Add the semolina in a slow, steady stream, whisking constantly to prevent lumps forming. Put the pan back over medium heat and whisk for 3 minutes, or until the mixture has boiled and is very thick (it will now be difficult to whisk). Turn off the heat. Working quickly and using a wooden spoon, beat in the egg yolk, parmesan and parsley and season to taste with sea salt and freshly ground black pepper.

2 Spread the mixture into a lightly oiled, shallow 2.5 litre (87 fl oz/10 cup) baking dish. Stand at room temperature for about an hour, or until firm.

3 Heat the grill (broiler) to medium. Turn the semolina out onto a board, but keep the baking dish handy. Using a wet knife, trim the edges of the semolina. Cut the semolina in half lengthways, then into eight long rectangles. Now cut each piece in half diagonally to form 16 triangles. Place on a lightly oiled baking tray and grill for 7 minutes on each side, or until nicely browned. Turn the grill up high.

4 Arrange the semolina triangles, in two slightly overlapping rows, back in the baking dish. Sprinkle with the gorgonzola and cheddar and drizzle with the cream.

5 Put the baking dish under the grill and cook for 5 minutes, or until the cheese is hot and bubbling. Serve warm, sprinkled with a good grind of black pepper.

ARANCINI
Makes 20

a large pinch of saffron threads
250 ml (9 fl oz/1 cup) dry white wine
750 ml (26 fl oz/3 cups) vegetable stock
100 g (3½ oz) butter
1 onion, finely chopped
1 large garlic clove, crushed
2 tablespoons thyme
220 g (7¾ oz/1 cup) risotto rice
50 g (1¾ oz/½ cup) grated parmesan cheese
100 g (3½ oz/⅔ cup) diced mozzarella or
  fontina cheese
70 g (2½ oz/¾ cup) dry breadcrumbs
vegetable oil, for deep-frying

1 Soak the saffron in the wine and leave to infuse. Pour the stock into a saucepan, bring to the boil, then reduce the heat, cover and keep at a gentle simmer.
2 Melt the butter in a large saucepan. Sauté the onion and garlic over low heat for 3–4 minutes, or until softened. Add the thyme and rice and stir until the rice is translucent. Add the saffron wine and stir until all the wine is absorbed. Add 125 ml (4 fl oz/½ cup) hot stock and stir constantly over medium heat until absorbed. Continue adding more stock, 125 ml (4 fl oz/½ cup) at a time, stirring constantly for 20–25 minutes, or until all the stock is absorbed and the rice is tender and creamy. (It doesn't matter if the rice becomes a little glutinous—it will actually stick together better.)
3 Remove from the heat, stir in the parmesan, then spread out on a tray covered with plastic wrap. Leave to cool, then refrigerate overnight to firm up.
4 Roll a small amount of the rice mixture into a walnut-sized ball. Press a hole in the middle with your thumb, push a cube of mozzarella inside and press the rice around it to enclose it in a ball. Repeat with the remaining rice and cheese, then roll each ball in the breadcrumbs, pressing down to coat well.
5 Heat enough oil in a deep-fryer or large heavy-based saucepan to fully cover the rice balls. Heat the oil to 180°C (350°F), or until a cube of bread dropped into the oil browns in 15 seconds. Cook the rice balls in batches, without crowding, for 3–4 minutes. Drain on paper towels and leave for a few minutes before eating. Serve hot or at room temperature.

SWEET POTATO AND SAGE RISOTTO

Serves 4

1.25 litres (44 fl oz/5 cups) vegetable stock
60 ml (2 fl oz/¼ cup) extra virgin olive oil,
   plus extra, for drizzling
1 red onion, cut into thin wedges
600 g (1 lb 5 oz) orange sweet potato,
   peeled and cut into 2 cm (¾ inch) dice
440 g (15½ oz/2 cups) risotto rice
75 g (2½ oz/¾ cup) shredded parmesan
   cheese, plus extra shaved parmesan,
   to serve
3 tablespoons shredded sage

1 Pour the stock into a saucepan. Bring to the boil, then reduce the heat, cover and keep at a gentle simmer.
2 Heat the olive oil in a large saucepan. Sauté the onion over medium heat for 5 minutes, or until softened. Add the sweet potato and rice and stir until well coated.
3 Add 125 ml (4 fl oz/½ cup) hot stock, stirring constantly over medium heat until the liquid is absorbed. Continue adding more stock, 125 ml (4 fl oz/½ cup) at a time, stirring constantly for 20–25 minutes, or until all the stock is absorbed, the sweet potato is cooked and the rice is tender and creamy.
4 Stir in the parmesan and most of the sage; season well. Serve drizzled with a little more olive oil and sprinkled with the remaining sage and shaved parmesan.

The cooler months sharpen the appetite and are when hungry tummies most demand a hearty, warming dinner. This is where the humble casserole or bake comes into its own. Casseroles in particular love beans of all descriptions, slow-cooked to creamy, tender perfection, simmering in and soaking up a flavoursome sauce while spreading delicious aromas into every corner of the house and promising sustenance to come. Another brilliant way to beat off the winter chill is with a fragrant curry. While curries are eaten year-round in seriously hot climates, there is something especially thrilling about their spicy life-giving warmth when the mercury dips. Whichever way your tastes run, things are bound to heat up...

CASSEROLES, CURRIES & BAKES

SPICY CHICKPEA AND VEGETABLE CASSEROLE

Serves 4

330 g (10½ oz/1½ cups) dried chickpeas
2 tablespoons olive oil
1 large onion, chopped
1 garlic clove, crushed
3 teaspoons ground cumin
½ teaspoon chilli powder
½ teaspoon allspice
400 g (14 oz) tin chopped tomatoes
375 ml (13 fl oz/1½ cups) vegetable stock
300 g (10½ oz) pumpkin (winter squash), peeled and cut into large dice
150 g (5½ oz) green beans, trimmed
200 g (7 oz) baby (pattypan) squash, quartered
2 tablespoons tomato paste (concentrated purée)
1 teaspoon dried oregano

1 Soak the chickpeas in enough cold water to cover overnight. Drain.
2 Heat the olive oil in a large saucepan. Add the onion and garlic and sauté for 3 minutes, or until softened. Add the cumin, chilli powder and allspice and cook, stirring, for 1 minute. Add the chickpeas, tomato and stock. Bring to the boil, then reduce the heat, cover and simmer for 1 hour, stirring occasionally.
3 Stir in the pumpkin, beans, squash, tomato paste and oregano. Cover and simmer for 15 minutes, then remove the lid and simmer, uncovered, for a further 10 minutes to reduce and thicken the sauce slightly. Serve hot.
Note A quick way to soak chickpeas is to place them in a large saucepan, cover with cold water, bring to the boil, then remove from the heat and leave to soak for 2 hours. If you're in a hurry, use tinned chickpeas—drain and rinse thoroughly before use.

THAI RED SQUASH CURRY

Serves 4

2 tablespoons vegetable oil
1–2 tablespoons Thai red curry paste (see Note)
400 ml (14 fl oz) tin coconut milk
2 tablespoons soy sauce
125 ml (4 fl oz/½ cup) light vegetable stock
2 teaspoons grated palm sugar (jaggery)
700 g (1 lb 9 oz) baby (pattypan) squash,
    halved (or quartered if large); or use the
    same quantity of zucchini (courgettes),
    cut into slices 2.5 cm (1 inch) thick
100 g (3½ oz) baby corn, halved lengthways
100 g (3½ oz) snow peas (mangetout), trimmed
2 teaspoons lime juice
50 g (1¾ oz/⅓ cup) unsalted roasted cashews,
    roughly chopped
steamed jasmine rice, to serve
lime wedges, to serve

1 Heat the oil in a large saucepan. Add the curry paste and stir over medium–high heat for 1–2 minutes, or until the paste separates. Add the coconut milk, soy sauce, stock and palm sugar and stir until the sugar has dissolved. Bring to the boil.
2 Add the squash and return to the boil. Stir in the baby corn, then cover and simmer for 12–15 minutes, or until the squash is just tender.
3 Add the snowpeas and lime juice and simmer, uncovered, for 1 minute. Serve scattered with the cashews, accompanied by steamed jasmine rice, and lime wedges for squeezing over.
Note Thai cookery uses several kinds of curry pastes, each with a distinct flavour and colour obtained from its particular blend of herbs and spices. Red curry paste is highly fragrant. Commercial brands vary from medium to hot in intensity, so add more or less to suit your taste.

GREEN CURRY WITH SWEET POTATO AND EGGPLANT

Serves 4–6

1 tablespoon vegetable oil
1 onion, chopped
1–2 tablespoons green curry paste
1 eggplant (aubergine), quartered and sliced
400 ml (14 fl oz) tin coconut milk
250 ml (9 fl oz/1 cup) vegetable stock
6 makrut (kaffir lime) leaves, plus extra shredded
    makrut leaves, to serve
1 orange sweet potato, peeled and diced
2 teaspoons soft brown sugar
2 teaspoons lime zest
2 tablespoons lime juice
coriander (cilantro) leaves, to garnish
steamed jasmine rice, to serve

1 Heat the oil in a large wok or frying pan. Add the onion and curry paste and cook, stirring, over medium heat for 3 minutes. Add the eggplant and cook for a further 4–5 minutes, or until softened.

2 Pour in the coconut milk and stock. Bring to the boil, then reduce the heat and simmer for 5 minutes. Add the lime leaves and sweet potato and cook, stirring occasionally, for 10 minutes, or until the vegetables are very tender.

3 Mix in the sugar, lime zest and lime juice until well combined. Season to taste with sea salt. Serve garnished with coriander leaves and shredded lime leaves, with steamed jasmine rice.

YELLOW CURRY WITH PUMPKIN, GREEN BEANS AND CASHEWS

Serves 4

500 ml (17 fl oz/2 cups) coconut cream
3 teaspoons yellow curry paste
125 ml (4 fl oz/½ cup) vegetable stock
500 g (1 lb 2 oz) jap or kent pumpkin
   (winter squash), peeled and diced
300 g (10½ oz) green beans, trimmed
   and halved
2 tablespoons soy sauce
2 tablespoons lime juice
1 tablespoon grated palm sugar (jaggery)
   or soft brown sugar
3 tablespoons coriander (cilantro) leaves
40 g (1½ oz/¼ cup) cashew nuts, toasted
steamed jasmine rice, to serve

1 Without shaking the tin of coconut cream, spoon the thick cream from the top of the tin into a wok and heat until boiling. Add the curry paste, then reduce the heat and simmer, stirring, for 5 minutes, until the cream begins to separate.
2 Stir in the remaining coconut cream, stock and pumpkin; simmer for 10 minutes. Add the beans and cook for a further 8 minutes, or until the vegetables are tender.
3 Gently stir in the soy sauce, lime juice and palm sugar until well combined. Serve scattered with the coriander leaves and cashews, with steamed jasmine rice.

INDIAN-STYLE SPINACH

Serves 4

2 tablespoons ghee or vegetable oil
1 onion, thinly sliced
2 garlic cloves, finely chopped
2 teaspoons finely grated fresh ginger
1 teaspoon brown mustard seeds
½ teaspoon ground cumin
¼ teaspoon ground coriander
1 teaspoon ground turmeric
½ teaspoon garam masala
350 g (12 oz) English spinach,
    washed and trimmed
60 ml (2 fl oz/¼ cup) pouring
    (whipping) cream
1 tablespoon lemon juice

1 Heat a wok until very hot. Add the ghee and swirl it around to coat the wok. Sauté the onion over medium heat for 2 minutes to soften. Add the garlic, ginger and all the spices and cook, stirring for 1 minute, or until fragrant.

2 Roughly tear the spinach leaves in half and add to the spice mixture. Cook for 1–2 minutes, or until wilted.

3 Add the cream, simmer for 2 minutes, then add the lemon juice and season with sea salt and freshly ground black pepper. Serve hot.

DRY POTATO AND PEA CURRY

Serves 4

2 teaspoons brown mustard seeds
2 tablespoons ghee or vegetable oil
2 onions, sliced
2 garlic cloves, crushed
2 teaspoons grated fresh ginger
1 teaspoon ground turmeric
½ teaspoon chilli powder
1 teaspoon ground cumin
1 teaspoon garam masala
750 g (1 lb 10 oz) all-purpose potatoes, peeled and diced
100 g (3½ oz/⅔ cup) frozen peas
2 tablespoons chopped mint

1 Heat the mustard seeds in a large dry saucepan until they start to pop. Add the ghee, onion, garlic and ginger and sauté over medium heat for 5 minutes, or until the onion has softened.

2 Add the turmeric, chilli powder, cumin, garam marsala and potato. Season with sea salt and freshly ground black pepper and stir to coat the potato with the spices.

3 Add 125 ml (4 fl oz/½ cup) water, bring to the boil, then reduce the heat, cover and simmer for 15–20 minutes, or until the potato is just tender, stirring occasionally.

4 Stir in the peas, then cover and simmer for 3–5 minutes, or until the potato is cooked and all the liquid is absorbed. Stir in the mint and season well. Serve hot.

CHICKPEA CURRY

Serves 4

1 tablespoon ghee or vegetable oil
2 onions, finely sliced
4 garlic cloves, crushed
1 teaspoon chilli powder
1 teaspoon sea salt
1 teaspoon turmeric
1 teaspoon paprika
1 tablespoon ground cumin
1 tablespoon ground coriander
2 x 425 g (15 oz) tins chickpeas, drained
   and rinsed
400 g (14 oz) tin chopped tomatoes
1 teaspoon garam masala

1 Heat the ghee in a saucepan. Sauté the onion and garlic over medium heat for 5 minutes, or until the onion has softened.
2 Add the chilli powder, salt, turmeric, paprika, cumin and coriander and cook, stirring, for 1 minute.
3 Stir in the chickpeas and tomato, then cover and simmer over low heat for 20 minutes, stirring occasionally.
4 Stir in the garam masala. Cover and simmer for a further 10 minutes. Serve hot.

DAL WITH VEGETABLES

Serves 6

150 g (5½ oz/⅔ cup) yellow lentils
150 g (5½ oz/scant ⅔ cup) red lentils
1 tablespoon ghee or vegetable oil
1 onion, chopped
2 garlic cloves, crushed
1 tablespoon fenugreek seeds
2 teaspoons ground cumin
2 teaspoons ground coriander
½ teaspoon ground turmeric
400 g (14 oz) tin chopped tomatoes
750 ml (26 fl oz/3 cups) vegetable stock
2 carrots, chopped
250 g (9 oz/2 cups) cauliflower florets
150 g (5½ oz) green beans, trimmed and halved
60 ml (2 fl oz/¼ cup) pouring (whipping) cream
2 tablespoons chopped coriander (cilantro)
    leaves
naan bread, to serve

1 Rinse the lentils separately under cold water until the water runs clear, then drain well. Put the yellow lentils in a small bowl, cover with water and leave to stand for 30 minutes, then drain well.

2 Heat the ghee in a saucepan. Sauté the onion and garlic over medium heat for 3 minutes, or until the onion is soft.

3 Add the spices and stir for 30 seconds, or until fragrant. Add all the lentils, tomato and stock, stirring well. Bring to the boil, then reduce the heat, cover and simmer for 20 minutes.

4 Stir in the carrot and cauliflower, then cover and cook for 10 minutes. Add the beans and cook, covered, for a further 5 minutes, or until the lentils are tender and the vegetables are cooked.

5 Stir in the cream and season to taste. Serve scattered with the coriander leaves, with naan bread.

POTATO CURRY WITH SESAME SEEDS

Serves 4

4 large all-purpose potatoes
1 tablespoon vegetable oil
1 teaspoon cumin seeds
1 teaspoon coriander seeds
2 teaspoons mustard seeds
2 tablespoons sesame seeds
½ teaspoon turmeric
1 teaspoon chopped red chilli
2 teaspoons finely grated lemon zest
2 tablespoons lemon juice

1 Boil, steam or microwave the potatoes until tender. Drain and allow to cool slightly, then peel and chop.
2 Heat the oil in a large heavy-based saucepan over medium heat. Add the cumin, coriander and mustard seeds and cook for 1 minute, stirring constantly.
3 Add the sesame seeds and cook for 1–2 minutes, stirring until golden. Add the turmeric, chilli, potatoes, lemon zest and lemon juice, then stir until well combined and heated through. Season to taste with sea salt and freshly ground black pepper and serve.

LENTIL BHUJA CASSEROLE

Serves 4–6

375 g (13 oz/2 cups) green lentils
1 large onion
1 large all-purpose potato
1 teaspoon ground cumin
1 teaspoon ground coriander
1 teaspoon ground turmeric
90 g (3¼ oz/⅗ cup) plain (all-purpose) flour
vegetable oil, for pan-frying
2 garlic cloves, crushed
1 tablespoon grated fresh ginger
250 ml (9 fl oz/1 cup) tomato passata
   (puréed tomatoes)
500 ml (17 fl oz/2 cups) vegetable stock
250 ml (9 fl oz/1 cup) pouring (whipping) cream
200 g (7 oz) green beans, trimmed
2 carrots, sliced
pitta bread, to serve

1 Put the lentils in a bowl, cover with cold water and leave to soak overnight. Drain well and place in a bowl.

2 Grate the onion and potato, place in a clean tea towel (dish towel) and squeeze out the excess moisture. Add to the lentils with the spices and flour and mix well. Using dry hands, roll the mixture into walnut-sized balls and place on a foil-lined tray. Cover and refrigerate for 30 minutes.

3 Heat about 2 cm (¾ inch) of oil in a heavy-based frying pan. Add the lentil balls in small batches and fry over high heat for 5 minutes, or until golden brown. Drain on paper towels.

4 Heat another 2 tablespoons oil in a large saucepan. Add the garlic and ginger and sauté over medium heat for 1 minute, then stir in the tomato passata, stock and cream. Bring to the boil, then reduce the heat and simmer for 10 minutes.

5 Add the lentil balls, beans and carrot. Cover and simmer for 35 minutes, stirring occasionally. Serve hot, with pitta bread.

Note The lentil balls can be made a day ahead and stored in an airtight container in the refrigerator.

BEAN AND CAPSICUM STEW

Serves 4–6

200 g (7 oz/1 cup) dried haricot beans
2 tablespoons olive oil
1 red onion, cut into thin wedges
2 large garlic cloves, crushed
1 red capsicum (pepper), cut into 1.5 cm
  (⅝ inch) squares
1 green capsicum (pepper), cut into 1.5 cm
  (⅝ inch) squares
2 x 400 g (14 oz) tins chopped tomatoes
2 tablespoons tomato paste (concentrated
  purée)
500 ml (17 fl oz/2 cups) vegetable stock
2 tablespoons chopped basil
125 g (4½ oz/¾ cup) kalamata olives, pitted
1–2 teaspoons soft brown sugar
crusty bread, to serve

1 Soak the beans in enough cold water to cover overnight.

2 Drain the beans, rinse well and place in a saucepan. Cover with fresh cold water and bring to the boil. Cook for 45 minutes, or until just tender. Drain and set aside.

3 Heat the olive oil in a saucepan. Sauté the onion and garlic over medium heat for 2–3 minutes, or until the onion is soft. Add the red and green capsicum and cook for a further 5 minutes.

4 Stir in the tomato, tomato paste, stock and beans, then cover and simmer for 40 minutes, or until the beans are tender. Stir in the basil, olives and sugar, season well with sea salt and freshly ground black pepper and serve with crusty bread.

CORN SPOONBREAD

Serves 4

3 cobs of sweet corn
250 g (9 oz/1 cup) crème fraîche
1 egg
30 g (1 oz/¼ cup) self-raising flour
a pinch of cayenne pepper
50 g (1¾ oz/½ cup) grated parmesan cheese
40 g (1½ oz) butter

1 Preheat the oven to 190°C (375°F/Gas 5). Slice the kernels off the corn cobs and place in a large bowl. Add the crème fraîche, egg, flour, cayenne pepper and half the parmesan. Season with sea salt and freshly ground black pepper and mix together well.

2 Spoon the mixture into a greased, shallow 18 cm (7 inch) baking dish. Sprinkle the remaining parmesan over the top, dot with the butter and bake for 30–35 minutes, or until firm and golden brown. Serve hot, straight from the dish.

HUNGARIAN CASSEROLE

Serves 4–6

1 tablespoon olive oil

30 g (1 oz) butter

4 large all-purpose potatoes, peeled and
cut into large chunks

1 onion, chopped

1 red capsicum (pepper), roughly chopped

1 green capsicum (pepper), roughly chopped

440 g (14 oz) tin chopped tomatoes

250 ml (9 fl oz/1 cup) vegetable stock

2 teaspoons caraway seeds

2 teaspoons paprika

Croutons

4 thick slices of white bread

250 ml (9 fl oz/1 cup) vegetable oil

1 Heat the olive oil and butter in a large heavy-based saucepan. Add the potatoes and cook over medium heat, turning regularly, until crisp on the edges.

2 Add the onion and red and green capsicum and sauté for 5 minutes. Stir in the tomato, stock, caraway seeds and paprika and season to taste with sea salt and freshly ground black pepper. Simmer, uncovered, for 10 minutes, or until the potatoes are tender.

3 Meanwhile, make the croutons. Cut the crusts off the bread and discard, then cut the bread into small cubes. Heat the oil in a frying pan over medium heat. Add the bread cubes and cook for 2 minutes, or until golden brown and crisp, turning often. Drain on paper towels, scatter over the casserole and serve immediately.

BORLOTTI BEAN MOUSSAKA

Serves 6

250 g (9 oz/1¼ cups) dried borlotti
  (cranberry) beans
2 large eggplants (aubergines), sliced
80 ml (2½ fl oz/⅓ cup) olive oil
1 onion, chopped
1 garlic clove, crushed
125 g (4½ oz/1⅓ cups) sliced button mushrooms
800 g (1 lb 12 oz) tin chopped tomatoes
250 ml (9 fl oz/1 cup) red wine
1 tablespoon tomato paste (concentrated purée)
1 tablespoon chopped oregano

Topping
250 g (9 oz/1 cup) plain yoghurt
4 eggs, lightly beaten
500 ml (17 fl oz/2 cups) milk
¼ teaspoon ground paprika
50 g (1¾ oz/½ cup) grated parmesan cheese
40 g (1½ oz/½ cup) fresh breadcrumbs

1 Soak the borlotti beans in enough cold
water to cover overnight.
2 Rinse and drain the beans, then place in
a large heavy-based saucepan, cover with
fresh water and bring to the boil. Reduce

the heat and simmer for 1½ hours, or until
tender. Drain and set aside.
3 Meanwhile, sprinkle the eggplant slices
with salt and set aside for 30 minutes. Rinse
and pat dry. Brush the eggplant slices with
a little olive oil and cook under a hot grill
(broiler) for 3 minutes on each side, or
until golden. Drain on paper towels.
4 Heat the remaining oil in a large heavy-
based saucepan. Sauté the onion and garlic
over medium heat for 3 minutes, or until
the onion is golden. Add the mushrooms
and cook for 3 minutes, or until browned.
Stir in the tomato, wine, tomato paste and
oregano. Bring to the boil, then reduce the
heat and simmer for 40 minutes, or until
the sauce has thickened.
5 Meanwhile, preheat the oven to 200°C
(400°F/Gas 6). Spoon the borlotti beans
into a large baking dish, then top with the
tomato sauce and eggplant slices.
6 To make the topping, whisk together the
yoghurt, eggs, milk and paprika. Pour over
the eggplant and set aside for 10 minutes.
Combine the parmesan and breadcrumbs in
a bowl. Sprinkle over the sauce, then bake
for 45–60 minutes, or until the moussaka is
heated through and the top is golden.

POTATO AND ZUCCHINI CASSEROLE

Serves 4–6

1 kg (2 lb 4 oz) ripe tomatoes
60 ml (2 fl oz/¼ cup) olive oil
2 onions, sliced
2 garlic cloves, crushed
400 g (14 oz) zucchini (courgettes),
    thickly sliced
400 g (14 oz) small waxy potatoes, such as
    pontiac or desiree, left unpeeled and cut
    into 1 cm (½ inch) slices
1 large red capsicum (pepper), cut into squares
1 teaspoon dried oregano
2 tablespoons chopped flat-leaf (Italian) parsley
2 tablespoons chopped dill
½ teaspoon ground cinnamon

1 Preheat the oven to 180°C (350°F/Gas 4). Score a cross in the base of each tomato. Place in a heatproof bowl and cover with boiling water. Leave for 30 seconds, then plunge into cold water and peel the skin away from the cross. Scoop out the seeds with a teaspoon, roughly chop the flesh and place in a large bowl.

2 Heat 2 tablespoons of the olive oil in a frying pan. Sauté the onion over medium heat for 10 minutes, then add the garlic and cook for a further 2 minutes. Add to the tomato with all the other ingredients. Season generously and mix well.

3 Transfer to a large baking dish and drizzle with the remaining oil. Cover and bake for 1–1½ hours, or until the vegetables are tender, stirring every 30 minutes. Serve hot.

ZUCCHINI PASTA BAKE

Serves 4

200 g (7 oz) risoni
40 g (1½ oz) butter
4 spring onions (scallions), thinly sliced
400 g (14 oz) zucchini (courgettes), grated
4 eggs
125 ml (4 fl oz/½ cup) pouring (whipping) cream
100 g (3½ oz/heaped ⅓ cup) ricotta cheese
  (see Note)
100 g (3½ oz/⅔ cup) grated mozzarella cheese
75 g (2½ oz/¾ cup) grated parmesan cheese

1 Preheat the oven to 180°C (350°F/Gas 4). Cook the risoni in a large saucepan of rapidly boiling salted water until *al dente*. Drain well.

2 Meanwhile, melt the butter in a frying pan. Sauté the spring onion for 1 minute, then add the zucchini and cook for a further 4 minutes, or until soft. Remove from the heat and leave to cool slightly.

3 Put the risoni in a bowl and mix in the eggs, cream, ricotta, mozzarella and half the parmesan. Stir in the zucchini mixture and season well.

4 Spoon into four 500 ml (17 fl oz/2 cup) greased ovenproof dishes, but not right up to the brim. Sprinkle with the remaining parmesan and bake for 25–30 minutes, or until firm and golden. Serve hot.

Note Because this dish has such simple flavours, it is important to use good-quality cheese for best results. Try to buy the ricotta off a wedge rather than in a tub.

WINTER VEGETABLE CASSEROLE

Serves 4

200 g (7 oz) pumpkin (winter squash)
2 all-purpose potatoes
1 parsnip
30 g (1 oz) butter
1 tablespoon plain (all-purpose) flour
375 ml (13 fl oz/1½ cups) milk
½ teaspoon ground nutmeg
cress or thyme leaves, to garnish

Crumble topping

80 g (2¾ oz/1 cup) fresh breadcrumbs
100 g (3½ oz/⅔ cup) roasted cashew nuts,
  roughly chopped
30 g (1 oz) butter

1 Preheat the oven to 180°C (350°F/Gas 4).
Bring a large saucepan of water to the boil.

Peel the pumpkin and cut into large
bite-sized pieces. Peel the potatoes and
parsnip and cut into smaller pieces. Add the
vegetables to the boiling water and cook for
8 minutes, or until just tender. Drain and
arrange in a large, deep baking dish.
2 Melt the butter in a saucepan over low
heat. Add the flour and stir for 1 minute,
then remove from the heat and gradually
stir in the milk. Return the pan to the heat.
Bring to the boil, stirring constantly, until
the sauce has thickened. Boil for a further
1 minute, then add the nutmeg and season
with sea salt and freshly ground black
pepper. Pour the sauce over the vegetables.
3 To make the crumble topping, mix
together the breadcrumbs and cashews and
sprinkle over the vegetables. Dot with the
butter, then bake for 30 minutes, or until
the topping is golden. Serve hot, garnished
with cress or thyme.

VEGETABLE CASSEROLE WITH HERB DUMPLINGS

Serves 4

1 tablespoon olive oil
1 large onion, chopped
2 garlic cloves, crushed
2 teaspoons sweet paprika
1 large all-purpose potato, chopped
1 large carrot, sliced
400 g (14 oz) tin chopped tomatoes
375 ml (13 fl oz/1½ cups) vegetable stock
400 g (14 oz) orange sweet potato, peeled
   and diced
150 g (5½ oz/2½ cups) broccoli florets
2 zucchini (courgettes), thickly sliced
2 tablespoons sour cream

Herb dumplings
125 g (4½ oz/1 cup) self-raising flour
20 g (¾ oz) cold butter, chopped
2 teaspoons chopped flat-leaf (Italian) parsley
1 teaspoon thyme
1 teaspoon chopped rosemary
80 ml (2½ fl oz/⅓ cup) milk

1 Preheat the oven to 200°C (400°F/Gas 6). Heat the olive oil in a large saucepan. Sauté the onion over medium heat for 5 minutes, or until soft. Add the garlic and paprika and cook, stirring, for 1 minute.
2 Add the potato, carrot, tomato and stock. Bring to the boil, then reduce the heat, cover and simmer for 10 minutes. Add the sweet potato, broccoli and zucchini and simmer for a further 10 minutes, or until all the vegetables are tender.
3 Meanwhile, make the dumplings. Sift the flour and a pinch of salt into a bowl. Lightly rub in the butter with your fingertips until the mixture resembles fine breadcrumbs. Stir in the herbs and make a well in the centre. Add the milk and mix using a flat-bladed knife until the mixture comes together in beads. Gather up the dough and lift onto a lightly floured surface. Divide into eight portions, then shape each into a ball.
4 Stir the sour cream into the casserole. Transfer to a 2 litre (70 fl oz/8 cup) baking dish and top with the dumplings. Bake for 20 minutes, or until the dumplings are golden and cooked. Serve hot.

BAKED POTATO CAKE

Serves 4–6

8 roasting potatoes, scrubbed
200 g (7 oz/2 cups) dry breadcrumbs
125 g (4½ oz/1 cup) grated cheddar cheese
50 g (1¾ oz/½ cup) grated parmesan cheese
30 g (1 oz) butter
2 tablespoons olive oil
1 garlic clove, crushed

1 Preheat the oven to 180°C (350°F/Gas 4). Grease a deep, 20 cm (8 inch) spring-form cake tin and line the base and side with baking paper.

2 Thinly slice the potatoes, leaving the skin on if desired. Mix the breadcrumbs, cheddar and parmesan in a bowl and set aside.
3 In a small saucepan, gently heat the butter and olive oil, then stir in the garlic and a good grind of black pepper. Remove from the heat.
4 Overlap some potato slices in the base of the cake tin. Brush with the butter mixture, then sprinkle with some of the breadcrumb mixture. Continue layering the ingredients, ending with a layer of cheese.
5 Press down firmly and bake for 1 hour, or until the topping is golden and the potato is tender. Serve hot.

FENNEL, TOMATO AND WHITE BEAN STEW

Serves 4–6

5 ripe tomatoes
2 leeks, white part only, sliced
2 garlic cloves, finely chopped
1 large fennel bulb, washed, halved,
    cored and sliced
60 ml (2 fl oz/¼ cup) extra virgin olive oil
60 ml (2 fl oz/¼ cup) Pernod
2 bay leaves
5 thyme sprigs
500 g (1 lb 2 oz) all-purpose potatoes,
    peeled and cut into large chunks
400 g (14 oz) tin cannellini beans, rinsed
    and drained
250 ml (9 fl oz/1 cup) vegetable stock
250 ml (9 fl oz/1 cup) dry white wine
ready-made pesto (see page 60), to serve

1 Preheat the oven to 180°C (350°F/Gas 4). Score a cross in the base of each tomato. Place in a heatproof bowl and cover with boiling water. Leave for 30 seconds, then plunge into cold water and peel the skin away from the cross. Scoop out the seeds with a teaspoon, chop the flesh and place in a large baking dish.

2 Stir in the leek, garlic, fennel, olive oil, Pernod, bay leaves and thyme. Mix well and set aside for at least 30 minutes, or preferably several hours if possible, to allow the flavours to develop.

3 Cover the dish and bake for 30 minutes. Add the potato, beans, stock and wine, mix well, then cover and bake for a further 35–45 minutes, or until the potato is cooked through. Remove the bay leaves and thyme sprigs.

4 Serve in warmed bowls, topped with a spoonful of pesto.

Slippery, slurpy noodles and ready-in-a-flash stir-fries: here is food that's so easy and quick to prepare, endlessly versatile, wonderfully healthy and also deliciously satisfying without being heavy. Aromatic with chilli, lemon grass, lime, tamarind, ginger and sesame, and starring those succulent Asian greens, this chapter is a culinary side street straight down Asia where exquisite, fragrant flavours linger— a great place to visit whenever jaded tastebuds need reviving or you need a simple zing of inspiration. Think of these recipes as a template to which you can add or vary your vegetables, herbs and flavourings at will, depending on the contents of your pantry and the promptings of fancy. Just have everything ready before you start cooking and dinner will be on the table before you know it.

NOODLES & STIR-FRIES

RICE NOODLES WITH GINGER AND SWEET CHILLI VEGETABLES

Serves 4

500 g (1 lb 2 oz) fresh rice noodle sheets, at room temperature
2 tablespoons vegetable oil
1 teaspoon sesame oil
3 tablespoons grated fresh ginger
1 onion, thinly sliced
1 red capsicum (pepper), sliced
100 g (3½ oz) shiitake mushrooms, sliced
200 g (7 oz) baby corn, halved
500 g (1 lb 2 oz) Chinese broccoli, sliced
200 g (7 oz) snow peas (mangetout)
60 ml (2 fl oz/¼ cup) sweet chilli sauce
2 tablespoons light soy sauce
2 tablespoons dark soy sauce
1 tablespoon lime juice
16 Thai basil leaves

1 Cut the noodle sheets into strips about 3 cm (1¼ inches) wide, then cut each strip into three. Gently separate the noodles—you may need to run a little cold water over them to do this.
2 Heat a wok until very hot. Add the vegetable and sesame oils and swirl to coat the side. Stir-fry the ginger and onion over medium–high heat for 4 minutes, or until the onion has softened. Add the vegetables and stir-fry until brightly coloured and just tender.
3 Add the noodles and stir-fry until they start to soften. Mix together the sweet chilli sauce, light and dark soy sauces and lime juice, then pour over the noodles, toss to coat and cook until heated through.
4 Remove from the heat, toss the Thai basil leaves through and serve.

BALTI EGGPLANT AND TOFU STIR-FRY

Serves 4

2 tablespoons vegetable oil
1 onion, finely chopped
70 g (2½ oz/¼ cup) balti curry paste (see Note)
300 g (10½ oz) slender eggplants (aubergines),
    cut diagonally into 1 cm (½ inch) slices
300 g (10½ oz) firm tofu, cut into 1.5 cm
    (⅝ inch) dice
3 ripe tomatoes, cut into wedges
60 ml (2 fl oz/¼ cup) vegetable stock
75 g (2½ oz/1⅔ cups) baby English spinach
    leaves
steamed rice, to serve
50 g (1¾ oz/⅓ cup) toasted cashew nuts

1 Heat a wok or deep frying pan until very hot. Add the oil and swirl to coat the side. Stir-fry the onion over high heat for 3–4 minutes, or until golden.
2 Stir in the curry paste and cook for 1 minute, then add the eggplant and cook for 5 minutes. Stir in the tofu and gently toss for 3–4 minutes, or until golden.
3 Add the tomato and stock and cook for 3 minutes, or until the tomato is soft. Stir in the spinach and cook until just wilted. Season to taste and serve on a bed of steamed rice, sprinkled with the cashews.
Note Originating in northern Pakistan, Balti is a type of Kashmiri cooking that has become highly popular in Britain, particularly in Birmingham. You can buy Balti curry paste from gourmet food stores and Asian markets. If you can't find it, you can use a Kashmiri or mild Indian curry paste in this recipe instead.

STIR-FRIED SPINACH WITH TOFU AND ASIAN GREENS

Serves 4

2 tablespoons lime juice
2 tablespoons vegetable oil
1 tablespoon soy sauce
1 teaspoon sambal oelek or chilli paste
½ teaspoon soft brown sugar
1 tablespoon peanut oil
200 g (7 oz) smoked tofu, cut into 2 cm (¾ inch) dice
450 g (1 lb/1 bunch) choy sum, trimmed and cut into 8 cm (3¼ inch) lengths
150 g (5½ oz) English spinach leaves, torn
2 teaspoons sesame seeds, toasted
a small handful of coriander (cilantro) leaves
steamed rice, to serve

1 Put the lime juice, vegetable oil, soy sauce, sambal oelek and sugar in a small bowl and mix well to make a dressing.
2 Heat a large wok until very hot. Add the peanut oil and swirl to coat the side. Stir-fry the tofu over medium heat for 2–3 minutes, or until golden brown. Add half the dressing and toss to coat. Remove the tofu from the wok and set aside.
3 Add the choy sum to the wok and stir-fry for 1 minute, then add the spinach and stir-fry for 1 minute. Return the tofu to the wok, add the sesame seeds and remaining dressing and toss lightly. Serve scattered with the coriander, with steamed rice.

TAMARI-ROASTED ALMONDS WITH SPICY GREEN BEANS AND JASMINE RICE

Serves 4–6

60 ml (2 fl oz/¼ cup) sesame oil
500 g (1 lb 2 oz/2½ cups) jasmine rice
1 long red chilli, seeded and finely chopped
2 cm (¾ inch) piece of ginger, peeled and grated
2 garlic cloves, crushed
375 g (13 oz) green beans, trimmed and cut
    into 5 cm (2 inch) lengths
125 ml (4 fl oz/½ cup) hoisin sauce
1 tablespoon soft brown sugar
2 tablespoons mirin
125 g (4½ oz/¾ cup) tamari-roasted almonds,
    roughly chopped (see Note)

1 Preheat the oven to 200°C (400°F/Gas 6). Heat 1 tablespoon of the sesame oil in a 1.5 litre (52 fl oz/6 cup) flameproof baking or casserole dish. Add the rice and stir until well coated, then stir in 1 litre (35 fl oz/ 4 cups) boiling water. Cover and bake for 20 minutes, or until the rice is tender and all the water has been absorbed. Keep warm.
2 Meanwhile, heat a wok until very hot, add the remaining oil and swirl to coat the side. Stir-fry the chilli, ginger and garlic over high heat for 1 minute.
3 Add the beans, hoisin sauce and sugar and stir-fry for 2 minutes. Stir in the mirin and cook for 1 minute, or until the beans are tender but still crunchy.
4 Divide the rice among serving bowls. Stir the almonds through the beans, divide the mixture among the bowls and serve.
Note Tamari-roasted almonds are sold in health food stores. If unavailable, soak raw almonds in tamari for 30 minutes, then drain and pat dry. Heat 1 tablespoon oil in a non-stick frying pan, add the almonds and toss over medium heat for 2–3 minutes. Drain and leave to dry before using.

SNAKE BEANS STIR-FRIED WITH THAI BASIL, GARLIC AND CHILLI

Serves 4 as a side dish

60 ml (2 fl oz/¼ cup) soy sauce
60 ml (2 fl oz/¼ cup) vegetable stock
2 tablespoons vegetable oil
1 teaspoon red curry paste
1 red Asian shallot, finely chopped
3 garlic cloves, finely sliced
1 small red chilli, seeded and sliced
500 g (1 lb 2 oz) snake (yard-long) beans, cut
    into 8 cm (3¼ inch) lengths on the diagonal
a handful of Thai basil leaves

1 In a small bowl, mix together the soy sauce, stock and 60 ml (2 fl oz/¼ cup) water. Set aside.

2 Heat a wok until very hot. Add the oil and swirl to coat the side. Add the curry paste, shallot, garlic and chilli and stir-fry over medium–high heat for 1 minute, or until fragrant. Add the snake beans and stir-fry for 5 minutes.

3 Stir in the sauce and cook, tossing gently, until the beans are tender. Remove from the heat and season to taste.

4 Stir half the Thai basil through the beans. Serve immediately, scattered with the remaining Thai basil.

ORANGE SWEET POTATO, SPINACH AND WATER CHESTNUT STIR-FRY

Serves 4

500 g (1 lb 2 oz) orange sweet potato, peeled
  and cut into 1.5 cm (⅝ inch) dice
1 tablespoon vegetable oil
2 garlic cloves, crushed
2 teaspoons sambal oelek or chilli sauce
225 g (8 oz) tin sliced water chestnuts
2 teaspoons grated palm sugar (jaggery) or
  soft brown sugar
500 g (1 lb 2 oz/1 bunch) English spinach,
  stems removed
2 tablespoons soy sauce
2 tablespoons vegetable stock
steamed rice, to serve

1 Boil, steam or microwave the sweet potato until tender. Drain well.

2 Heat a wok until very hot. Add the oil and swirl to coat the side. Stir-fry the garlic and sambal oelek over medium–high for 1 minute, or until fragrant. Add the sweet potato and water chestnuts and stir-fry for 2 minutes.

3 Reduce the heat to medium, add the palm sugar and cook for 2 minutes, or until the sugar has dissolved.

4 Add the spinach, soy sauce and stock and toss until the spinach has just wilted. Serve on a bed of steamed rice.

ASIAN GREENS WITH TERIYAKI TOFU DRESSING

Serves 6

650 g (1 lb 7 oz) baby bok choy (pak choy)
450 g (1 lb/1 bunch) choy sum
450 g (1 lb) snake (yard-long) beans, trimmed
60 ml (2 fl oz/¼ cup) vegetable oil
1 onion, thinly sliced
60 g (2¼ oz/⅓ cup) soft brown sugar
½ teaspoon ground chilli
2 tablespoons grated fresh ginger
250 ml (9 fl oz/1 cup) teriyaki sauce
1 tablespoon sesame oil
600 g (1 lb 5 oz) silken firm tofu, drained
steamed rice, to serve

1 Cut the baby bok choy and choy sum widthways into thirds. Cut the snake beans into long lengths.

2 Heat a wok until very hot. Add 1 tablespoon of the oil and swirl to coat the side. Stir-fry the onion over medium–high heat for 3–5 minutes, or until crisp. Remove using a slotted spoon and drain on paper towels.

3 Heat another tablespoon of the oil in the wok. Add the greens and stir-fry in batches for 2–3 minutes, or until just cooked, adding the remaining oil as needed. Remove and keep warm.

4 Drain any liquid from the wok. Mix together the sugar, chilli, ginger and teriyaki sauce, then add to the wok and bring to the boil. Simmer for 1 minute.

5 Add the sesame oil and tofu and simmer for 2 minutes, turning once—the tofu will break up. Divide the greens among serving plates, then top with the tofu mixture and fried onion. Serve with steamed rice.

POTATO NOODLES WITH VEGETABLES

Serves 4

30 g (1 oz) dried black fungus
300 g (10½ oz) dried potato starch noodles
4 spring onions (scallions)
2 tablespoons vegetable oil
60 ml (2 fl oz/¼ cup) sesame oil
3 garlic cloves, finely chopped
4 cm (1½ inch) piece of fresh ginger,
    peeled and grated
2 carrots, cut into short matchsticks
500 g (1 lb 2 oz/1 bunch) baby bok choy
    (pak choy), leaves separated, or 250 g
    (9 oz) English spinach, roughly chopped
60 ml (2 fl oz/¼ cup) shoyu
2 tablespoons mirin
1 teaspoon sugar
1 toasted nori sheet, cut into thin, short strips
toasted sesame seeds, to garnish

1 Soak the dried black fungus in warm water for 15–30 minutes, or until soft. Drain, then roughly chop and set aside.
2 Meanwhile, cook the noodles in a saucepan of boiling water for 5 minutes, or until translucent. Drain and rinse under cold running water to remove the excess starch. Chop into 15 cm (6 inch) lengths and set aside.
3 Finely chop two spring onions and cut the others into short lengths. Set aside.
4 Heat a wok until very hot. Add the vegetable oil and 1 tablespoon of the sesame oil and swirl to coat the side. Stir-fry the garlic, ginger and finely chopped spring onion over medium heat for 3 minutes. Add the carrot and stir-fry for 1 minute.
5 Add the noodles, remaining sesame oil, remaining spring onion, bok choy, shoyu, mirin and sugar. Toss well, then cover and cook over low heat for 2 minutes.
6 Add the black fungus, then cover and cook for a further 2 minutes. Serve scattered with the nori strips and sesame seeds.

PHAD THAI
Serves 4

400 g (14 oz) dried flat rice stick noodles
2 tablespoons peanut oil
2 eggs, lightly beaten
1 onion, cut into thin wedges
2 garlic cloves, crushed
1 small red capsicum (pepper), cut into thin strips
100 g (3½ oz) fried tofu, cut into strips 5 mm
   (¼ inch) wide
6 spring onions (scallions), thinly sliced on the
   diagonal
a handful of chopped coriander (cilantro) leaves
60 ml (2 fl oz/¼ cup) soy sauce
2 tablespoons lime juice
1 tablespoon soft brown sugar
2 teaspoons sambal oelek or chilli sauce
90 g (3¼ oz/1 cup) bean sprouts, tails trimmed
40 g (1½ oz/¼ cup) chopped roasted unsalted
   peanuts

1 Cook the noodles in a saucepan of boiling water for 5–10 minutes, or until tender. Drain and set aside.
2 Heat a wok over high heat and swirl in enough peanut oil to coat the bottom and side. When the oil is smoking, add the egg and swirl to form a thin omelette. Cook for 30 seconds, or until just set. Roll up, remove from the pan and thinly slice.
3 Heat the remaining sesame oil in the wok. Stir-fry the onion, garlic and capsicum over high heat for 2–3 minutes, or until the onion has softened. Add the noodles, tossing well. Stir in the omelette, tofu, spring onion and half the coriander.
4 Mix together the soy sauce, lime juice, sugar and sambal oelek, then pour it over the noodles and toss to coat. Sprinkle the bean shoots over the top and garnish with the peanuts and the remaining coriander. Serve immediately.

CHINESE BROCCOLI WITH GINGER, LIME AND PEANUTS

Serves 4 as a side dish

40 g (1½ oz) tamarind pulp
1 tablespoon peanut oil
600 g (1 lb 5 oz) Chinese broccoli, trimmed
　and cut in half
1 small red chilli, seeded and finely chopped
2 garlic cloves, finely chopped
3 teaspoons finely grated fresh ginger
1 tablespoon sugar
1 tablespoon lime juice
1 teaspoon sesame oil
1 tablespoon finely chopped roasted
　unsalted peanuts

1 Put the tamarind pulp in a bowl and pour in 60 ml (2 fl oz/¼ cup) boiling water. Allow to steep for 5 minutes, then strain, discarding the solids.

2 Heat a wok until very hot. Add the peanut oil and swirl to coat the side. Stir-fry the Chinese broccoli over medium–high for 2–3 minutes, or until just wilted.

3 Add the chilli, garlic and ginger and toss for 1 minute, then stir in the sugar, lime juice and 1 tablespoon of tamarind liquid. Simmer for 1 minute.

4 Remove the Chinese broccoli to a serving plate and drizzle with the sesame oil. Scatter with the peanuts, season to taste and serve.

SICHUAN-STYLE EGGPLANT

Serves 4

3 teaspoons chilli paste
2 tablespoons Chinese rice wine
2 tablespoons soy sauce
½ teaspoon sugar
2 teaspoons Chinese black vinegar
250 ml (9 fl oz/1 cup) vegetable stock
½ teaspoon sesame oil
2 tablespoons vegetable oil
500 g (1 lb 2 oz) eggplant (aubergine),
　　cut into large dice
4 garlic cloves, finely sliced
1 tablespoon julienned fresh ginger
4 spring onions (scallions), finely sliced
　　on the diagonal
1 red chilli, finely chopped
steamed jasmine rice, to serve

1 Put the chilli paste, rice wine, soy sauce, sugar, vinegar, stock and sesame oil in a small bowl with 125 ml (4 fl oz/½ cup) water. Mix together well to make a sauce. Set aside.

2 Heat a wok until very hot. Add the vegetable oil and swirl to coat the side. Stir-fry the eggplant, garlic, ginger, spring onion and chilli over medium–high heat for 3 minutes.

3 Pour in the sauce and stir to coat the eggplant. Reduce the heat, then cover and simmer for 20 minutes, or until the eggplant is tender and the sauce has been absorbed, stirring occasionally. Serve hot, with steamed jasmine rice.

TOFU WITH CHILLI RELISH AND CASHEWS

Serves 4

Chilli relish

80 ml (2½ fl oz/⅓ cup) peanut oil
12 red Asian shallots, chopped
8 garlic cloves, chopped
8 long red chillies, chopped
2 red capsicums (peppers), chopped
1 tablespoon tamarind concentrate
1 tablespoon soy sauce
100 g (3½ oz/¾ cup) grated palm sugar (jaggery),
    or soft brown sugar

2 tablespoons kecap manis
1 tablespoon peanut oil
6 spring onions (scallions), cut into 3 cm
    (1¼ inch) lengths
750 g (1 lb 10 oz) silken firm tofu, cut into
    3 cm (1¼ inch) dice
a large handful of Thai basil
100 g (3½ oz/⅔ cup) roasted salted cashew nuts
steamed rice, to serve

1 To make the chilli relish, heat half the peanut oil in a frying pan and sauté the shallot and garlic over medium heat for 2 minutes. Transfer to a food processor, add the chilli and capsicum and process until smooth. Heat the remaining oil in the pan, add the shallot mixture and cook over medium heat for 2 minutes. Stir in the tamarind, soy sauce and sugar and cook for 20 minutes, stirring occasionally.

2 Put 2–3 tablespoons of the relish in a small bowl (store the remainder in a small airtight jar in the fridge). Add the kecap manis, mix well and set aside.

3 Heat a wok until very hot. Add the peanut oil and swirl to coat the side. Stir-fry the spring onion over medium–high heat for 30 seconds, then remove from the wok.

4 Stir-fry the tofu for 1 minute, then stir in the relish mixture. Cook for 3 minutes, or until the tofu is coated and heated through. Toss the spring onion, Thai basil and cashews through and stir-fry just until the basil has wilted. Serve with steamed rice.

UDON NOODLE STIR-FRY

Serves 4

500 g (1 lb 2 oz) fresh udon noodles
1 tablespoon sesame oil
6 spring onions (scallions), cut into short lengths
3 garlic cloves, crushed
1 tablespoon grated fresh ginger
2 carrots, cut into short lengths
150 g (5½ oz) snow peas (mangetout),
    cut in half on the diagonal
100 g (3½ oz/heaped 1 cup) bean sprouts,
    tails trimmed
450 g (1 lb/1 bunch) choy sum, chopped
2 tablespoons shoyu
2 tablespoons mirin
2 tablespoons kecap manis
2 roasted nori sheets, cut into thin strips

1 Cook the noodles in a saucepan of boiling water for 5 minutes, or until they are tender and not clumped together. Drain, rinse under hot water and set aside.
2 Heat a wok until very hot. Add the sesame oil and swirl to coat the side. Stir-fry the spring onion, garlic and ginger over high heat for 1–2 minutes, or until softened. Add the carrot, snow peas and 1 tablespoon water and toss well. Cover and cook for 1–2 minutes, or until the vegetables are just tender.
3 Add the noodles, bean sprouts, choy sum, shoyu, mirin and kecap manis, then toss until the choy sum is just wilted and coated with the sauce. Stir in the nori just before serving.

TEMPEH STIR-FRY

Serves 4

1 teaspoon sesame oil
1 tablespoon peanut oil
2 garlic cloves, crushed
1 tablespoon grated fresh ginger
1 red chilli, finely sliced
4 spring onions (scallions), sliced on the diagonal
300 g (10½ oz) tempeh, diced
500 g (1 lb 2 oz/1 bunch) baby bok choy (pak choy), leaves separated
800 g (1 lb 12 oz) Chinese broccoli, chopped
125 ml (4 fl oz/½ cup) mushroom oyster sauce
2 tablespoons rice vinegar
2 tablespoons coriander (cilantro) leaves
40 g (1½ oz/¼ cup) cashew nuts, toasted
steamed rice, to serve

1 Heat a wok until very hot. Add the sesame and peanut oils and swirl to coat the side. Stir-fry the garlic, ginger, chilli and spring onion over medium heat for 1–2 minutes, or until softened. Add the tempeh and cook for 5 minutes, or until golden. Remove the mixture from the wok and keep warm.

2 Add half the greens and 1 tablespoon water to the wok. Cover and cook for 3–4 minutes, or until wilted. Remove from the wok and cook the remaining greens with a little more water.

3 Return the greens and tempeh to the wok. Add the mushroom oyster sauce and vinegar and toss to warm through. Sprinkle with the coriander and nuts and serve with steamed rice.

FRAGRANT GREENS

Serves 4 as a side dish

2 tablespoons vegetable oil
300 g (10½ oz) broccoli, cut into small florets
150 g (5½ oz) snake (yard-long) beans, trimmed and cut into short lengths
3 spring onions (scallions), sliced
250 g (9 oz/3⅓ cups) finely shredded cabbage
1 green capsicum (pepper), cut into strips
2 tablespoons lime juice
1 tablespoon soft brown sugar
a small handful of Thai basil leaves, shredded

1 Heat a wok until very hot. Add the oil and swirl to coat the side. Stir-fry the broccoli and snake beans over medium–high heat for 3–4 minutes, or until bright green and just tender. Add the spring onion, cabbage and capsicum and continue stir-frying until just softened.

2 Mix together the lime juice and sugar, stirring until the sugar has dissolved. Add to the wok with the Thai basil, then toss together and serve.

Note You can use any green vegetable in this dish, including Asian greens such as choy sum or bok choy (pak choy). If you can't find Thai basil, use sweet basil or coriander (cilantro).

MUSHROOM LONG-LIFE NOODLES

Serves 4

125 g (4½ oz) dried black fungus, sliced
400 g (14 oz) pancit canton noodles,
 or other dried yellow egg noodles
1 tablespoon peanut oil
60 ml (2 fl oz/¼ cup) soy sauce
1½ tablespoons mushroom soy sauce
1 teaspoon sesame oil
1 teaspoon sugar
250 ml (9 fl oz/1 cup) vegetable stock
1 tablespoon grated fresh ginger
2 garlic cloves, crushed
250 g (9 oz) fresh shiitake mushrooms, sliced
250 g (9 oz) shimeji mushrooms, separated
250 g (9 oz) enoki mushrooms, separated
4 spring onions (scallions), finely sliced
 on the diagonal

1 Soak the dried black fungus in warm water for 15–30 minutes, or until soft. Drain well and set aside.

2 Cook the noodles in a saucepan of boiling water for 3 minutes, or until tender. Drain, rinse under cold water, then drain again. Toss the noodles with 1 teaspoon of the peanut oil.

3 Put the soy sauce, mushroom soy sauce, sesame oil, sugar and stock in a small bowl and mix together well. Set aside.

4 Heat a wok until very hot. Add the remaining peanut oil and swirl to coat the side. Stir-fry the ginger and garlic over medium–high heat for 1 minute, then add the black fungus, shiitake and shimeji mushrooms and stir-fry for 3 minutes.

5 Add the noodles, enoki mushrooms, spring onion and soy sauce mixture and gently toss, cooking until the noodles have absorbed the sauce. Serve immediately.

STIR-FRIED CAULIFLOWER WITH TOASTED NUTS

Serves 4 as a side dish

2 tablespoons vegetable oil
2 tablespoons mild curry paste
1 tablespoon currants
1 tablespoon grated fresh ginger
4 spring onions (scallions), sliced on
   the diagonal
500 g (1 lb 2 oz) cauliflower, cut into
   bite-sized florets
2 teaspoons sesame oil
150 g (5½ oz/1½ cups) walnuts, toasted
150 g (5½ oz/1 cup) cashew nuts, toasted
1 tablespoon sesame seeds

1 Heat a wok until very hot. Add the vegetable oil and swirl to coat the side. Stir-fry the curry paste over medium–high heat for 3 minutes, or until fragrant.
2 Add the currants, ginger, spring onion and cauliflower and stir-fry for 4–5 minutes, adding about 80 ml (2½ fl oz/⅓ cup) water to moisten. Cover and steam for 1 minute, or until the cauliflower is tender. Season to taste and drizzle with the sesame oil.
3 Toss the nuts through the cauliflower mixture and serve sprinkled with the sesame seeds.

CHILLI NOODLE AND NUT STIR-FRY

Serves 4

1½ tablespoons vegetable oil

1 tablespoon sesame oil

1 large onion, cut into thin wedges

4 garlic cloves, very thinly sliced

2–3 small red chillies, finely chopped

1 red capsicum (pepper), cut into strips

1 green capsicum (pepper), cut into strips

2 large carrots, cut into batons

100 g (3½ oz) green beans, trimmed

2 celery stalks, cut into batons

2 teaspoons honey

500 g (1 lb 2 oz) hokkien (egg) noodles, separated

100 g (3½ oz/⅔ cup) dry-roasted peanuts

100 g (3½ oz/⅔ cup) honey-roasted cashew nuts

3 tablespoons chopped garlic chives, or 4 spring onions (scallions), chopped

sweet chilli sauce, to serve

1 Heat a wok until very hot. Add the vegetable and sesame oils and swirl to coat the side. Stir-fry the onion, garlic and chilli over high heat for 1 minute, or until the onion just starts to soften.

2 Add the red and green capsicum, carrot and beans and stir-fry for 1 minute.

3 Add the celery, honey and 1 tablespoon water, toss well, then cover and cook for 1–2 minutes, or until the vegetables are just tender.

4 Add the noodles and nuts. Toss together well, then cover and cook for a further 1–2 minutes, or until the noodles are heated through. Mix the garlic chives through and serve drizzled with sweet chilli sauce.

STIR-FRIED MUSHROOMS WITH BASIL

Serves 4 as a side dish

1 tablespoon sesame oil

2.5 cm (1 inch) piece of galangal, peeled and thinly sliced

2 garlic cloves, chopped

2 red chillies, thinly sliced

200 g (7 oz) button mushrooms, halved

100 g (3½ oz) oyster mushrooms, halved

1 tablespoon soy sauce

2 handfuls of basil, chopped

1 Heat a wok until hot. Add the sesame oil and swirl to coat the side. Add the galangal, garlic and chilli and stir-fry over medium–high heat for 2 minutes.
2 Add the button mushrooms and stir-fry for a further 2 minutes, then add the oyster mushrooms and stir-fry for 30 seconds, tossing constantly until the mushrooms start to soften. Add the soy sauce and basil, toss well and serve.

PUMPKIN AND CASHEW STIR-FRY

Serves 4–6

2 tablespoons vegetable oil
155 g (5½ oz/1 cup) cashew nuts
1 leek, white part only, sliced
2 teaspoons ground coriander
2 teaspoons ground cumin
2 teaspoons brown mustard seeds
2 garlic cloves, crushed
1 kg (2 lb 4 oz) butternut pumpkin (squash), peeled and diced
185 ml (6 fl oz/¾ cup) orange juice
1 teaspoon soft brown sugar
steamed rice, to serve

1 Heat a large wok until very hot. Add half the oil and swirl to coat the side. Stir-fry the cashews over medium heat until golden, then remove using a slotted spoon and drain on paper towels.

2 Stir-fry the leek for 2–3 minutes, or until softened. Remove from the wok.

3 Reheat the wok, add the remaining oil and stir-fry the spices and garlic for 2 minutes, or until the spices are fragrant and the mustard seeds begin to pop.

4 Add the pumpkin and stir to coat well. Stir-fry for 5 minutes, or until the pumpkin is brown and tender.

5 Add the orange juice and sugar, bring to the boil, then reduce the heat and cook for 5 minutes. Return the leek to the wok, add most of the cashews and toss well. Sprinkle with the remaining cashews and serve with steamed rice.

SOMEN NESTS WITH EGGPLANT AND SHIITAKE MUSHROOMS

Serves 4

2 small eggplants (aubergines),
   cut into slices 1 cm (½ inch) thick
12 dried shiitake mushrooms
60 ml (2 fl oz/¼ cup) vegetable oil
100 g (3½ oz) enoki mushrooms
1 tablespoon sugar
1 tablespoon white miso paste
1 tablespoon mirin
60 ml (2 fl oz/¼ cup) shoyu
300 g (10½ oz) dried somen noodles

1 Blanch the eggplant slices in boiling water for 5 minutes. Drain, transfer to a plate and weigh down with a plate for 15 minutes to press out any remaining liquid. Pat dry with paper towels.

2 Soak the dried shiitake mushrooms in 250 ml (9 fl oz/1 cup) boiling water for 10 minutes. Drain, reserving the liquid.
3 Heat the oil in a large frying pan. Cook the eggplant in batches over medium heat until golden brown on both sides. Remove from the pan and keep warm.
4 Add the enoki mushrooms to the pan, cook for 10 seconds, then remove.
5 Add the sugar, miso, mirin and shoyu to the pan with the shiitake mushrooms, reserved mushroom liquid and 125 ml (4 fl oz/½ cup) water. Stir well, bring to the boil, then reduce the heat, cover and simmer for 10 minutes, or until reduced to a sauce.
6 Meanwhile, cook the noodles in boiling water for 3 minutes, or until tender.
7 Drain the noodles, divide among serving plates and swirl into nests. Top with the eggplant and mushrooms, drizzle with the sauce and serve immediately.

IDIYAPPAM

Serves 4

225 g (8 oz) rice stick noodles
80 ml (2½ fl oz/⅓ cup) vegetable oil
50 g (1¾ oz/⅓ cup) cashew nuts
½ onion, chopped
150 g (5½ oz/1 cup) fresh or frozen peas
10 curry leaves
2 carrots, grated
2 leeks, white part only, finely shredded
1 red capsicum (pepper), diced
2 tablespoons tomato sauce (ketchup)
1 tablespoon soy sauce
1 teaspoon sea salt
3 hard-boiled eggs, peeled and cut
   into wedges

1 Soak the noodles in cold water for 30 minutes, then drain and place in a saucepan of boiling water. Remove from the heat and stand for 3 minutes, then drain and refresh in cold water.

2 Heat 1 tablespoon of the oil in a wok. Add the cashews and fry over medium heat until golden. Remove and set aside.

3 Add the onion to the wok and stir-fry for 7 minutes, or until dark golden. Remove and drain on paper towels.

4 Meanwhile, cook the peas in boiling water until tender. Drain and keep warm.

5 Heat the remaining oil in the wok over medium heat. Briefly fry the curry leaves, then add the carrot, leek and capsicum and stir for 1 minute.

6 Add the tomato sauce, soy sauce, salt and noodles and cook until heated through, stirring constantly so the noodles don't stick. Pile the noodles onto a platter and serve garnished with the peas, cashews, fried onion and egg.

STIR-FRIED CRISP TOFU IN A HOT BEAN SAUCE

Serves 4

500 g (1 lb 2 oz) firm tofu, cut into small dice
2 tablespoons peanut oil
60 ml (2 fl oz/¼ cup) soy sauce
2 teaspoons finely grated fresh ginger
125 g (4½ oz/¾ cup) rice flour
vegetable oil, for pan-frying
2 onions, cut into thin wedges
2 garlic cloves, finely chopped
2 teaspoons soft brown sugar
½ red capsicum (pepper), cut into thin strips
5 spring onions (scallions), cut into short lengths
2 tablespoons dry sherry
2 teaspoons finely grated orange zest
2 tablespoons hot bean paste, or to taste
  (see Note)
steamed rice, to serve

1 Put the tofu in a non-metallic bowl. Mix together the peanut oil, soy sauce and ginger, then pour over the tofu and toss to coat. Cover and refrigerate for 30 minutes.

2 Drain the tofu, reserving the marinade, then toss several pieces at a time in the rice flour to coat heavily.
3 Heat a wok until very hot. Add about 60 ml (2 fl oz/¼ cup) vegetable oil and swirl to coat the side. Working in batches, stir-fry the tofu over medium heat for 1½ minutes, or until golden all over, adding more oil as needed. Remove from the wok, drain on paper towels and keep warm.
4 Drain any oil from the wok. Reheat the wok, add 1 tablespoon of fresh oil and stir-fry the onion, garlic and sugar for 3 minutes, or until the onion is golden. Add the capsicum, spring onion, sherry, orange zest, bean paste and reserved tofu marinade. Stir and bring to the boil, then add the tofu and toss to heat through. Serve with steamed rice.
Note Hot bean pastes are sold in Asian grocery stores. These salty, intensely flavoured pastes are made from fermented soya beans or black beans, with chilli and other spices added. They vary quite widely in heat, so adjust the quantity to suit.

HOKKIEN NOODLES WITH ASIAN GREENS AND GLAZED TOFU

Serves 4

Marinade
60 ml (2 fl oz/¼ cup) kecap manis
1 tablespoon mushroom soy sauce
1 tablespoon vegetarian oyster sauce

300 g (10½ oz) firm tofu, cut into slices
   1 cm (½ inch) thick
1 teaspoon sesame oil
60 ml (2 fl oz/¼ cup) peanut oil
1 onion, cut into wedges
2 garlic cloves, crushed
1 tablespoon grated fresh ginger
450 g (1 lb/1 bunch) choy sum, chopped
500 g (1 lb 2 oz/1 bunch) baby bok choy
   (pak choy), chopped
450 g (1 lb) hokkien (egg) noodles, separated

1 In a small bowl, mix together the marinade ingredients. Spread the tofu slices in a shallow non-metallic dish and pour the marinade over, tossing to coat. Cover and leave to marinate for at least 15 minutes. Drain the tofu, reserving the marinade.
2 Heat a wok until very hot. Add the sesame oil and 1 tablespoon of the peanut oil and swirl to coat the side. Stir-fry the onion, garlic and ginger over medium heat for 5 minutes, or until the onion has softened. Remove and set aside.
3 Add the vegetables to the wok and stir-fry until just wilted. Remove and keep warm.
4 Toss the noodles and reserved marinade in the wok and stir-fry until heated through. Divide among serving plates.
5 Heat the remaining peanut oil in the wok and quickly stir-fry the tofu until browned all over. Arrange the tofu, greens and onion mixture over the noodles and serve.

The very essence of simplicity, salads showcase nature's goodness and are a colourful way to add crunch, texture and vitality to a plate. Because they're so simply constructed, when it comes to salads fresh is definitely best: using premium produce and ingredients will make all the difference between a dull, boring salad and one that really sings. Some salads are substantial enough to enjoy on their own as a lovely light lunch or supper—and when they taste this fabulous it's easy to forget how very good they are for you too! This chapter brings together some much-loved salads from around the globe, as well as fresh twists on a few time-honoured classics. So grab those tongs, get thee to the crisper and start tossing...

SALADS

WARM POTATO SALAD WITH GREEN OLIVE DRESSING

Serves 6

1.5 kg (3 lb 5 oz) small boiling potatoes,
    such as nicola, scrubbed
90 g (3¼ oz/½ cup) green olives,
    pitted and finely chopped
2 teaspoons capers, finely chopped
a handful of flat-leaf (Italian) parsley, chopped
1 teaspoon finely grated lemon zest
2 tablespoons lemon juice
2 garlic cloves, crushed
125 ml (4 fl oz/½ cup) extra virgin olive oil

1 Boil the potatoes for 15 minutes, or until just tender when pierced with the tip of a sharp knife. Drain and cool slightly.
2 Meanwhile, put the remaining ingredients in a small bowl and whisk together with a fork.
3 Cut the warm potatoes in half and place in a serving bowl. Pour the dressing over and gently toss. Season to taste with freshly ground black pepper and a little sea salt if desired. Serve warm.

ASPARAGUS ORANGE SALAD

Serves 4

300 g (10½ oz) thin asparagus spears
50 g (1¾ oz/1⅔ cups) watercress sprigs
½ small red onion, very thinly sliced
1 orange, cut into 12 segments
1 teaspoon finely grated orange zest
1 tablespoon orange juice
1 teaspoon sugar
1 tablespoon red wine vinegar
2 teaspoons poppy seeds
2 tablespoons olive oil
60 g (2¼ oz/½ cup) crumbled goat's cheese

1 Cook the asparagus in boiling water for 1–2 minutes, or until just tender. Refresh under cold running water and drain well.
2 Arrange the asparagus on a platter with the watercress, onion and orange segments.
3 Put the orange zest, orange juice, sugar, vinegar and poppy seeds in a small bowl. Whisk in the olive oil with a fork until well combined, then drizzle over the salad.
4 Scatter the goat's cheese over the salad, season to taste with sea salt and freshly ground black pepper and serve.

SWEET POTATO AND SPINACH SALAD

Serves 4

1 pitta bread
60 ml (2 fl oz/¼ cup) olive oil
500 g (1 lb 2 oz) orange sweet potato
1 small orange
150 g (5½ oz/3⅓ cups) baby English
   spinach leaves

Orange sesame dressing
60 ml (2 fl oz/¼ cup) olive oil
1 teaspoon sesame oil
2 tablespoons orange juice
1 teaspoon finely grated orange zest
1 teaspoon lemon juice
1 garlic clove, crushed
2 teaspoons dijon mustard

1 Heat the grill (broiler) to high. Cut off and discard the edge of the pitta bread. Split the bread into two thin halves, then lightly brush all over with some of the olive oil. Toast under the grill until crisp and lightly browned. Set aside.

2 Scrub the sweet potato, leave the skin on and cut into slices 1 cm (½ inch) thick. Toss in the remaining oil and cook under the grill for 10 minutes, or until soft and golden, turning once. Place in a salad bowl.

3 Using a sharp knife, cut a thin slice off the top and bottom of the orange. Slice off the skin, removing as much pith as possible. Slice down the side of an orange segment, between the flesh and membrane. Repeat on the other side and lift the segment out. Repeat to remove all the segments. Lightly toss the orange segments through the salad, along with the spinach.

4 Break the pitta crisps into small shards and scatter over the salad.

5 Put all the orange sesame dressing ingredients in a small bowl and whisk together well. Season to taste and pour over the salad just before serving.

CHERRY AND PEAR TOMATO SALAD WITH WHITE BEANS

Serves 4

60 ml (2 fl oz/¼ cup) olive oil
2 red Asian shallots, finely diced
1 large garlic clove, crushed
1½ tablespoons lemon juice
250 g (9 oz) red cherry tomatoes, halved
250 g (9 oz) yellow pear tomatoes, halved
425 g (15 oz) tin white beans, drained
    and rinsed
a handful of basil leaves, torn
2 tablespoons chopped parsley

1 Put the olive oil, shallot, garlic and lemon juice in a small bowl and whisk to make a dressing.
2 Place the tomatoes and beans in a serving bowl. Drizzle with the dressing and scatter the basil and parsley over the top. Gently toss together and serve.

TUNISIAN EGGPLANT SALAD

Serves 4

2 large eggplants (aubergines), cut into
    2 cm (¾ inch) dice
125 ml (4 fl oz/½ cup) olive oil
1 teaspoon cumin seeds
2 garlic cloves, very thinly sliced
1 tablespoon currants
1 tablespoon slivered almonds
6 small roma (plum) tomatoes, quartered
    lengthways
1 teaspoon dried oregano
4 bird's eye chillies, halved lengthways
    and seeded
2 tablespoons lemon juice
4 tablespoons chopped parsley
½ preserved or salted lemon
extra virgin olive oil, for drizzling

1 Put the eggplant in a large colander and sprinkle well with sea salt. Set aside to drain in the sink for 2–3 hours. Dry with paper towels.

2 Heat half the olive oil in a large heavy-based saucepan over medium–high heat. Fry the eggplant in batches for 5–6 minutes at a time, or until golden, turning halfway through and adding more oil as needed. Drain on paper towels and set aside.

3 Reduce the heat and add any remaining oil to the pan, along with the cumin, garlic, currants and almonds. Sauté for 30 seconds, or until the garlic starts to colour. Add the tomato and oregano and cook for 1 minute.

4 Remove from the heat and add the eggplant, chilli, lemon juice and parsley. Discard the salty flesh from the preserved lemon, cut the rind into thin strips and add to the salad. Toss gently and season with freshly ground black pepper.

5 Set aside at room temperature for several hours for the flavours to develop. Just before serving, check the seasoning and drizzle with extra virgin olive oil.

Note The eggplant may be salted for up to 24 hours to extract all the moisture, so that less oil is required for frying.

MOROCCAN CARROT SALAD WITH GREEN OLIVES AND MINT

Serves 4

1½ teaspoons cumin seeds
½ teaspoon coriander seeds
1 tablespoon red wine vinegar
2 tablespoons olive oil
1 garlic clove, crushed
2 teaspoons harissa
¼ teaspoon orange flower water
600 g (1 lb 5 oz) baby (Dutch) carrots
8 large green olives, pitted and finely sliced
2 tablespoons shredded mint
30 g (1 oz/1 cup) watercress sprigs

1 Put the cumin and coriander seeds in a small frying pan and toast over medium–high heat for 30 seconds, or until fragrant. Tip the seeds into a small bowl to cool, then grind to a powder using a mortar and pestle or spice grinder.
2 Put the spice mix in a large bowl. Add the vinegar, olive oil, garlic, harissa and orange flower water. Whisk to make a dressing.
3 Scrub the carrots well and trim the tops. Blanch the carrots in boiling salted water for 5 minutes, or until almost tender. Drain in a colander and allow to dry for a few minutes.
4 Add the hot carrots to the dressing and toss gently to coat. Allow to cool to room temperature, for the dressing to infuse into the carrots.
5 Just before serving, add the green olives and mint. Season well and toss gently to combine. Serve on a bed of watercress.

TABOULEH

Serves 6

130 g (4½ oz/¾ cup) burghul (bulgur)
3 ripe tomatoes
1 telegraph (long) cucumber
4 spring onions (scallions), sliced
1 bunch (150 g/5½ oz) flat-leaf (Italian)
    parsley, chopped
a handful of chopped mint
80 ml (2½ fl oz/⅓ cup) lemon juice
1½ teaspoons sea salt
60 ml (2 fl oz/¼ cup) olive oil
1 tablespoon extra virgin olive oil

1 Put the burghul in a bowl, cover with 500 ml (17 fl oz/2 cups) water and leave to soak for 1½ hours.

2 Drain the burghul and squeeze out any excess water. Spread out on paper towels and leave to dry for 30 minutes.

3 Cut the tomatoes in half and squeeze out any excess seeds. Cut the flesh into 1 cm (½ inch) dice and place in a salad bowl. Cut the cucumber in half lengthways and scoop out the seeds. Cut the flesh into 1 cm (½ inch) dice and add to the tomatoes.

4 Add the burghul, spring onion, parsley and mint and toss together well.

5 In a small bowl, whisk together the lemon juice and sea salt until the salt has dissolved. Season well with freshly ground black pepper and slowly whisk in the olive oils to make a dressing.

6 Pour the dressing over the salad, toss well and serve.

FATTOUSH

Serves 4

1 large pitta bread, split
2 baby cos (romaine) lettuces, torn into
  bite-sized pieces
2 tomatoes, chopped
2 small Lebanese (short) cucumbers, chopped
1 green capsicum (pepper), chopped
4 spring onions (scallions), chopped
a large handful of mint, roughly chopped
a large handful of coriander (cilantro) leaves,
  roughly chopped

Dressing
60 ml (2 fl oz/¼ cup) lemon juice
60 ml (2 fl oz/¼ cup) olive oil
1 tablespoon sumac

1 Preheat the oven to 180°C (350°F/Gas 4).
Place the pitta bread on a baking tray and
bake for 5 minutes, or until golden and
crisp. Remove from the oven and set aside
to cool. Break into 2 cm (¾ inch) pieces.
2 Mix together the dressing ingredients
and season to taste with sea salt and
freshly ground black pepper.
3 Put the lettuce, tomato, cucumber,
capsicum, spring onion and herbs in a
salad bowl and toss together.
4 Crumble the pitta bread pieces over
the salad. Drizzle with the dressing and
serve immediately so the bread doesn't
become soggy.

CHARGRILLED CAULIFLOWER SALAD WITH TAHINI DRESSING

Serves 4

Tahini dressing
65 g (2¼ oz/¼ cup) tahini
1 garlic clove, crushed
60 ml (2 fl oz/¼ cup) seasoned rice vinegar
1 tablespoon vegetable oil
1 teaspoon lime juice
¼ teaspoon sesame oil

1 head of cauliflower
12 garlic cloves, crushed
2 tablespoons vegetable oil
2 baby cos (romaine) lettuces, leaves separated
50 g (1¾ oz/1⅔ cups) watercress sprigs
2 teaspoons sesame seeds, toasted
1 tablespoon chopped flat-leaf (Italian) parsley

1 Heat a chargrill pan or barbecue grill plate to medium.

2 Put all the tahini dressing ingredients in a non-metallic bowl with 1 tablespoon water. Whisk together well and season to taste with sea salt and freshly ground black pepper.

3 Cut the cauliflower in half, then into 1 cm (½ inch) wedges. Place on a tray and gently rub with the garlic and oil. Season well, then chargrill, in batches if necessary, until golden on both sides and cooked through. Remove from the heat.

4 Arrange the lettuce and watercress in a salad bowl and top with the cauliflower. Drizzle the dressing over the cauliflower, sprinkle with the sesame seeds and parsley and serve.

SALATA BALADI
(ARABIC VEGETABLE SALAD)

Serves 4–6

2 tablespoons extra virgin olive oil

2 tablespoons lemon juice

1 cos (romaine) lettuce, torn into
   bite-sized pieces

3 ripe tomatoes, each cut into 8 wedges

1 green capsicum (pepper), cut into
   bite-sized pieces

1 telegraph (long) cucumber, cut in half
   lengthways, then seeded and sliced

6 radishes, sliced

1 small salad onion, thinly sliced (see Note)

2 tablespoons chopped flat-leaf (Italian) parsley

2 tablespoons chopped mint

1 In a small bowl, whisk together the olive oil and lemon juice. Season well with sea salt and freshly ground black pepper.
2 Put the remaining ingredients in a salad bowl and toss well.
3 Just before serving, drizzle the dressing over the salad and toss together well.
Note Salad onions are sweeter than regular onions. They are readily available, but if you can't find them you could use a red onion instead.

BABY BEETROOT, BROAD BEAN AND TATSOI SALAD

Serves 4

1.6 kg (3 lb 8 oz/2 bunches) baby beetroot (beets), with leaves attached
500 g (1 lb 2 oz) fresh broad (fava) beans, shelled
200 g (7 oz/1 bunch) tatsoi, leaves separated

Honey mustard dressing
80 ml (2½ fl oz/⅓ cup) olive oil
1 tablespoon lemon juice
1 tablespoon wholegrain mustard
1 tablespoon honey

1 Bring a large saucepan of water to the boil. Wearing rubber gloves to stop your hands staining, trim the beetroot, discarding the stalks and reserving any unblemished leaves. Add the beetroot to the saucepan, then cover and simmer for 8–10 minutes, or until tender. Drain and leave to cool.
2 When the beetroot are cool enough to handle, slip off the skins, pat the beetroot dry with paper towels and place in a large shallow bowl.
3 Bring a small saucepan of salted water to the boil. Add the broad beans and simmer for 2–3 minutes, then drain. When cool enough to handle, slip the beans out of their skins and add to the beetroot. Add the reserved beetroot leaves and the small inner leaves of the tatsoi.
4 Put the honey mustard dressing ingredients in a small bowl and whisk together well. Season to taste with sea salt and freshly ground black pepper.
5 Pour the dressing over the salad and toss gently. Serve warm or at room temperature.

CUCUMBER, FETA, MINT AND DILL SALAD

Serves 4

125 g (4½ oz) feta cheese
4 Lebanese (short) cucumbers
1 small red onion, thinly sliced
1½ tablespoons chopped dill
1 tablespoon dried mint
60 ml (2 fl oz/¼ cup) olive oil
1½ tablespoons lemon juice

1 Crumble the feta into 1 cm (½ inch) chunks, into a salad bowl. Peel the cucumbers, cut in half lengthways, then scoop out the seeds with a teaspoon. Cut the flesh into 1 cm (½ inch) dice and add to the bowl with the onion and dill.
2 Grind the mint using a mortar and pestle, or force it through a sieve until powdered. Tip into a small bowl, add the olive oil and lemon juice and whisk well. Season with sea salt and freshly ground black pepper.
3 Just before serving, pour the dressing over the salad and toss together well.

INSALATA CAPRESE
Serves 4

3 large vine-ripened tomatoes
250 g (9 oz) bocconcini (fresh baby
  mozzarella cheese)
12 basil leaves
60 ml (2 fl oz/¼ cup) extra virgin olive oil

1 Cut each tomato into four slices about
1 cm (½ inch) thick. Cut the bocconcini into
24 slices the same thickness as the tomato.
2 Arrange the tomato slices on a serving
plate, alternating them with two slices of
the bocconcini and the basil leaves.
3 Drizzle with the olive oil, sprinkle with
sea salt and freshly ground black pepper
and serve.
Variation Use whole cherry tomatoes and
toss them with the bocconcini and basil.

ROASTED FENNEL AND ORANGE SALAD

Serves 4

8 baby fennel bulbs, with fronds attached
100 ml (3½ fl oz) olive oil
2 oranges
1 red onion, halved and thinly sliced
100 g (3½ oz/⅔ cup) pitted kalamata olives
1 tablespoon lemon juice
2 tablespoons chopped mint
1 tablespoon chopped flat-leaf (Italian) parsley

1 Preheat the oven to 200°C (400°F/Gas 6). Trim the fronds off the fennel and reserve. Remove the stalks and cut a slice from the base of each fennel bulb 5 mm (¼ inch) thick. Slice each bulb into six wedges, place in a baking dish and drizzle with 60 ml (2 fl oz/¼ cup) of the olive oil. Season well. Bake for 40–45 minutes, or until tender and slightly caramelised, turning once or twice during cooking. Remove from the oven and allow to cool.
2 Using a sharp knife, cut a thin slice off the top and bottom of each orange. Slice off the skin, removing as much pith as possible. Working over a bowl to catch the juices, slice down the side of an orange segment, between the flesh and membrane. Repeat on the other side and lift the segment out. Repeat with all the segments, then squeeze out and reserve any orange juice remaining in the membranes. Place the segments in another bowl with the onion and olives.
3 In a small bowl, whisk together the lemon juice, reserved orange juice and remaining oil until emulsified. Season well.
4 Pour half the dressing over the salad, mix well and transfer to a serving dish. Top with the fennel, drizzle with the remaining dressing and scatter the parsley and mint over the top. Chop the reserved fennel fronds, sprinkle over the salad and serve.

MEDITERRANEAN LENTIL SALAD

Serves 4–6

1 large red capsicum (pepper)
1 large yellow capsicum (pepper)
250 g (9 oz/1 cup) red lentils
1 red onion, finely chopped
1 Lebanese (short) cucumber, chopped

Dressing
80 ml (2½ fl oz/⅓ cup) olive oil
2 tablespoons lemon juice
1 teaspoon ground cumin
2 garlic cloves, crushed

1 Cut the capsicums into large flat pieces and remove the seeds and membranes. Cook, skin side up, under a hot grill (broiler) until the skins blister and blacken. Leave to cool in a plastic bag, then peel away the skin and cut the flesh into thin strips. Place in a salad bowl and set aside.
2 Meanwhile, cook the lentils in a saucepan of boiling water for 10 minutes, or until tender; do not overcook or they will become mushy. Drain well.
3 Add the lentils to the capsicum with the onion and cucumber. Toss to combine.
4 Put the dressing ingredients in a small bowl and whisk together. Season well with sea salt and freshly ground black pepper, pour over the salad and mix well.
5 Cover and refrigerate for 4 hours to allow the flavours to develop. Serve at room temperature.

AVOCADO AND BLACK BEAN SALAD

Serves 4

250 g (9 oz/scant 1¼ cups) dried black (turtle) beans
1 red onion, chopped
4 roma (plum) tomatoes, chopped
1 red pepper (capsicum), chopped
375 g (13 oz/heaped 1¾ cups) drained tinned corn kernels
90 g (3¼ oz/1 bunch) coriander (cilantro), roughly chopped
2 avocados, peeled and chopped
1 mango, peeled and chopped
150 g (5½ oz) rocket (arugula), trimmed

Lime and chilli dressing
1 garlic clove, crushed
1 small red chilli, finely chopped
2 tablespoons lime juice
60 ml (2 fl oz/¼ cup) olive oil

1 Soak the beans in enough cold water to cover overnight.

2 Drain the beans and rinse well. Place in a large saucepan, cover with water and bring to the boil. Reduce the heat and simmer for 1½ hours, or until tender. Drain and allow to cool slightly.

3 Put the beans in a large serving bowl. Add the remaining salad ingredients and toss together well.

4 Put all the lime and chilli dressing ingredients in a small bowl and whisk together well. Season to taste with sea salt and freshly ground black pepper. Pour the dressing over the salad, toss well and serve.

RED POTATO SALAD WITH DILL AND MUSTARD

Serves 4

6 red-skinned boiling potatoes, such as
  desiree
1 tablespoon wholegrain mustard
1½ tablespoons chopped dill
2 teaspoons soft brown sugar
60 ml (2 fl oz/¼ cup) red wine vinegar
80 ml (2½ fl oz/⅓ cup) olive oil

1 Steam or boil the potatoes for 20 minutes, or until tender. Drain and leave to cool slightly. When cool enough to handle, cut the potatoes into 3 cm (1¼ inch) chunks and place in a salad bowl.

2 Mix the mustard, dill, sugar and vinegar together in a small bowl. Using a fork, whisk in the olive oil to make a dressing. Season to taste with sea salt and freshly ground black pepper. Toss the dressing through the warm potatoes and serve.

WARM ARTICHOKE SALAD

Serves 4

juice of 1 lemon
8 young globe artichokes, about 200 g
(7 oz) each
a handful of finely shredded basil
50 g (1¾ oz/½ cup) shaved parmesan cheese

Dressing
1 garlic clove, finely chopped
½ teaspoon sugar
1 teaspoon dijon mustard
2 teaspoons finely chopped lemon zest
60 ml (2 fl oz/¼ cup) lemon juice
80 ml (2½ fl oz/⅓ cup) extra virgin olive oil

1 Put half the lemon juice in a large bowl of water. Working with one artichoke at a time, remove the tough outer leaves until you get to the pale green leaves. Cut across the top of the artichoke, halfway down the tough leaves, then trim the stem to 4 cm (1½ inches) long and lightly peel it. Cut the artichoke in half lengthways and remove the hairy choke with a teaspoon. Brush the artichokes with lemon while you work, then place in the lemon water as you go to stop them turning brown.
2 Place the artichokes in a large saucepan of boiling water and cover with a plate or heatproof bowl to keep them immersed. Cook for 25 minutes, or until tender when pierced through the thickest part with a skewer. Drain and leave to cool slightly, then cut the artichokes in half again and arrange on a serving platter.
3 To make the dressing, whisk the garlic, sugar, mustard, lemon zest and lemon juice in a small bowl. Season to taste with sea salt and freshly ground black pepper, then whisk in the olive oil.
4 Pour the dressing over the artichoke and serve scattered with the basil and parmesan.

ASIAN-STYLE COLESLAW

Serves 4

200 g (7 oz/2⅔ cups) finely shredded
  red cabbage
175 g (6 oz/3¾ cups) finely shredded
  Chinese cabbage
1 large carrot, peeled and shaved using
  a vegetable peeler
1 small red onion, thinly sliced
1 red chilli, seeded and sliced lengthways
  (optional)
80 g (2¾ oz/¾ cup) thinly sliced snow peas
  (mangetout)
a small handful of Thai basil leaves, torn
50 g (1¾ oz/⅓ cup) chopped roasted peanuts

Creamy ginger dressing
2 tablespoons lime juice
1½ teaspoons finely grated fresh ginger
90 g (3¼ oz/⅓ cup) light sour cream
1 teaspoon soy sauce
1 garlic clove

1 Put all the cabbage in a large salad bowl. Add the carrot, onion, chilli (if using), snow peas, Thai basil and half the roasted peanuts and toss well.
2 Put all the creamy ginger dressing ingredients in a small bowl and whisk together. Season to taste with sea salt.
3 Pour the dressing over the coleslaw and toss well. Serve at room temperature, scattered with the remaining peanuts.

VIETNAMESE NOODLE SALAD

Serves 4–6

200 g (7 oz) dried rice vermicelli
a handful of torn Vietnamese mint
a handful of coriander (cilantro) leaves
½ red onion, cut into thin wedges
1 green mango, peeled and cut into thin strips
1 Lebanese (short) cucumber, halved
    lengthways and thinly sliced on the diagonal
155 g (5½ oz/1 cup) cashew nuts, roughly
    chopped

Lemon grass dressing

125 ml (4 fl oz/½ cup) lime juice
1 tablespoon shaved palm sugar (jaggery)
    or soft brown sugar
60 ml (2 fl oz/¼ cup) seasoned rice vinegar
2 lemon grass stems, white part only,
    finely chopped
2 red chillies, seeded and finely chopped
3 makrut (kaffir lime) leaves, shredded

1 Put the noodles in a bowl and cover with boiling water. Leave to stand for 10 minutes, or until soft. Drain, rinse under cold running water and drain again. Cut the noodles into short lengths and place in a large salad bowl.
2 Add the mint, coriander, onion, mango, cucumber and most of the cashews, then gently toss together.
3 Put all the lemon grass dressing ingredients in a small bowl and whisk together well. Season to taste with sea salt.
4 Toss the dressing through the salad, then cover and refrigerate for 30 minutes. Sprinkle with the remaining nuts just before serving.

GREEN PAPAYA SALAD

Serves 4

500 g (1 lb 2 oz) green papaya
1–2 small red chillies, thinly sliced
1 tablespoon grated palm sugar (jaggery)
  or soft brown sugar
1 tablespoon soy sauce
2 tablespoons lime juice
1 tablespoon fried garlic (see Note)
1 tablespoon fried Asian shallots (see Note)
10 green beans, trimmed and cut into 1 cm
  (½ inch) lengths
8 cherry tomatoes, quartered
2 tablespoons chopped roasted unsalted
  peanuts (optional)

1 Peel the papaya, cut it in half and scoop out the seeds using a teaspoon. Grate the papaya into long, fine shreds using a zester or a knife.

2 Place the papaya in a large mortar with the chilli, palm sugar, soy sauce and lime juice. Lightly pound with a pestle until combined.

3 Add the fried garlic and fried Asian shallots, beans and tomatoes and lightly pound until combined. Transfer to a salad bowl and serve immediately, sprinkled with the peanuts, if desired.

Note Packets of fried garlic and fried Asian shallots are sold in Asian food stores.

STEAMED CORN SALAD

Serves 4

1 large red capsicum (pepper)
3 corn cobs, husks and silky threads removed
90 g (3¼ oz/1 cup) bean sprouts, tails trimmed
4 spring onions (scallions), thinly sliced on
   the diagonal

Soy and ginger dressing

½ teaspoon crushed garlic
½ teaspoon finely grated fresh ginger
1 teaspoon sugar
1 tablespoon rice vinegar
1 tablespoon soy sauce
1 tablespoon lemon juice
2 teaspoons sesame oil
2 tablespoons peanut oil

1 Cut the capsicum into large flat pieces and remove the seeds and membranes. Cook, skin side up, under a hot grill (broiler) until the skin blisters and blackens. Leave to cool in a plastic bag, then peel away the skin and cut the flesh into large strips.
2 Using a heavy knife, cut each corn cob into six 2.5 cm (1 inch) slices. Steam for 5–8 minutes, or until tender. Divide among serving plates and arrange the capsicum and bean shoots over the top.
3 To make the soy and ginger dressing, put the garlic, ginger, sugar, vinegar, soy sauce and lemon juice in a small bowl and mix to dissolve the sugar. Whisk in the sesame and peanut oils and season to taste.
4 Drizzle the dressing over the corn, garnish with the spring onion and serve.

SNOW PEA SALAD

Serves 4–6

250 g (9 oz) snow peas (mangetout), trimmed
50 g (1¾ oz) snow pea (mangetout) sprouts
1 small red capsicum (pepper), julienned
1 tablespoon tamari
1 tablespoon mirin
1 teaspoon soft brown sugar
1 garlic clove, crushed
1 teaspoon very finely chopped fresh ginger
¼ teaspoon sesame oil
1 tablespoon vegetable oil
1 tablespoon toasted sesame seeds

1 Bring a saucepan of water to the boil, add the snow peas and cook for 1 minute. Drain, then plunge into a bowl of iced water for 2 minutes. Drain well.

2 Put the snow peas in a salad bowl with the snow pea sprouts and capsicum.

3 In a small bowl, whisk together the tamari, mirin, sugar, garlic, ginger, sesame and vegetable oils and half the toasted sesame seeds.

4 Pour the dressing over the salad and toss well. Season to taste with sea salt and freshly ground black pepper and serve sprinkled with the remaining sesame seeds.

GADO GADO

Serves 4

2 small carrots, thinly sliced
100 g (3½ oz/heaped ¾ cup) small
  cauliflower florets
12 snow peas (mangetout), trimmed
90 g (3¼ oz/1 cup) bean sprouts, tails trimmed
8 large iceberg lettuce-leaf cups
4 small potatoes, cooked and thinly sliced
1 Lebanese (short) cucumber, thinly sliced
2 hard-boiled eggs, peeled and cut into
  quarters
2 ripe tomatoes, cut into wedges

Peanut sauce
1 tablespoon vegetable oil
1 small onion, finely chopped
125 g (4½ oz/½ cup) crunchy peanut butter
185 ml (6 fl oz/¾ cup) coconut milk
1 teaspoon sambal oelek or chilli sauce
1 tablespoon lemon juice
1 tablespoon kecap manis

1 Bring a saucepan of water to the boil. Add the carrots and cauliflower and steam for 5 minutes, or until nearly tender. Add the snow peas and cook for 2 minutes, then add the bean sprouts and cook for a further 1 minute. Refresh under cold running water and set aside to cool.

2 To make the peanut sauce, heat the oil in a saucepan and sauté the onion for 5 minutes over low heat, or until softened. Stir in the peanut butter, coconut milk, sambal oelek, lemon juice, kecap manis and 60 ml (2 fl oz/ ¼ cup) water. Bring to the boil, stirring constantly, then reduce the heat and simmer for 5 minutes, or until the sauce has reduced and thickened. Remove from the heat.

3 Place two lettuce leaves one inside the other to make four lettuce cups.

4 In each lettuce cup, arrange one-quarter of the potato, carrot, cauliflower, snow peas, bean sprouts and cucumber. Drizzle with the peanut sauce and serve garnished with the egg quarters and tomato wedges.

Packed with antioxidants, enzymes, fibre, vitamins and minerals, vegetables should take up the lion's share of our plates, rather than being relegated to the side as an afterthought. Love your vegetables, cook them with the care and respect they deserve and you can throw away those vitamin pills for good. Today we are fortunate to have in our supermarkets and greengrocers a vast array of produce from the mighty vegetable kingdom, but where possible do seek out vegetables that are grown locally in your area and are in season: not only will they be cheaper, but they'll most likely be much fresher, and by this virtue more flavoursome and nutritious too. Nutritionists tell us we need to eat at least five serves of vegetables a day for abundant good health. Here are just a few ideas to help you on your way.

VEGETABLES ON THE SIDE

SAUTÉED BABY BEANS WITH ARTICHOKES AND GREEN OLIVES

Serves 4

200 g (7 oz) baby beans, trimmed
8 spring onions (scallions)
1 tablespoon olive oil
6 rosemary sprigs
8 green olives
2 quartered artichoke hearts in brine, drained
1 tablespoon salted baby capers, rinsed
 and drained
1 tablespoon extra virgin olive oil
2 teaspoons tarragon vinegar

1 Blanch the beans in boiling salted water for 2 minutes, then drain.
2 Trim the spring onions to roughly the same length as the beans.
3 Heat the olive oil in a large frying pan. Sauté the beans, spring onion and rosemary sprigs over medium heat for 1–2 minutes, or until the spring onion is lightly browned. Remove from the heat.
4 Add the olives, artichoke, capers, extra virgin olive oil and vinegar. Season with sea salt and freshly ground black pepper and toss to coat the vegetables.
5 Pile into a bowl and serve warm or at room temperature.

PEPPERONATA

Serves 4

3 red capsicums (peppers)
3 yellow capsicums (peppers)
2 tablespoons olive oil
1 large red onion, thinly sliced
3 large tomatoes, finely chopped
1 tablespoon sugar
2 tablespoons balsamic vinegar
4 tablespoons chopped flat-leaf
 (Italian) parsley
2 garlic cloves, finely chopped

1 Slice the capsicums into 2 cm (¾ inch) wide strips and set aside.
2 Heat the olive oil in a large frying pan and sauté the onion over low heat for 5 minutes, or until softened. Add the capsicum and cook for a further 5 minutes.
3 Add the tomatoes, cover and simmer over low–medium heat for 10 minutes, or until the vegetables are soft. Remove the lid and simmer for a further 2 minutes, then stir in the sugar and vinegar.
4 Transfer the mixture to a serving bowl and scatter with the parsley and garlic. Season with sea salt and freshly ground black pepper and serve.

HONEY-ROASTED ROOT VEGETABLES

Serves 4

60 g (2¼ oz) butter
2 tablespoons honey
4 thyme sprigs
3 carrots
2 parsnips
1 orange sweet potato
1 white sweet potato
8 small pickling onions
8 Jerusalem artichokes
1 garlic bulb

1 Preheat the oven to 200°C (400°F/Gas 6). Line a baking dish or roasting tin with baking paper.

2 Gently melt the butter in a small saucepan, then stir in the honey and thyme sprigs. Set aside.

3 Peel the carrots, parsnips and sweet potatoes and cut them into chunks. Spread them in the baking dish.

4 Peel the onions and Jerusalem artichokes and add them to the baking dish. Sprinkle generously with sea salt and freshly ground black pepper, drizzle with the butter mixture and toss gently to coat.

5 Trim the base of the garlic bulb and wrap the garlic in foil. Add to the baking dish and bake for 1 hour, or until the vegetables are tender, turning them occasionally.

6 Remove the garlic from the foil and slip the cloves from their skins. Arrange over the vegetables and serve.

SPICED BABY TURNIPS

Serves 4

8 small roma (plum) tomatoes
60 ml (2 fl oz/¼ cup) olive oil
3 small onions, sliced
3 teaspoons ground coriander
1 teaspoon sweet paprika
8 baby turnips, trimmed
1 teaspoon soft brown sugar
600 g (1 lb 5 oz/½ bunch) silverbeet (Swiss chard)
a handful of flat-leaf (Italian) parsley, chopped

1 Score a cross in the base of each tomato. Place in a heatproof bowl and cover with boiling water. Leave for 30 seconds, then plunge into cold water and peel the skin away from the cross. Cut the tomatoes into 1.5 cm (⅝ inch) slices and gently squeeze out most of the juice and seeds.

2 Heat the olive oil in a large frying pan and sauté the onion over medium heat for 5 minutes, or until soft.
3 Stir in the coriander and paprika, cook for 1 minute, then add the tomato, turnips, sugar and 80 ml (2½ fl oz/⅓ cup) hot water. Season well with sea salt and freshly ground black pepper and cook for 5 minutes.
4 Cover the pan, reduce the heat to low and cook for a further 4–5 minutes, or until the turnips are tender.
5 Meanwhile, strip the silverbeet leaves off the stalks, discarding the stalks. Rinse the leaves under cold water and shake off the excess.
6 Add the silverbeet and parsley to the pan and stir well. Cover and cook for 4 minutes, or until the silverbeet has wilted. Check the seasoning and serve.

CHARGRILLED EGGPLANT WITH LEMON PESTO

Serves 4–6

8 slender eggplants (aubergines), halved
  lengthways, or 2 large eggplants,
  cut into 1.5 cm (⅝ inch) slices
2 tablespoons olive oil

Lemon pesto

2 large handfuls of basil
a large handful of parsley
50 g (1¾ oz/⅓ cup) pine nuts, toasted
2 small garlic cloves
60 g (2¼ oz/heaped ½ cup) grated
  parmesan cheese
grated zest of 1 lemon
60 ml (2 fl oz/¼ cup) lemon juice
125 ml (4 fl oz/½ cup) extra virgin olive oil

1 Heat a chargrill pan or barbecue grill plate to high. Brush both sides of the eggplant slices with the olive oil and chargrill, in batches if necessary, for 3 minutes, or until golden and cooked through on both sides. If you are using slender eggplants, only grill them on the cut side, then finish off in a 200°C (400°F/Gas 6) oven for 5–8 minutes, or until soft. Cover and keep warm.
2 To make the lemon pesto, put the basil, parsley, pine nuts, garlic, parmesan, lemon zest and lemon juice in a food processor. Pulse until combined. Slowly add the olive oil and process until the mixture forms a smooth paste. Season to taste with sea salt and freshly ground black pepper.
3 Stack the eggplant on a platter, drizzling some of the pesto between each layer. Serve immediately.

FENNEL WITH WALNUT PARSLEY CRUST

Serves 4

2 tablespoons lemon juice
1 teaspoon sea salt
8 small fennel bulbs, halved lengthways
1 teaspoon fennel seeds
100 g (3½ oz/1 cup) grated parmesan cheese
100 g (3½ oz/heaped ¾ cup) chopped walnuts
160 g (5¾ oz/2 cups) fresh breadcrumbs
1 tablespoon chopped parsley
2 teaspoons lemon zest
2 garlic cloves, chopped
250 ml (9 fl oz/1 cup) vegetable stock
45 g (1½ oz) butter, chopped

1 Bring a large saucepan of water to the boil. Add the lemon juice, salt and fennel. Cook for 5–10 minutes, or until the fennel is tender, then drain and leave to cool.
2 Put the fennel seeds in a small frying pan and toast over medium heat for 1 minute to release their flavour. Tip the seeds into a food processor. Add the parmesan, walnuts, breadcrumbs, parsley, lemon zest and garlic and pulse gently to combine. Stir in 2 tablespoons of the stock to moisten.
3 Place the fennel, cut side up, in a ceramic baking dish. Spoon the walnut mixture over the fennel, spreading it to completely cover each piece. Pour the remaining stock around the fennel and dot each piece with butter.
4 Bake for 25 minutes, or until the crust is golden and the fennel is tender, basting from time to time. Serve hot, drizzled with the basting juices.

MASHED CARROTS WITH CUMIN SEEDS

Serves 4

6 carrots, peeled and cut into 2.5 cm
  (1 inch) chunks
1 tablespoon olive oil
2 garlic cloves, finely chopped
1 teaspoon ground turmeric
2 teaspoons finely grated fresh ginger
60 g (2¼ oz/¼ cup) Greek-style yoghurt
2 teaspoons harissa
2 tablespoons chopped coriander (cilantro)
  leaves
2 teaspoons lime juice
1 teaspoon cumin seeds

1 Put the carrots in a large saucepan and cover with cold water. Bring to the boil, then reduce the heat and simmer for 3 minutes. Drain and allow to dry.

2 Heat the olive oil in a saucepan. Sauté the garlic, turmeric and ginger over medium heat for 1 minute, or until fragrant.

3 Add the carrot and cook for 3 minutes. Stir in 1 tablespoon water, then cover and cook over low heat for 10–15 minutes, or until the carrot is soft.

4 Transfer the mixture to a bowl and roughly mash. Stir in the yoghurt, harissa, coriander and lime juice, then season to taste with sea salt and freshly ground black pepper.

5 Put the cumin seeds in a small frying pan and toast over medium–high heat for 30 seconds, or until fragrant. Scatter over the mashed carrot and serve.

MUSHROOMS WITH STICKY BALSAMIC SYRUP

Serves 4

80 ml (2½ fl oz/⅓ cup) olive oil
750 g (1 lb 10 oz) small button mushrooms
2 large garlic cloves, finely chopped
45 g (1½ oz/¼ cup) soft brown sugar
60 ml (2 fl oz/¼ cup) balsamic vinegar
3 teaspoons thyme

1 Heat the olive oil in a large frying pan. Add the mushrooms, season with sea salt and cook over high heat for 5 minutes, or until slightly softened and golden.
2 Add the garlic and cook for 1 minute. Stir in the sugar, vinegar and 1 tablespoon water and boil for 5 minutes, or until the liquid has reduced by one-third. Season to taste with freshly ground black pepper.
3 Pile the mushrooms into a serving bowl. Reduce the remaining pan juices for 1 minute, or until thick and syrupy.
4 Pour the syrup over the mushrooms, sprinkle with the thyme and serve.

ZUCCHINI WITH MINT AND FETA

Serves 4

6 zucchini (courgettes)
1 tablespoon olive oil
75 g (2½ oz/½ cup) crumbled feta cheese
1 teaspoon finely grated lemon zest
1 tablespoon lemon juice
½ teaspoon chopped garlic
1 tablespoon extra virgin olive oil
2 tablespoons finely shredded mint
2 tablespoons finely shredded parsley

1 Slice each zucchini lengthways into four thick batons. Heat the olive oil in a large frying pan and sauté the zucchini over medium heat for 3–4 minutes, or until just tender and lightly golden.

2 Arrange the zucchini on a serving platter and sprinkle with the feta.

3 Put the lemon zest, lemon juice and garlic in a small bowl and mix well. Whisk in the extra virgin olive oil with a fork to make a dressing.

4 Pour the dressing over the zucchini. Scatter with the mint and parsley and season with sea salt and freshly ground black pepper. Serve warm.

DIAMOND-CUT ROAST SWEET POTATO AND SLIVERED GARLIC

Serves 4

2 small orange sweet potatoes,
    about 14 cm (5½ inches) long and
    6 cm (2½ inches) thick
juice of ½ orange
1 tablespoon olive oil
8–10 rosemary sprigs
2 garlic cloves, sliced into fine slivers

1 Preheat the oven to 190°C (375°F/Gas 5). Peel the sweet potatoes and cut them in half lengthways. Using a strong, sharp knife, make 1 cm (½ inch) deep cuts in a diamond pattern into the sweet potato, about 1.5 cm (⅝ inch) apart—be careful not to cut all the way through. Place on a lightly oiled baking tray, cut side up.
2 In a small bowl, whisk together the orange juice and olive oil. Season well with sea salt and freshly ground black pepper and brush all over the sweet potato. Scatter the rosemary sprigs over the top.
3 Roast for 20 minutes, then scatter the garlic slivers over the sweet potato and bake for a further 20–30 minutes, or until the sweet potato is tender.

BALSAMIC MIXED ONIONS

Serves 4

250 ml (9 fl oz/1 cup) dry white wine
125 ml (4 fl oz/½ cup) good-quality balsamic
    vinegar
1 tablespoon olive oil
2 tablespoons light brown sugar
2 dried bay leaves
1 kg (2 lb 4 oz) assorted small onions,
    such as pearl, red and pickling (see Note)
30 g (1 oz/¼ cup) raisins

1 Put the wine, vinegar, olive oil, sugar
and bay leaves in a large saucepan with
2 tablespoons water. Stir to dissolve the
sugar, then bring to the boil.
2 Cut any roots off the onions, then peel
them, leaving the ends intact. Add them
to the saucepan and return to the boil.
3 Add the raisins and simmer gently, tossing
occasionally, for 50 minutes, or until the
onions are tender and the liquid is thick
and syrupy.
4 Transfer to a serving dish and allow to
cool. Serve at room temperature.
Note Select onions of a similar size so they
cook at the same rate. The cooked onions
can be stored in an airtight container in the
refrigerator for up to 2 weeks.

SWEET CORN WITH LIME AND CHILLI BUTTER

Serves 4

4 corn cobs
80 g (2¾ oz) butter
2 tablespoons olive oil
1 lemon grass stem, white part only,
    bruised and cut in half
3 small bird's eye chillies, seeded and
    finely chopped
2 tablespoons finely grated lime zest
2 tablespoons lime juice
2 tablespoons finely chopped coriander
    (cilantro) leaves

1 Remove the husks and silky threads from the corn. Wash well, then use a heavy knife to cut each cob into 2 cm (¾ inch) slices.
2 Heat the butter and olive oil in a large saucepan. Add the lemon grass and gently sauté over low heat for 5 minutes, then remove from the pan using a slotted spoon.
3 Add the chilli to the pan and cook for 2 minutes, then stir in the lime zest, lime juice and 60 ml (2 fl oz/¼ cup) water. Add the corn, then cover and cook for 5–8 minutes, or until the corn is tender, shaking the pan frequently.
4 Season to taste, then stir in the coriander. Serve hot, with plenty of napkins.

CREAMED SPINACH

Serves 4–6

1.5 kg (3 lb 5 oz) English spinach
10 g (¼ oz) butter
1 garlic clove, crushed
¼ teaspoon freshly grated nutmeg
80 ml (2½ fl oz/⅓ cup) thick (double/heavy)
    cream, plus extra, to serve
1 tablespoon grated parmesan cheese

1 Trim the tough ends from the spinach stalks and wash the leaves well. Shake the spinach to remove any excess water, but do not dry completely.

2 Melt the butter in a large frying pan. Add the spinach, garlic and nutmeg and season with sea salt and freshly ground black pepper. Cook over medium heat for 4 minutes, or until the spinach has just wilted.
3 Transfer the spinach to a sieve and press down well with the back of a spoon to squeeze out the excess moisture. Place the spinach on a chopping board and finely chop using a mezzaluna or sharp knife.
4 Gently heat the cream in the frying pan. Add the spinach and stir to warm through.
5 Pile the spinach into a serving dish. Top with another dollop of cream, sprinkle with the parmesan and serve.

ROASTED BEETROOT WITH HORSERADISH CREAM

Serves 4

8 beetroot (beets)
2 tablespoons olive oil
2 teaspoons honey
1½ tablespoons bottled creamed horseradish
100 g (3½ oz/heaped ⅓ cup) sour cream
chopped flat-leaf (Italian) parsley, to garnish

1 Preheat the oven to 200°C (400°F/Gas 6). Scrub the beetroot. Wearing gloves, trim the ends, then peel and cut into quarters. Place on a large square sheet of foil.

2 In a small bowl, mix together the olive oil and honey. Season with sea salt and freshly ground black pepper.

3 Drizzle the honey mixture over the beetroot, coating well. Loosely enclose the beetroot in the foil and bake for 1 hour, or until tender when pierced with a skewer. Remove the beetroot from the oven and leave in the foil for 5 minutes.

4 In a small serving bowl, mix together the horseradish and sour cream. Season lightly.

5 Remove the beetroot from the foil and arrange on a serving platter. Scatter the parsley over the top and serve with the horseradish cream.

BRUSSELS SPROUTS WITH CHESTNUT AND SAGE BUTTER

Serves 4

25 g (1 oz) butter, softened
25 g (1 oz) peeled, cooked chestnuts,
　finely chopped (see Note)
1 teaspoon chopped sage
700 g (1 lb 9 oz) brussels sprouts, trimmed

1 Put the butter, chestnuts and sage in a bowl and mix together well. Scrape the mixture onto a large piece of baking paper and shape into a log, using the paper to help you. Wrap and refrigerate until firm.

2 Cook the brussels sprouts in a saucepan of salted boiling water for 10 minutes, or until just tender—take care not to overcook them or they will become soggy. Drain well and place in a serving bowl.

3 Cut the chilled chestnut and sage butter into thin slices. Toss four of the slices through the brussels sprouts until evenly coated. Season well with sea salt and freshly ground black pepper.

4 Arrange the remaining butter slices over the sprouts and serve immediately.

Note Frozen, vacuum-packed or tinned chestnuts are available from gourmet food stores and large supermarkets. Toasted walnuts can be substituted in this recipe.

ROASTED RED ONION AND ROMA TOMATOES WITH BALSAMIC VINAIGRETTE

Serves 4

8 roma (plum) tomatoes
2 red onions
2 garlic cloves, unpeeled
1½ tablespoons balsamic vinegar
1 teaspoon dijon mustard
60 ml (2 fl oz/¼ cup) extra virgin olive oil

1 Preheat the oven to 150°C (300°F/ Gas 2). Cut the tomatoes into quarters lengthways and place them on a lightly oiled baking tray.

2 Cut the tops off the onions and peel away the skin, leaving the onions attached at the base. Cut each onion into eight wedges and place on the baking tray. Put the garlic cloves in the middle of the tray and season all the vegetables well with sea salt and freshly ground black pepper.
3 Roast for 1 hour, then transfer the tomatoes and onions to a serving plate.
4 Slip the roasted garlic cloves out of their skins, into a small bowl. Mash the garlic, then mix in the vinegar and mustard. Using a small wire whisk, slowly beat in the olive oil to make a vinaigrette. Season well.
5 Drizzle the vinaigrette over the roasted vegetables and serve.

POTATOES COOKED IN SPARKLING WINE

Serves 4

16 new red potatoes
750 ml (26 fl oz/3 cups) dry sparkling
   white wine
3 teaspoons fennel seeds
2 teaspoons grated lemon zest
2 bay leaves
30 g (1 oz) butter, melted

1 Using a vegetable peeler, peel off a strip of skin from around the middle of each potato.

2 Put the potatoes in a saucepan and pour in the sparkling wine. Add the fennel seeds, lemon zest, bay leaves and a good pinch of sea salt. Partially cover and bring to the boil over medium–high heat, then reduce the heat and simmer for 30 minutes, or until the potatoes are tender when pierced with the tip of a sharp knife. Drain and transfer to a serving dish.

3 Drizzle the potatoes with the melted butter and toss gently. Serve hot.

GREEN BEANS WITH FETA AND TOMATOES

Serves 4

1 tablespoon olive oil

1 onion, chopped

2 garlic cloves, crushed

1½ tablespoons chopped oregano

125 ml (4 fl oz/½ cup) white wine

400 g (14 oz) tin chopped tomatoes

250 g (9 oz) green beans, trimmed

1 tablespoon balsamic vinegar

200 g (7 oz) feta cheese, cut into 1.5 cm
(⅝ inch) dice

1 Heat the olive oil in a saucepan and sauté the onion over medium heat for 5 minutes, or until softened.

2 Add the garlic and half the oregano and cook for a further minute. Pour in the wine and cook for 3 minutes, or until the liquid has reduced by one-third.

3 Stir in the tomato and cook for about 10 minutes. Add the beans, then cover and cook for a further 10 minutes.

4 Stir in the vinegar, then pile into a serving dish. Scatter with the feta and remaining oregano, season with sea salt and freshly ground black pepper and serve.

JERUSALEM ARTICHOKES ROASTED WITH RED WINE AND GARLIC

Serves 4

1 tablespoon lemon juice
800 g (1 lb 12 oz) Jerusalem artichokes
2 tablespoons red wine
2 tablespoons olive oil
1 tablespoon tamari
2 garlic cloves, crushed
a dash of Tabasco sauce
2 tablespoons vegetable stock
2 tablespoons chopped parsley

1 Preheat the oven to 200°C (400°F/Gas 6). Put the lemon juice in a bowl of water. Scrub the Jerusalem artichokes well, then cut them in half lengthways and quickly place in the lemon water to stop them turning brown.

2 In a small bowl, mix together the wine, olive oil, tamari, garlic, Tabasco sauce and stock, then pour the mixture into a roasting tin. Drain the artichokes and quickly dry them with paper towels, then place in the roasting tin and toss to coat. Season with sea salt and freshly ground black pepper.

3 Cover with foil and bake for 40 minutes, or until the Jerusalem artichokes are tender. Remove the foil and bake for a further 5 minutes, or until the pan juices have formed a reduced glaze. Serve hot, sprinkled with the parsley.

KOHLRABI MASH WITH CIDER

Serves 4

300 ml (10½ fl oz) apple cider
600 g (1 lb 5 oz) kohlrabi (see Note)
300 g (10½ oz) boiling potatoes, peeled
   and cut into chunks
2 tablespoons pouring (whipping) cream
ground white pepper, to taste

Parsley oil
a small handful of parsley
1 scant teaspoon dijon mustard
1 teaspoon white wine vinegar
125 ml (4 fl oz/½ cup) extra virgin olive oil

1 Put 250 ml (9 fl oz/1 cup) of the cider in a saucepan with 250 ml (9 fl oz/1 cup) water. Thickly peel the kohlrabi, cutting off a good 5 mm (¼ inch) of the skin, then cut the flesh into small dice and add to the saucepan. Bring to the boil, then reduce the heat and simmer for 30 minutes.

2 Add the potato and 500 ml (17 fl oz/ 2 cups) boiling water and simmer for a further 20 minutes, or until the kohlrabi and potato are very tender. Drain well.
3 Meanwhile, put all the parsley oil ingredients in a small food processor and blend for 45 seconds, or until smooth. Season to taste with sea salt and freshly ground black pepper.
4 Purée the kohlrabi and potato using a potato ricer or mouli—don't use a food processor or the mixture will become gluey.
5 Transfer to a bowl and add the cream and remaining cider. Season to taste with sea salt and white pepper and mix well. Serve immediately, drizzled with the parsley oil.
Note Kohlrabi is a member of the cabbage family, with a mildly sweet flavour and a dense, solid flesh. When fresh, it has a hard body with a satiny skin. Once peeled, keep it in acidulated water (a bowl of water to which lemon juice or vinegar has been added) if not cooking it immediately; this will stop the kohlrabi discolouring.

BRAISED RED CABBAGE

Serves 4–6

60 g (2¼ oz) butter
1 onion, chopped
2 garlic cloves, crushed
900 g (2 lb) red cabbage, sliced
2 green apples, peeled, cored and diced
4 cloves
¼ teaspoon nutmeg
1 fresh bay leaf
2 juniper berries
1 cinnamon stick
80 ml (2½ fl oz/⅓ cup) red wine
50 ml (1½ fl oz) red wine vinegar
2 tablespoons soft brown sugar
1 tablespoon redcurrant jelly
500 ml (17 fl oz/2 cups) vegetable stock

1 Preheat the oven to 150°C (300°F/Gas 2). Melt 40 g (1½ oz) of the butter in a large flameproof casserole dish. Sauté the onion and garlic over medium heat for 5 minutes, or until softened.

2 Add the cabbage and cook for a further 10 minutes, stirring frequently.

3 Add the apple, cloves, nutmeg, bay leaf, juniper berries and cinnamon stick, then pour in the wine and cook for 5 minutes. Stir in the vinegar, sugar, redcurrant jelly and stock and bring to the boil.

4 Cover the dish, transfer to the oven and bake for 2 hours. Check the liquid level—there should be only about 125 ml (4 fl oz/½ cup) left. If there is a lot of liquid left, bake the cabbage a little longer until the liquid has reduced.

5 Stir in the remaining butter, season well with sea salt and freshly ground black pepper and serve.

BAKED SWEET POTATO WITH SAFFRON AND PINE NUT BUTTER

Serves 4–6

1 kg (2 lb 4 oz) white sweet potatoes
2 tablespoons olive oil
1 tablespoon milk
a pinch of saffron threads
100 g (3½ oz) butter, softened
40 g (1½ oz/¼ cup) pine nuts, toasted
2 tablespoons finely chopped parsley
2 garlic cloves, crushed

1 Preheat the oven to 180°C (350°F/Gas 4). Peel the sweet potatoes and chop them into large chunks. Place on a baking tray, drizzle with the olive oil and toss to coat. Cover with foil and bake for 20 minutes.
2 Meanwhile, warm the milk, stir in the saffron and leave to infuse for 5 minutes.

3 Transfer the saffron milk to a food processor and add the butter, pine nuts, parsley and garlic. Pulse until just combined, taking care not to overprocess the mixture—the nuts should still have some texture.
4 Place a sheet of plastic wrap on a work surface, put the butter in the centre and roll up to form a neat log, about 4 cm (1½ inches) in diameter. Refrigerate for 30 minutes.
5 Remove the foil from the baking tray and bake the sweet potato for a further 30 minutes, or until tender when pierced with the tip of a sharp knife. Transfer to a serving plate.
6 Unwrap the butter and cut into 1 cm (½ inch) slices. Arrange the butter slices over the sweet potato, season well with sea salt and freshly ground black pepper and serve immediately.

An old adage says we cannot live by bread alone, but it sure is scrumptiously delicious and has played a huge role in keeping humanity alive throughout the ages. These days supermarket shelves bulge with breads of all descriptions, and while the ready-made stuff is incredibly convenient, there's nothing as wholesome, satisfying, soul-gladdening and therapeutic as pulling a hot crusty loaf fresh from the oven. And don't let anyone tell you breads are difficult to make: most are surprisingly forgiving. Home-made breads have an earthy, naturally rustic quality and are free of the stabilisers and emulsifiers that commercially baked goods typically contain. From savoury little muffins, cute as a button, to scones and pizza breads and handsome gourmet loaves, the world of bread is vast indeed. Come break some bread with us!

BREADS, SCONES
& SAVOURY
MUFFINS

CHEESE PINWHEEL SCONES
Makes 10

250 g (9 oz/2 cups) plain (all-purpose) flour
1 tablespoon baking powder
a pinch of cayenne pepper
30 g (1 oz) cold unsalted butter, chopped
185 ml (6 fl oz/¾ cup) milk

Filling
40 g (1½ oz/⅓ cup) crumbled goat's cheese
40 g (1½ oz/heaped ⅓ cup) grated parmesan
   cheese
40 g (1½ oz/⅓ cup) grated mature cheddar
   cheese
2 tablespoons chopped flat-leaf (Italian) parsley

1 Preheat the oven to 220°C (425°F/Gas 7).
Line a baking tray with baking paper.

2 Sift the flour, baking powder, cayenne
pepper and a pinch of sea salt into a large
bowl. Using your fingertips, rub in the
butter until the mixture resembles
breadcrumbs. Add the milk and mix to a
soft dough using a flat-bladed knife. Add
a little extra flour if the dough is too sticky.
3 Turn out onto a floured work surface
and roll out to a 20 x 25 cm (8 x 10 inch)
rectangle. Sprinkle the goat's cheese over
the top, then the parmesan, cheddar and
parsley, leaving a bit of a border. Starting
from the long side, roll the dough into a
cylinder, then cut into 10 slices about 2 cm
(¾ inch) thick. Transfer to the baking tray,
spacing them 2 cm (¾ inch) apart.
4 Bake for 10–12 minutes, or until golden
and cooked through. Cool slightly on a
wire rack and serve warm.

POLENTA MUFFINS WITH PECORINO AND BASIL

Makes 12 muffins or 48 mini muffins

150 g (5½ oz/1¼ cups) self-raising flour
110 g (3¾ oz/¾ cup) polenta
60 g (2¼ oz/⅔ cup) grated pecorino cheese
1 egg, lightly beaten
250 ml (9 fl oz/1 cup) milk
80 ml (2½ fl oz/⅓ cup) olive oil
45 g (1½ oz/⅓ cup) chopped semi-dried
  (sun-blushed) tomatoes
a small handful of chopped basil

1 Preheat the oven to 180°C (350°F/Gas 4). Grease a 12-hole standard muffin tin or two 24-hole mini muffin tins, or line the holes with paper cases.

2 Sift the flour into a large bowl. Stir in the polenta and pecorino, season with freshly ground black pepper and make a well in the centre. Combine the egg, milk and olive oil in a bowl, then pour into the well in the flour. Add the tomatoes and basil and stir quickly until just combined. Do not overmix —the batter should be slightly lumpy.

3 Spoon the mixture into the muffin holes. Bake for 20–25 minutes (or 10–12 minutes for mini muffins), or until the muffins are golden and come away from the side of the tin. Remove from the oven and leave to cool in the tin for 2 minutes before transferring to a wire rack. Serve warm.

ZUCCHINI AND CARROT MUFFINS

Makes 12

250 g (9 oz/2 cups) self-raising flour
1 teaspoon ground cinnamon
½ teaspoon ground nutmeg
2 carrots, peeled and grated
2 zucchini (courgettes), grated
60 g (2¼ oz/½ cup) chopped pecans
2 eggs
250 ml (9 fl oz/1 cup) milk
90 g (3¼ oz) unsalted butter, melted

1 Preheat the oven to 210°C (415°F/ Gas 6–7). Grease a 12-hole standard muffin tin.

2 Sift the flour, cinnamon, nutmeg and a pinch of sea salt into a large bowl. Add the carrot, zucchini and pecans and stir well.
3 Put the eggs, milk and melted butter in a separate bowl and whisk together well.
4 Make a well in the centre of the flour mixture, then add the egg mixture all at once. Mix quickly using a fork until all the ingredients are just moistened. Do not overmix—the batter should still be lumpy.
5 Spoon the batter into the muffin holes and bake for 15–20 minutes, or until golden. Remove from the oven and loosen the muffins with a flat-bladed knife or spatula. Leave to cool in the tin for 2 minutes before turning out onto a wire rack to cool slightly. Serve warm.

PUMPKIN AND SAGE SCONES

Makes 8

250 g (9 oz/2 cups) self-raising flour
250 g (9 oz/1 cup) cooked and puréed
    pumpkin (winter squash)
20 g (¾ oz) cold unsalted butter, chopped
1 tablespoon chopped sage
1–2 tablespoons milk

1 Preheat the oven to 180°C (350°F/Gas 4). Line a baking tray with baking paper.

2 Sift the flour into a bowl with a pinch of sea salt. Using your fingertips, rub the pumpkin and butter into the flour, then stir in the sage.

3 Bring the mixture together with a little milk, then turn out onto the baking tray. Shape into a round and roll out to about 3 cm (1¼ inches) thick.

4 Gently mark or cut the scone into eight wedges. Bake for 15–20 minutes, or until lightly browned and cooked through. Serve warm.

MARSALA AND FENNEL SEED RINGS

Makes 24

375 g (13 oz/3 cups) plain (all-purpose) flour
55 g (2 oz/¼ cup) caster (superfine) sugar
1½ teaspoons baking powder
1 tablespoon fennel seeds
1 teaspoon sea salt flakes
80 ml (2½ fl oz/⅓ cup) sweet marsala
125 ml (4 fl oz/½ cup) extra virgin olive oil
1 egg yolk
parmesan or pecorino cheese, to serve

1 Preheat the oven to 180°C (350°F/Gas 4). Lightly grease a baking tray.
2 Put the flour, sugar, baking powder, fennel seeds and sea salt flakes in a bowl and mix together well. In another bowl, whisk together the marsala, olive oil and 80 ml (2½ fl oz/⅓ cup) water. Add to the dry ingredients and stir until a dough forms.
3 Turn the dough out onto a work surface (the dough shouldn't stick, so there is no need to flour it) and divide in half. Cut each half into 12 even pieces, then roll each into a log about 10 cm (4 inches) long. Form each log into a ring, pressing the joins firmly to seal. Place on the baking tray.
4 Mix the egg yolk with 1 tablespoon water and brush the rings with the glaze. Bake for 20 minutes, then reduce the oven temperature to 150°C (300°F/Gas 2) and bake for a further 15–20 minutes, or until golden and crisp. Cool on a wire rack.
5 Serve with chunks of parmesan or pecorino. Store in an airtight container in a cool place for up to 2 weeks.

PLUM AND ROSEMARY FLAT BREAD

Makes 1

60 ml (2 fl oz/¼ cup) warm milk
2 teaspoons instant dried yeast
115 g (4 oz/½ cup) caster (superfine) sugar
2 eggs, lightly beaten
grated zest of 1 lemon
2 teaspoons finely chopped rosemary
185 g (6½ oz/1½ cups) white strong (bread) flour
150 g (5½ oz) unsalted butter, softened
10 plums, halved and pitted, or 800 g
    (1 lb 12 oz) tinned plums, drained
whipped cream or mascarpone cheese, to serve

1 Grease a 25 cm (10 inch) spring-form cake tin or a loose-based flan (tart) tin.
2 Put the milk and yeast in the bowl of an electric mixer. Stir in 55 g (2 oz/¼ cup) of the sugar, the eggs, lemon zest and 1 teaspoon of the rosemary, then add the flour. Using the beater attachment, mix for

1 minute, or until a soft dough forms. Add the butter, then continue mixing for a further minute, or until the dough is smooth, shiny and thick. Alternatively, mix the dough by hand, using a wooden spoon.
3 Spoon into the cake tin and cover with plastic wrap. Leave in a draught-free place for 1½–2 hours, or until doubled in size.
4 Gently punch down the dough. Moisten the palms of your hands with water and press the dough into the edge of the tin. Arrange the plums, cut side up, over the top, pressing them gently into the dough. Leave for 30 minutes.
5 Meanwhile, preheat the oven to 200°C (400°F/Gas 6). Sprinkle the plums with the remaining sugar and scatter with the remaining rosemary. Bake for 10 minutes, then reduce the temperature to 180°C (350°F/Gas 4) and bake for a further 20 minutes, or until light golden and slightly spongy when pressed in the centre. Serve warm, with cream or mascarpone.

TAHINI SPIRALS

Makes 10

1 teaspoon active dried yeast
1 teaspoon caster (superfine) sugar
1 tablespoon olive oil
335 g (11¾ oz/2⅔ cups) white strong (bread) flour
90 g (3¼ oz/⅓ cup) tahini
60 g (2¼ oz/⅓ cup) soft brown sugar
2 teaspoons vegetable oil

1 Pour 250 ml (9 fl oz/1 cup) warm water into a large bowl. Sprinkle with the yeast and caster sugar and leave in a draught-free place for 10 minutes, or until foamy.
2 Stir in the olive oil, then place in the bowl of an electric mixer with a dough hook attachment and add one-third of the flour. With the mixer set to the lowest speed, gradually add the remaining flour, 60 g (2¼ oz/½ cup) at a time, mixing until a dough forms. Increase the speed to medium and knead for 7 minutes, or until the dough is smooth and elastic. Alternatively, mix the dough by hand, using a wooden spoon, then turn out onto a floured work surface and knead for 7 minutes, or until smooth and elastic.
3 Transfer to a large oiled bowl, turning to coat in the oil. Cover with plastic wrap and leave to rise in a draught-free place for 2 hours, or until doubled in size.
4 Preheat the oven to 190°C (375°F/Gas 5). Lightly grease two baking trays. Put the tahini, sugar and oil in a small bowl, stirring to mix well.
5 Gently punch down the dough, turn out onto a floured surface and divide into 10 portions. Roll out each portion to form a 20 x 10 cm (8 x 4 inch) rectangle. Spread about 1 tablespoon of the tahini mixture over the dough, spreading it to the edges. Starting at the long edge of the rectangle, roll it up into a long cylinder. Tightly coil the cylinder to form a round, then tuck the end underneath.
6 Place on the baking trays and flatten slightly with the palm of your hand. Bake for 12–15 minutes, or until golden. Serve warm or at room temperature.

SOURDOUGH BREAD

Makes 2 loaves

Starter
125 g (4½ oz/1 cup) white strong (bread) flour
2 teaspoons fresh yeast

Sponge
125 g (4½ oz/1 cup) white strong (bread) flour

Dough
375 g (13 oz/3 cups) white strong (bread) flour
1 teaspoon sea salt
2 teaspoons fresh yeast

1 To make the starter, sift the flour into a bowl and make a well in the centre. Cream the yeast with 250 ml (9 fl oz/1 cup) warm water, pour into the flour and gradually work in the flour to form a thick smooth paste. Cover with plastic wrap and leave at room temperature for 24 hours to ferment.
2 To make the sponge, stir the flour into the starter mixture and gradually whisk in 125 ml (4 fl oz/½ cup) warm water until smooth. Cover with plastic wrap and leave for 24 hours.

3 To make the dough, sift the flour and salt into a large bowl and make a well in the centre. Cream the yeast with 80 ml (2½ fl oz/⅓ cup) warm water and add to the flour with the starter and sponge mixture. Gradually incorporate the flour into the well. Turn out onto a floured surface and knead for 10 minutes, or until smooth and elastic, incorporating extra flour if needed.
4 Place in a lightly oiled bowl, cover and leave in a draught-free place for 1 hour, or until doubled in size. Lightly grease two baking trays and dust with flour. Gently punch down the dough and knead for 1 minute, or until smooth. Divide in half and shape each portion into a 20 cm (8 inch) round. Using a sharp knife, score diagonal cuts 1 cm (½ inch) deep along the loaves.
5 Place on the baking trays, cover and leave in a draught-free place for 45 minutes, or until doubled in size. Meanwhile, preheat the oven to 190°C (375°F/Gas 5).
6 Bake for 35–40 minutes, or until the loaves are golden and crusty and sound hollow when tapped, changing the trays around halfway through baking. Cool on a wire rack before cutting.

DRIED TOMATO AND ROSEMARY FOUGASSE

Makes 8

1½ teaspoons active dried yeast
a pinch of caster (superfine) sugar
1½ teaspoons sea salt flakes
2 teaspoons finely chopped rosemary
150 g (5½ oz/1 cup) sun-dried tomatoes, drained well and patted dry (reserve the oil)
2½ tablespoons of oil reserved from the sun-dried tomatoes (or use extra virgin olive oil), plus extra, for brushing
450 g (1 lb/3⅔ cups) plain (all-purpose) flour

1 Pour 125 ml (4 fl oz/½ cup) warm water into a small bowl. Sprinkle with the yeast and sugar and leave in a draught-free place for 10 minutes, or until foamy.
2 Transfer to the bowl of an electric mixer. Add the remaining ingredients and another 185 ml (6 fl oz/¾ cup) warm water. Using a low speed, mix for 7 minutes, or until the dough is smooth and elastic (it will be quite soft). Alternatively, mix the dough by hand, using a wooden spoon, then turn out onto a floured surface and knead for 7 minutes, or until smooth and elastic. Cover with plastic wrap and leave in a draught-free place for 1½–2 hours, or until doubled in size.
3 Gently punch down the dough, then turn out onto a floured work surface and cut into eight even portions. Using a floured rolling pin, roll out each piece to form an 18 x 9 cm (7 x 3½ inch) oval. Place on a board and, using a sharp knife, cut angled slits down each half of each oval, cutting through to the board (but not through the edges of the dough). Gently pull the cuts apart to form long gaps.
4 Transfer to two greased baking trays, brush with olive oil, then cover with a damp cloth. Leave for 20–25 minutes, or until slightly risen and puffy.
5 Meanwhile, preheat the oven to 200°C (400°F/Gas 6). Bake for 20 minutes, or until golden and crisp. Transfer to a wire rack to cool.

RYE BREAD

Makes 1 loaf

185 ml (6 fl oz/¾ cup) warm milk
2 teaspoons active dried yeast
1 teaspoon sugar
200 g (7 oz/2 cups) rye flour, plus extra,
   for dusting
165 g (5½ oz/1⅓ cups) white strong (bread) flour
1 teaspoon sea salt

1 Pour the milk into a small bowl, sprinkle with the yeast and sugar and leave in a draught-free place for 10 minutes, or until foamy.
2 Sift the flours and salt into a large bowl and make a well in the centre. Add the yeast mixture and 185 ml (6 fl oz/¾ cup) warm water and, using your fingers, mix to form a dough.

3 Turn out onto a lightly floured work surface and knead for 10 minutes, or until smooth and elastic. Place in a large oiled bowl, turning to coat in the oil. Cover with plastic wrap and leave in a draught-free place for 1 hour, or until doubled in size.
4 Grease a baking tray and lightly dust with flour. Gently punch down the dough, then turn out onto a floured surface. Knead for 1 minute, or until smooth. Shape into an 18 cm (7 inch) circle and place on the baking tray. Using a sharp knife, score a shallow criss-cross pattern over the loaf. Lightly dust with rye flour. Cover with plastic wrap and leave in a draught-free place for 1 hour, or until doubled in size.
5 Meanwhile, preheat the oven to 180°C (350°F/Gas 4). Bake for 40–45 minutes, or until the bread sounds hollow when tapped. Cool completely before cutting.

MINI WHOLEMEAL LOAVES

Makes 4 small loaves

125 ml (4 fl oz/½ cup) warm milk
2 teaspoons active dried yeast
1 tablespoon caster (superfine) sugar
600 g (1 lb 5 oz/4 cups) wholemeal
    (whole-wheat) strong (bread) flour
1 teaspoon sea salt
60 ml (2 fl oz/¼ cup) olive oil
1 egg, lightly beaten

1 Pour the milk into a small bowl, sprinkle with the yeast and sugar and leave in a draught-free place for 10 minutes, or until foamy.
2 Put the flour and salt in a large bowl and make a well in the centre. Add the yeast mixture, olive oil and 250 ml (9 fl oz/1 cup) warm water to the well and mix to a soft dough. Gather into a ball, turn out onto a lightly floured work surface and knead for 10 minutes, adding extra flour if the dough is too sticky. Place in a large oiled bowl, turning to coat in the oil. Cover with plastic wrap and leave in a draught-free place for 1 hour, or until well risen.
3 Grease four 13 x 6½ x 5 cm (5 x 2¾ x 2 inch) loaf (bar) tins. Gently punch down the dough, then turn out onto a floured surface and knead for 1 minute, or until smooth. Divide into four portions, knead into shape and place in the tins. Cover with plastic wrap and leave in a draught-free place for 45 minutes, or until risen.
4 Meanwhile, preheat the oven to 210°C (415°F/Gas 6–7). Brush the loaves with beaten egg and bake for 10 minutes. Reduce the temperature to 180°C (350°F/Gas 4) and bake for a further 30–35 minutes, or until the loaves sound hollow when tapped. Transfer to a wire rack to cool.

POTATO BREAD

Makes 1 loaf

2 teaspoons active dried yeast
500 g (1 lb 2 oz/4 cups) plain (all-purpose) flour
2 tablespoons full-cream milk powder
1 teaspoon sea salt
235 g (8½ oz/1 cup) warm cooked mashed
    potato
a handful of snipped chives
1 egg white, mixed with 2 teaspoons cold water
sunflower seeds and pepitas (pumpkin seeds),
    for sprinkling

1 Pour 60 ml (2 fl oz/¼ cup) warm water into a small bowl and sprinkle with the yeast. Leave in a draught-free place for 10 minutes, or until foamy.

2 Sift 440 g (15½ oz/3½ cups) of the flour, the milk powder and salt into a large bowl. Using a fork, mix the potato and chives through. Add the yeast mixture and 250 ml (9 fl oz/1 cup) warm water and mix until combined. Add enough of the remaining flour to make a soft dough.

3 Turn out onto a lightly floured work surface and knead for 10 minutes, or until smooth and elastic. Place in an oiled bowl, turning to coat in the oil. Cover with plastic wrap and leave in a draught-free place for 1 hour, or until well risen.

4 Grease a 25 cm (10 inch) round cake tin and line the base with baking paper. Gently punch down the dough, then knead for 1 minute. Divide into 12 even pieces and form each into a smooth ball. Place evenly spaced balls in a daisy pattern in the cake tin, piling two balls in the centre. Cover and leave for 45 minutes, or until risen to the top of the tin.

5 Meanwhile, preheat the oven to 210°C (415°F/Gas 6–7). Brush the loaf with the egg white and sprinkle with sunflower seeds and pepitas. Bake for 15 minutes, then reduce the temperature to 180°C (350°F/Gas 4) and bake for a further 20 minutes, or until a skewer inserted into the centre comes out clean. Remove from the oven and leave in the tin for 10 minutes, before turning out onto a wire rack to cool.

MALT BREAD

Makes 1 loaf

2½ teaspoons active dried yeast
1 teaspoon sugar
300 g (10½ oz/2 cups) wholemeal
   (whole-wheat) flour
125 g (4½ oz/1 cup) plain (all-purpose) flour
2 teaspoons ground cinnamon
60 g (2¼ oz/½ cup) raisins
30 g (1 oz) unsalted butter, melted
1 tablespoon treacle or molasses
1 tablespoon liquid malt extract, plus
   ½ teaspoon, extra
1 tablespoon hot milk

1 Pour 250 ml (9 fl oz/1 cup) lukewarm water into a small bowl. Sprinkle with the yeast and sugar and leave in a draught-free place for 10 minutes, or until foamy.
2 Sift the flours, cinnamon and a pinch of sea salt into a large bowl, then stir in the raisins and make a well in the centre. Add the butter, treacle, malt extract and the yeast mixture and mix to a soft dough using a flat-bladed knife.
3 Turn out onto a lightly floured surface and knead for 10 minutes, or until smooth. Shape into a ball, place in a lightly oiled bowl and turn to coat in the oil. Cover with plastic wrap and leave in a draught-free place for 1 hour, or until well risen.
4 Grease a 21 x 14 x 7 cm (8¼ x 5½ x 2¾ inch) loaf (bar) tin and line the base with baking paper. Gently punch down the dough, then knead for 3 minutes, or until smooth. Roll out to a 20 cm (8 inch) square, then roll up and place in the loaf tin, seam side down. Cover and leave in a draught-free place for 40 minutes, or until well risen.
5 Meanwhile, preheat the oven to 180°C (350°F/Gas 4). Mix together the milk and extra malt and brush over the loaf. Bake for 40 minutes, or until a skewer inserted into the centre comes out clean.
6 Remove from the oven and leave in the tin for 3 minutes, before turning out onto a wire rack to cool.

WALNUT AND CHEDDAR SODA BREAD

Makes 1 loaf

250 g (9 oz/2 cups) plain (all-purpose) flour
225 g (8 oz/1½ cups) wholemeal
  (whole-wheat) flour
1 tablespoon baking powder
1 teaspoon bicarbonate of soda (baking soda)
1 tablespoon soft brown sugar
60 g (2¼ oz/½ cup) walnut pieces, chopped
175 g (6 oz/1½ cups) grated mature cheddar
  cheese
40 g (1½ oz) unsalted butter, melted and cooled
2 eggs, lightly beaten
250 ml (9 fl oz/1 cup) buttermilk

1 Preheat the oven to 180°C (350°F/Gas 4). Line a baking tray with baking paper.

2 Sift the flours, baking powder and bicarbonate of soda into a large bowl (tip any husks from the wholemeal flour left in the sieve back into the bowl). Stir in the sugar, walnuts and cheese and make a well in the centre.

3 In another bowl, whisk together the butter, eggs and buttermilk, then pour into the well in the flour. Stir with a wooden spoon until a soft dough forms, then turn out onto a lightly floured work surface.

4 Using lightly floured hands, briefly knead just until smooth, then shape into a 20 cm (8 inch) round. Place on the baking tray.

5 Using a sharp, lightly floured knife, cut a 1 cm (½ inch) deep cross into the top of the loaf. Bake for 30–40 minutes, or until golden. Cool on a wire rack, then serve warm or at room temperature.

SOY AND LINSEED LOAF

Makes 1 loaf

110 g (3¾ oz/½ cup) pearl barley
2 teaspoons active dried yeast
1 teaspoon caster (superfine) sugar
1 tablespoon linseeds (flax seeds)
1 teaspoon sea salt
2 tablespoons soy flour
2 tablespoons gluten flour
150 g (5½ oz/1 cup) wholemeal (whole-wheat) strong (bread) flour
310 g (11 oz/2½ cups) white strong (bread) flour
2 tablespoons olive oil

1 Put the barley in a saucepan with 500 ml (17 fl oz/2 cups) water, bring to the boil and boil for 20 minutes, or until softened. Drain.
2 Pour 150 ml (5 fl oz) warm water into a small bowl. Stir in the yeast and sugar and leave in a draught-free place for 10 minutes, or until foamy.
3 Put the barley, linseeds and salt in a large bowl with the soy, gluten and wholemeal flours. Stir in 250 g (9 oz/2 cups) of the white flour. Make a well in the centre and add the yeast mixture, olive oil and 150 ml (5 fl oz) warm water. Mix to a soft dough using a wooden spoon. Turn out onto a floured surface and knead for 10 minutes, or until smooth and elastic. Incorporate enough of the remaining flour until the dough is no longer sticky.
4 Place in an oiled bowl, turning to coat in the oil. Cover with plastic wrap and leave in a draught-free place for 45 minutes, or until doubled in size.
5 Brush a 10 x 26 cm (4 x 10½ inch) loaf (bar) tin with oil. Gently punch down the dough and knead for 2–3 minutes, then pat into a 20 x 24 cm (8 x 9½ inch) rectangle. Roll up firmly from the long side and place in the loaf tin, seam side down. Cover and leave in a draught-free place for 1 hour, or until risen to the top of the tin.
6 Meanwhile, preheat the oven to 200°C (400°F/Gas 6). Brush the loaf with water and make two slits on top. Bake for 30 minutes, or until golden. Turn out onto a wire rack to cool.

GREEK LEMON, DILL
AND FETA BREAD

Makes 2 loaves

375 g (13 oz/3 cups) white strong (bread) flour
125 g (4½ oz/1 cup) fine semolina
4 teaspoons active dried yeast
1 teaspoon caster (superfine) sugar
2 tablespoons olive oil
60 g (2¼ oz/1 bunch) dill, finely chopped
grated zest of 1 lemon
200 g (7 oz/1⅓ cups) coarsely crumbled
   feta cheese, well drained

1 Put the flour, semolina, yeast, sugar and 1½ teaspoons salt in the bowl of an electric mixer with a dough hook attachment. Make a well in the centre and pour 250 ml (9 fl oz/1 cup) warm water and the olive oil into the well. With the mixer set to the lowest speed, mix for 3 minutes, or until a dough forms. Increase the speed to medium, add the dill and lemon zest and knead for a further 8 minutes, or until the dough is smooth and elastic. Add the feta and knead for 2 minutes, or until incorporated. Alternatively, mix the dough by hand, using a wooden spoon, then turn out onto a floured work surface, sprinkle with the dill and lemon zest and knead for 8 minutes, or until the dill and zest are incorporated and the dough is smooth and elastic. Pat the dough into a 20 x 10 cm (8 x 4 inch) rectangle and sprinkle the feta over. Fold the dough over several times, then knead for 2 minutes, or until the feta is well incorporated.

2 Place in a large oiled bowl, turning to coat in the oil. Cover with plastic wrap and leave to rise in a draught-free place for 1½–2 hours, or until doubled in size.

3 Grease two 20 x 10 cm (8 x 4 inch) loaf (bar) tins. Gently punch down the dough, then turn out onto a floured work surface. Divide the dough in half and form each into a loaf shape. Place seam side down into the loaf tins. Cover with plastic wrap and leave in a draught-free place for 30 minutes, or until doubled in size.

4 Meanwhile, preheat the oven to 200°C (400°F/Gas 6). Bake the loaves for 10 minutes, then reduce the oven temperature to 180°C (350°F/Gas 4) and bake for a further 20 minutes, or until they are golden and sound hollow when tapped. Transfer to a wire rack to cool.

PIZZA-TOPPED FOCACCIA

Serves 4

2½ teaspoons active dried yeast
1 teaspoon caster (superfine) sugar
310 g (11 oz/2½ cups) plain (all-purpose) flour
1 teaspoon sea salt
2 tablespoons olive oil

Topping
1 tablespoon tomato paste (concentrated purée)
1 large red capsicum (pepper), thinly sliced
4 marinated artichoke hearts, quartered
12 black olives, pitted
200 g (7 oz) bocconcini (fresh baby mozzarella cheese), thickly sliced

1 Pour 185 ml (6 fl oz/¾ cup) warm water into a large bowl. Sprinkle with the yeast and sugar, then leave in a draught-free place for 10 minutes, or until foamy.
2 Sift the flour into a large bowl and add the salt, olive oil and yeast mixture. Mix to a soft dough, then turn out onto a lightly floured work surface and knead for 10 minutes, or until smooth and elastic.
3 Place in a large oiled bowl, turning to coat in the oil. Cover with plastic wrap and leave to rise in a draught-free place for 1 hour, or until doubled in size.
4 Gently punch down the dough, then turn out onto a floured surface and knead for 1 minute. Roll into a flat disc large enough to fit into a greased 23 cm (9 inch) spring-form cake tin. Press the dough into the tin, cover with a damp cloth and leave to rise for 20 minutes.
5 Meanwhile, preheat the oven to 180°C (350°F/Gas 4). Spread the tomato paste over the dough and arrange all the other topping ingredients, except the bocconcini, over the top. Bake for 20 minutes.
6 Remove the pizza from the oven and spread the bocconcini over the top, then bake for a further 20 minutes, or until the dough is well risen and firm to the touch in the centre. Cool slightly on a wire rack before cutting and serving.

ZUCCHINI, THYME AND BOCCONCINI PIZZA

Makes 2

500 g (1 lb 2 oz/4 cups) plain (all-purpose) flour
2 teaspoons active dried yeast
1 teaspoon sea salt
1 teaspoon sugar
1 tablespoon olive oil

Topping

8 zucchini (courgettes), cut into fine rounds
2 teaspoons grated lemon zest
3 tablespoons finely chopped parsley
2 teaspoons thyme sprigs
4 garlic cloves, crushed
80 ml (2½ fl oz/⅓ cup) olive oil
500 g (1 lb 2 oz) bocconcini cheese, finely diced
50 g (1¾ oz/½ cup) grated parmesan cheese
1 tablespoon extra virgin olive oil

1 Preheat the oven to 220°C (425°F/Gas 7). Put the flour, yeast, salt and sugar in a large bowl. Stir together and make a well in the centre. Pour the olive oil and 310 ml (10¾ fl oz/1¼ cups) lukewarm water into the well and mix until a soft dough forms. Turn out onto a lightly floured surface and knead for 10 minutes, or until smooth and elastic.
2 Place in a large oiled bowl, turning to coat in the oil. Cover with plastic wrap and leave to rise in a draught-free place for 40 minutes, or until doubled in size.
3 Gently punch down the dough, then knead for 1 minute. Divide in half and roll each portion out to a 5 mm (¼ inch) thickness. Place on two pizza trays.
4 To make the topping, put the zucchini, lemon zest, parsley, thyme, garlic and olive oil in a bowl and mix together. Top each pizza base with half the bocconcini and half the parmesan, then spoon on the zucchini mixture. Arrange the remaining bocconcini and parmesan over the top, season well and drizzle with the extra virgin olive oil.
5 Bake for 15–20 minutes, or until the pizza bases are crisp, and the topping is warmed through and golden. Serve hot.

Everyone loves a party, whether it's an informal get-together, a boisterous knees-up or a leisurely, languid picnic out in the great outdoors on a sunny day, lounging about on a picnic rug with a hamper packed with yummies. Here you'll find a collection of finger foods, nibbles and delicious little somethings for occasions big and small, including some trusty old favourites, some modern classics to pick at, and lots of fabulous fare for the buffet table. Many recipes can be prepared ahead, leaving plenty of time for you to kick back and relax. And don't forget that the fritters, savoury pies, tarts and pastries in other chapters also make fabulous party or picnic fare, as do some of the starters, so roam widely through this book in your quest to assemble the perfect little assortment of victuals. Pop the corks and get the party rolling… don't forget the napkins!

PARTIES &
PICNICS

CUMIN SEED WAFERS

Makes 48

250 g (9 oz/2 cups) plain (all-purpose) flour
1 teaspoon baking powder
1 teaspoon sea salt
60 g (2¼ oz) cold Copha (white vegetable
    shortening)
1 tablespoon cumin seeds, toasted

1 Preheat the oven to 180°C (350°F/Gas 4). Lightly grease two baking trays.
2 Sift the flour, baking powder and salt into a bowl. Using your fingertips, rub in the Copha until the mixture resembles fine breadcrumbs. Stir in the cumin seeds and make a well in the centre, then gradually add 125 ml (4 fl oz/½ cup) water to the well, stirring with a wooden spoon until a rough dough forms. Turn the dough out onto a lightly floured work surface and gently knead until just smooth. Cover with plastic wrap and refrigerate for 30 minutes.
3 Divide the dough into quarters and roll out each portion on a floured work surface until 1–2 mm (¹⁄₁₆ inch) thick, then trim to form a 20 x 30 cm (8 x 12 inch) rectangle. Cut in half lengthways, then cut across the width into fingers 5 cm (2 inches) wide. You should end up with 12 fingers from each dough quarter.
4 Place the wafers on the baking trays and bake in batches for 10–12 minutes, or until light golden. Transfer to a wire rack to cool. Store in an airtight container for up to 1 week.

ROASTED EGGPLANT DIP

Serves 4

1 large eggplant (aubergine)
2 teaspoons ground cumin
1 garlic clove, crushed
juice of ½ lemon
2 tablespoons extra virgin olive oil
2 tablespoons chopped coriander
   (cilantro) leaves
toasted pitta bread strips, to serve

1 Preheat the oven to 220°C (425°F/Gas 7).
2 Prick the eggplant several times with a
fork and place on a baking tray. Bake for
40–50 minutes, or until the skin is wrinkled
and the eggplant has collapsed. Remove
from the oven and set aside to cool.
3 Put the cumin in a small frying pan and
toast over medium heat for 1–2 minutes,
or until the colour deepens and the cumin
is fragrant. Set aside to cool.
4 Cut open the eggplant, scoop the
flesh into a sieve and leave to drain for
5 minutes. Finely dice the eggplant and
place in a serving bowl. Stir in the toasted
cumin, garlic, lemon juice, olive oil and
coriander and season to taste with sea salt
and freshly ground black pepper.
5 Serve with toasted pitta bread strips.

LABNEH
(YOGHURT CHEESE)

Makes 24

1 kg (2 lb 4 oz/4 cups) Greek-style yoghurt
2 teaspoons sea salt
1 teaspoon ground white pepper
375 ml (13 fl oz/1½ cups) extra virgin olive oil
2 garlic cloves, chopped
2 tablespoons rosemary leaves
6–8 thyme sprigs

1 Put the yoghurt in a bowl and stir in the salt and pepper. Line a bowl with a piece of muslin (cheesecloth) folded in half to make a 45 cm (18 inch) square. Spoon the yoghurt into the centre. Bring the fabric corners together and, using a long piece of kitchen string, tie as closely as possible to the yoghurt, leaving a loop at the end.
2 Thread the loop through the handle of a wooden spoon and hang the yoghurt over a bowl. Leave to drain in the refrigerator for 3 days.
3 Rinse a large, wide-necked jar with boiling water and dry in a warm oven.
4 In a small bowl, mix together the olive oil, garlic, rosemary and thyme sprigs. Set aside.
5 Untie the muslin and roll tablespoons of the drained yoghurt into balls (they won't be completely smooth). Make sure your hands are cool, and wash them often.
6 Place the labneh balls in the dried jar and pour the herbed olive oil over the top. Seal with a lid, then refrigerate for 24 hours, or up to 1 week. Serve at room temperature.

DOLMADES
Makes 42

275 g (9¾ oz) vine leaves in brine
(see Note)
185 ml (6 fl oz/¾ cup) olive oil
2 onions, finely chopped
165 g (5¾ oz/¾ cup) short-grain white rice
6 spring onions (scallions), finely chopped
4 tablespoons chopped dill
1 tablespoon chopped mint
1 tablespoon lemon juice
lemon wedges, to serve

1 Rinse the vine leaves in cold water, then soak in warm water for 1 hour. Drain well.
2 Heat 125 ml (4 fl oz/½ cup) of the olive oil in a heavy-based saucepan. Sauté the onion over low heat for 5 minutes, or until softened. Remove from the heat, cover and leave for 5 minutes, then mix in the rice, spring onion, herbs and lemon juice.

3 Lay a vine leaf on a plate, vein side up. Place 3 teaspoons of the rice mixture in the centre. Fold the sides of the leaf over the filling, then roll up towards the tip of the leaf, to make a little parcel. Repeat to make 42 dolmades.
4 Use five or six left-over vine leaves to line the base of a large heavy-based saucepan. Pack the dolmades in the saucepan in two layers and drizzle with the remaining oil. Sit a plate on top of the dolmades, to keep them in place, then pour in 375 ml (13 fl oz/1½ cups) water.
5 Bring to the boil, then reduce the heat, cover and simmer for 45 minutes. Carefully remove the plate (it will be hot), lift out the dolmades using a slotted spoon and place on a serving plate. Serve warm or at room temperature, with lemon wedges.
Note Fresh vine leaves can also be used, if available. Use small leaves and blanch them briefly in boiling water first.

BEETROOT HUMMUS

Serves 8

500 g (1 lb 2 oz) beetroot (beets)
80 ml (2½ fl oz/⅓ cup) olive oil
1 large onion, chopped
1 tablespoon ground cumin
400 g (14 oz) tin chickpeas, drained
1 tablespoon tahini
80 g (2¾ oz/⅓ cup) plain yoghurt
3 garlic cloves, crushed
60 ml (2 fl oz/¼ cup) lemon juice
125 ml (4 fl oz/½ cup) vegetable stock
pitta or pide (Turkish/flat bread), to serve

1 Scrub the beetroot well. Bring a large saucepan of water to the boil, add the beetroot and cook for 35–40 minutes, or until tender when pierced with the point of a sharp knife. Drain and cool slightly before peeling.

2 Meanwhile, heat 1 tablespoon of the olive oil in a frying pan. Sauté the onion over medium heat for 5 minutes, or until softened. Add the cumin and cook for a further 1 minute, or until fragrant. Set aside and leave to cool slightly.

3 Chop the beetroot and place in a food processor or blender with the onion mixture, chickpeas, tahini, yoghurt, garlic, lemon juice and stock. Blend until smooth. With the motor running, add the remaining oil in a thin, steady stream. Blend until thoroughly combined. Serve with pitta bread or pide.

Note You can use 500 g (1 lb 2 oz) of any vegetable to make this hummus. Try carrot or pumpkin (winter squash).

CUMIN AND GOUDA GOUGERES

Makes about 40

100 g (3½ oz) butter
140 g (5 oz/scant 1¼ cups) plain
　(all-purpose) flour
½ teaspoon cumin seeds, lightly crushed
3 eggs
150 g (5½ oz) aged gouda cheese,
　finely grated

1 Preheat the oven to 200°C (400°F/Gas 6). Line a baking tray with baking paper.
2 Put the butter in a small saucepan with a good pinch of sea salt and 250 ml (9 fl oz/ 1 cup) water. Place over medium heat until the butter has melted and the mixture has just come to the boil.

3 Add the flour and cumin seeds and stir until the mixture comes away from the side of the saucepan.
4 Transfer the mixture to the bowl of an electric mixer and allow to cool a little (alternatively, place in a bowl and mix using a hand mixer or wooden spoon). Beating continuously, add the eggs one at a time, beating well after each addition. Stir in the cheese.
5 Put teaspoonfuls of the mixture on the baking tray, about 4 cm (1½ inches) apart. Bake for 20 minutes, then reduce the oven temperature to 160°C (315°F/Gas 2–3) and bake for a further 20 minutes, or until the gougères are puffed, golden and dry.
6 Turn off the oven, open the door slightly and leave the gougères to cool a little. Serve warm or at room temperature.

PARMESAN-CRUSTED CARROTS

Serves 6

500 g (1 lb 2 oz) baby (Dutch) carrots
60 g (2¼ oz/½ cup) plain (all-purpose) flour
2 teaspoons ground cumin
2 eggs
250 g (9 oz/3 cups) fine fresh white breadcrumbs
1 tablespoon chopped parsley
65 g (2¼ oz/⅔ cup) grated parmesan cheese
vegetable oil, for deep-frying

1 Trim the leafy carrot tops, leaving about 2 cm (¾ inch) attached, then wash the carrots. Bring a large saucepan of salted water to the boil, add the carrots and cook for 5 minutes, or until tender when pierced with a metal skewer. Drain, dry well with paper towels and leave to cool.

2 Sift the flour and cumin onto a sheet of baking paper, then beat the eggs together in a wide, shallow bowl. In another bowl, mix together the breadcrumbs, parsley and parmesan and season well. Roll the carrots in the flour, then the eggs and finally the breadcrumbs. For an extra-crispy coating, repeat this process.

3 Fill a deep, heavy-based saucepan one-third full of oil and heat to 170°C (325°F), or until a cube of bread dropped into the oil browns in 20 seconds. Deep-fry the carrots in batches until golden and crisp. Serve immediately.

BAKED HERBED FETA

Serves 6

300 g (10½ oz) piece of feta cheese
1 tablespoon chopped rosemary
1 tablespoon chopped oregano
1 tablespoon chopped thyme
2 teaspoons freshly cracked black pepper,
  or to taste
2 tablespoons olive oil

1 Preheat the oven to 180°C (350°F/ Gas 4). Put the feta on a sheet of foil about 30 cm (12 inches) square.
2 In a small bowl, mix together the rosemary, oregano, thyme and pepper, then firmly press the mixture onto each side of the feta. Drizzle with the olive oil, then gently fold the sides of the foil over the cheese to make a parcel.
3 Place the parcel on a baking tray and bake for 10–15 minutes, or until the feta is soft.
4 Unwrap the feta and drain off any excess liquid. Serve warm or at room temperature, with crusty bread or as part of a cheese platter or salad.
Note If the piece of feta is very thick, it may need an extra 5 minutes in the oven to heat through. Cover any leftovers with plastic wrap and store in the refrigerator for up to 2 days.

TEMPURA VEGETABLES WITH WASABI MAYONNAISE

Serves 4–6

Wasabi mayonnaise

2 tablespoons whole-egg mayonnaise

3 teaspoons wasabi paste

½ teaspoon grated lime zest

2 egg yolks

250 ml (9 fl oz/1 cup) cold soda water

30 g (1 oz/¼ cup) cornflour (cornstarch)

115 g (4 oz/scant 1 cup) plain (all-purpose) flour

40 g (1½ oz/¼ cup) sesame seeds, toasted

vegetable oil, for deep-frying

1 small eggplant (aubergine), about 250 g (9 oz), cut into thin rounds

1 large onion, cut into thin rounds, keeping the rings intact

300 g (10½ oz) orange sweet potato, peeled and cut into thin rounds

1 In a small serving bowl, mix together the wasabi mayonnaise ingredients. Cover with plastic wrap and refrigerate until required.

2 Put the egg yolks and soda water in a bowl and mix lightly with a whisk.

3 Sift the cornflour and flour into a bowl. Add the sesame seeds and a good pinch of sea salt and mix well. Pour in the soda water mixture and stir lightly with chopsticks or a fork until just combined but still lumpy.

4 Fill a deep heavy-based saucepan or wok one-third full of oil and heat to 180°C (350°F), or until a cube of bread dropped into the oil browns in 15 seconds. Dip pairs of the vegetables into the batter and cook in batches for 3–4 minutes, or until golden brown and cooked through. Drain on paper towels and sprinkle with sea salt. Keep warm in a low oven, but do not cover or the tempura coating will become soggy.

5 Transfer all the tempura vegetables to a warmed serving platter. Serve immediately, with the wasabi mayonnaise.

SALT AND PEPPER TOFU PUFFS

Serves 4–6

125 ml (4 fl oz/½ cup) sweet chilli sauce
2 tablespoons lemon juice
2 x 200 g (7 oz) packets of fried tofu puffs
250 g (9 oz/2 cups) cornflour (cornstarch)
2 tablespoons sea salt
1 tablespoon ground white pepper
2 teaspoons caster (superfine) sugar
4 egg whites
peanut oil, for deep-frying (see Note)
lemon wedges, to serve

1 Put the sweet chilli sauce and lemon juice in a small serving bowl and mix together to make a dipping sauce. Cover and set aside.
2 Cut the tofu puffs in half and pat dry with paper towels.
3 Mix the cornflour, salt, pepper and sugar together in a large bowl. In another bowl, lightly beat the egg whites.
4 Working in batches, dip the tofu pieces into the beaten egg white, then toss them in the cornflour mixture, shaking off any excess.
5 Fill a deep heavy-based saucepan or wok one-third full of peanut oil and heat to 180°C (350°F), or until a cube of bread dropped into the oil browns in 15 seconds. Cook the tofu in batches for 1–2 minutes, or until crisp. Drain well on paper towels and serve immediately, with the dipping sauce and lemon wedges.
Note For best results, use a good-quality peanut oil for deep-frying the tofu puffs—the flavour will be slightly nutty.

CALIFORNIA ROLLS

Makes 30

500 g (1 lb 2 oz/2¼ cups) short-grain white rice
60 ml (2 fl oz/¼ cup) rice vinegar
1 tablespoon caster (superfine) sugar
1 teaspoon sea salt
125 g (4½ oz/½ cup) mayonnaise
3 teaspoons wasabi paste
2 teaspoons soy sauce
5 nori sheets
1 large Lebanese (short) cucumber, cut
    lengthways into long batons
1 avocado, thinly sliced
1 tablespoon black sesame seeds, toasted
30 g (1 oz) pickled ginger slices

1 Wash the rice under cold running water until the water runs clear, tossing frequently. Place in a saucepan with 750 ml (26 fl oz/3 cups) water. Bring to the boil over low heat and cook for 5 minutes, or until tunnels form in the rice. Remove from the heat, cover and stand for 15 minutes.

2 Put the vinegar, sugar and salt in a small saucepan and stir over low heat until the sugar and salt have dissolved. Set aside.
3 In a small bowl, mix together the mayonnaise, wasabi and soy sauce. Set aside until required.
4 Put the rice in a non-metallic bowl and separate the grains with a wooden spoon. Make a slight well in the centre, slowly stir in the vinegar dressing, then cool a little.
5 Lay a nori sheet on a bamboo mat or flat surface, shiny side down. Spread one-fifth of the rice over, leaving a narrow border at one end. Arrange one-fifth of the cucumber, avocado, sesame seeds and ginger lengthways over the rice, keeping clear of the border. Spread with some of the mayonnaise mixture, then roll to cover the filling. Continue rolling tightly to join the edge over, then hold in place for a few seconds. Trim the ends and cut into six slices.
6 Repeat with the remaining ingredients to make 30 rolls. Serve with the remaining mayonnaise mixture.

VIETNAMESE SPRING ROLLS

Serves 4

75 g (2½ oz) dried rice vermicelli
1 teaspoon sesame oil
1 tablespoon peanut oil
200 g (7 oz) firm tofu, cut into 4 slices
1 packet of 15 cm (6 inch) square rice paper
  wrappers (see Note)
½ small Lebanese (short) cucumber, cut into
  julienne strips
½ carrot, cut into julienne strips
a handful of mint leaves
50 g (1¾ oz/⅓ cup) roasted salted cashew
  nuts, roughly chopped

Dipping sauce
60 ml (2 fl oz/¼ cup) hoisin sauce
2 tablespoons kecap manis
1 tablespoon lime juice

1 Place the noodles in a bowl, cover with boiling water and leave to soak for 10 minutes. Drain well.
2 Put the dipping sauce ingredients in a bowl and mix together well. Set aside.
3 Heat the sesame and peanut oils in a large frying pan and cook the tofu over medium heat for 3 minutes on each side, or until golden. Drain on paper towels, then cut each slice into four widthways.
4 Fill a bowl with warm water. Dip a rice paper wrapper into the water for 15 seconds, or until it softens and becomes pliable.
5 Place the wrapper on a work surface. Put a narrow strip of noodles down the middle, then some tofu, cucumber, carrot, mint and cashews. Fold in the sides of the wrapper and roll it up tightly. Place on a plate, seam side down, and cover with a damp cloth.
6 Repeat with the remaining ingredients and serve with the dipping sauce.
Note Sheets of paper-thin dried rice paper wrappers are sold in Asian grocery stores and large supermarkets.

CAYENNE SPICED ALMONDS

Makes 250 g (9 oz/1⅔ cups)

1½ teaspoons cayenne pepper
1 teaspoon ground cumin
½ teaspoon smoked paprika
½ teaspoon caster (superfine) sugar
2 teaspoons sea salt flakes
1 tablespoon olive oil
250 g (9 oz/1⅔ cups) blanched almonds

1 In a large bowl, mix together the cayenne pepper, cumin, paprika, sugar and sea salt flakes. Set aside.
2 Heat the olive oil in a saucepan. Add the almonds and stir for 10 minutes over medium heat, or until the almonds are golden.
3 Remove the almonds using a slotted spoon, add to the spice mix and toss to coat well. Allow to cool to room temperature, tossing occasionally. Store in an airtight container until ready to serve.
Variation Try this recipe using your favourite nut mix.

WASABI POPCORN

Makes 1 large bowl

80 ml (2½ fl oz/⅓ cup) peanut oil
115 g (4 oz/½ cup) popcorn kernels
(popping corn)
1 teaspoon sea salt
40 g (1½ oz) butter
3 teaspoons wasabi paste
2 teaspoons caster (superfine) sugar

1 Heat the peanut oil in a large saucepan over medium–high heat. Drop a few popcorn kernels into the oil: if they spin, the oil is hot enough to cook the popcorn. Add the kernels and salt and cover with the saucepan lid.
2 When you start to hear the corn pop, shake the pan occasionally until the popping increases, then slows down dramatically. Remove from the heat but keep the lid on until the popping stops completely.
3 Meanwhile, melt the butter in a small saucepan, then stir in the wasabi and sugar.
4 Tip the popcorn into a large bowl. Drizzle with half the butter mixture, toss, then add the remaining butter mixture and season with more salt, if needed. Serve warm.

SPINACH PIE DIAMONDS

Makes 15

250 g (9 oz/2 cups) plain (all-purpose) flour
30 g (1 oz) unsalted butter, chopped
60 ml (2 fl oz/¼ cup) olive oil, plus extra,
    for brushing
125 ml (4 fl oz/½ cup) warm water

Filling
425 g (15 oz/1 small bunch) English spinach
1 leek, white part only, finely chopped
¼ teaspoon freshly grated nutmeg
2 teaspoons chopped dill
200 g (7 oz/1⅓ cups) crumbled feta cheese
1 tablespoon dry breadcrumbs
3 eggs, lightly beaten
2 tablespoons olive oil

1 Sift the flour and a good pinch of sea
salt into a bowl. Using your fingertips, rub
in the butter until the mixture resembles fine
breadcrumbs. Rub in the olive oil, make a
well in the centre and add enough of the
warm water to form a dough. Gather the
dough together, then cover with plastic
wrap and refrigerate for 1 hour.
2 Meanwhile, preheat the oven to
220°C (425°F/Gas 7). Grease a 3 cm

(1¼ inch) deep, 17 x 26 cm (6½ x 10½ inch)
baking tin.
3 To make the filling, trim off the bottom
quarter of each spinach stalk. Wash and
shred the leaves and attached stalks. Place
in a tea towel (dish towel) and wring out
the excess moisture. Tip into a bowl and
add the leek, nutmeg, dill, feta, breadcrumbs
and plenty of cracked black pepper. Using
your hands, mix in the eggs and olive oil,
but do not overmix.
4 Roll out just over half the dough on a
floured surface until large enough to line
the base and sides of the prepared tin. Lift
the dough into the tin, pressing it in.
Spoon the filling over the top.
5 Roll out the remaining pastry until large
enough to cover the pie. Place over the
filling and press the edges together to seal.
Trim the excess pastry, then brush the top
with a little extra olive oil. Using a knife,
mark into three strips lengthways, then
diagonally into diamonds. Cut two or three
slits through the top pastry layer to allow
steam to escape.
6 Bake for 45–50 minutes, or until well
browned. Turn out onto a wire rack to cool
for 10 minutes, then transfer to a cutting
board and cut into diamonds. Serve hot.

MEDITERRANEAN COB LOAF

Serves 6

2 eggplants (aubergines)
2 large red capsicums (peppers)
500 g (1 lb 2 oz) orange sweet potato,
   peeled and thinly sliced
4 zucchini (courgettes), sliced lengthways
80 ml (2½ fl oz/⅓ cup) olive oil
23 cm (9 inch) round cob loaf
160 g (5½ oz/⅔ cup) pesto (see page 60)
200 g (7 oz/heaped ¾ cup) ricotta cheese
35 g (1¼ oz/⅓ cup) grated parmesan cheese

1 Slice the eggplants lengthways and place in a colander in the sink. Sprinkle with salt and leave for 30 minutes, then rinse well and pat dry with paper towels.
2 Cut the capsicums into large flat pieces and remove the seeds and membranes. Cook, skin side up, under a hot grill (broiler) until the skins blister and blacken. Leave to cool in a plastic bag, then peel away the skin.
3 Brush the eggplant, sweet potato and zucchini with the olive oil and chargrill or grill (broil) in batches until well browned.
4 Slice the top off the loaf. Scoop out the soft bread from inside, leaving a thin shell. Brush the inside of the loaf and underneath the top with the pesto. Layer the zucchini and capsicum inside the loaf, then spread with the combined ricotta and parmesan. Layer the sweet potato and eggplant, lightly pressing down. Replace the top of the loaf.
5 Cover with plastic wrap and place on a baking tray. Set a tray on top of the loaf and weigh it down with tins of food. Refrigerate overnight.
6 Heat the oven to 250°C (500°F/Gas 9). Unwrap the loaf, place back on the baking tray and bake for 10 minutes, or until the cob is crisp. Cut into wedges to serve.

OLIVE AND ALMOND PALMIERS

Makes 24

75 g (2½ oz/½ cup) pitted and chopped black olives
95 g (3¼ oz/1 cup) ground almonds
25 g (1 oz/¼ cup) grated parmesan cheese
2 tablespoons chopped basil
60 ml (2 fl oz/¼ cup) olive oil
2 teaspoons wholegrain mustard
¼ teaspoon sea salt
½ teaspoon cracked black pepper
2 sheets of frozen puff pastry, thawed
60 ml (2 fl oz/¼ cup) milk

1 Preheat the oven to 200°C (400°F/Gas 6). Line two baking trays with baking paper.

2 Put the olives, ground almonds, parmesan, basil, olive oil, mustard, salt and pepper in a food processor. Blend to form a paste.
3 Lay out one sheet of pastry and cover evenly with half the olive mixture. Fold two opposite ends into the centre to meet. Fold the same way again. Brush the pastry with the milk, then repeat with the remaining pastry and filling.
4 Cut the pastry into slices 1.5 cm (⅝ inch) thick. Shape the slices into a V-shape, with the two sides curving out slightly. Place on the baking trays, leaving room for spreading.
5 Bake for 15–20 minutes, or until puffed and golden. Remove from the oven and turn out onto a wire rack to cool. Serve at room temperature.
Note Palmiers can be cooked up to 6 hours ahead and stored in an airtight container.

ORANGE SWEET POTATO WEDGES WITH TANGY CUMIN MAYONNAISE

Serves 4

2½ tablespoons olive oil
1 kg (2 lb 4 oz) orange sweet potatoes
200 g (7 oz/heaped ¾ cup) mayonnaise
60 ml (2 fl oz/¼ cup) lime juice
1 teaspoon honey
1 heaped tablespoon roughly chopped
  coriander (cilantro)
1½ teaspoons ground cumin

1 Preheat the oven to 200°C (400°F/Gas 6). Pour the olive oil into a large roasting tin and heat in the oven for 5 minutes.
2 Peel the sweet potatoes and cut into wedges about 6 cm (2½ inches) long. Add them to the roasting tin, season with sea salt and freshly ground black pepper and toss to coat. Spread them out in the tin in a single layer and bake for 35 minutes, turning occasionally.
3 Meanwhile, put the mayonnaise, lime juice, honey, coriander and cumin in a food processor and blend until smooth.
4 Drain the sweet potato wedges on paper towels and serve hot, with the tangy cumin mayonnaise on the side.

VEGETABLE PLATTER WITH SAFFRON AIOLI

Serves 4–6

Saffron aïoli

a pinch of saffron threads
2 egg yolks
3 garlic cloves, crushed
2 tablespoons lemon juice
310 ml (10¾ fl oz/1¼ cups) canola oil

12 baby (Dutch) carrots, scrubbed and
    trimmed, leaving some stem attached
155 g (5½ oz/1 bunch) asparagus spears,
    trimmed
100 g (3½ oz) baby corn
100 g (3½ oz) green beans, trimmed
2 witlof (chicory/Belgian endive), base trimmed
    and leaves separated
300 g (10½ oz) radishes, cut in half down
    the middle

1 To make the aïoli, mix the saffron in a small bowl with 1 tablespoon water. In a food processor, blend the egg yolks, garlic and lemon juice until smooth. With the motor running, add the oil, a few drops at a time, then in a thin, steady stream until thoroughly combined. Slowly add 2 tablespoons warm water to thin slightly. Season well with sea salt, then spoon into a small bowl and stir in the saffron water. Cover and refrigerate until required.

2 Blanch the carrots, asparagus, corn and beans separately in a saucepan of boiling salted water until just tender but still crisp, then drain and refresh in cold water. The carrots will take about 3 minutes (or serve them raw), the asparagus 2 minutes, the corn 1 minute, and the beans 30 seconds.

3 Arrange all the vegetables on a platter, sprinkle lightly with sea salt and serve with the aïoli.

FRIED GREEN TOMATOES WITH A CORNMEAL CRUST

Serves 4–6

750 g (1 lb 10 oz) unripe green tomatoes
60 g (2¼ oz/½ cup) plain (all-purpose) flour
225 g (8 oz/1½ cups) polenta
2 teaspoons finely chopped thyme
2 teaspoons finely chopped marjoram
50 g (1¾ oz/½ cup) grated parmesan cheese
2 eggs, beaten with 1 tablespoon water
olive oil, for pan-frying

1 Preheat the oven to 180°C (350°F/Gas 4). Cut the tomatoes into 1 cm (½ inch) slices and season with sea salt.
2 Put the flour in a shallow bowl and season well with sea salt and freshly ground black pepper. In another shallow bowl, mix together the polenta, thyme, marjoram and parmesan.
3 Dip the tomato slices in the flour, coating all over. Dip them in the beaten egg, then the polenta mixture. Set aside in a single layer.
4 Fill a large, heavy-based frying pan with olive oil to a depth of 5 mm (¼ inch). Heat to 170°C (325°F), or until a cube of bread dropped in the oil browns in 20 seconds. Cook the tomato slices in batches for 2–3 minutes on each side, or until golden. Remove with tongs and drain on paper towels.
5 Transfer the tomato slices to a baking dish and keep warm in a low oven while cooking the remainder, adding more oil to the pan as needed. Serve hot.

Sometimes there's nothing nicer than settling down to a dainty cup of tea or a steaming hot mug of coffee and tucking into a little sweet treat—a slice of warm, moist cake, a crispy crunchy biscuit (cookie), a delectable cakey muffin, a chewy chunky brownie or a chocolatey slice of something nice… and all the more so when it's something you've pulled fresh from the oven yourself, greeted by a rush of warm, sweet, comforting aromas and gasps of appreciation and joyous wonder from family and friends. None of the treats in this chapter are very fussy, difficult or too time-consuming to make. So warm up the oven, get out those mixing bowls and spoons and get ready to bake: something yummy will be ready in a shake. Go on, you know you want to—and everyone will love you for it!

CAKES &
BISCUITS

ORANGE AND WALNUT BISCOTTI

Makes about 40

310 g (11 oz/2½ cups) plain (all-purpose) flour,
   plus extra, for rolling
1 teaspoon baking powder
½ teaspoon bicarbonate of soda (baking soda)
170 g (6 oz/¾ cup) caster (superfine) sugar
3 eggs, lightly beaten
grated zest of 3 oranges
2 teaspoons natural vanilla extract
250 g (9 oz/2½ cups) walnut halves,
   lightly toasted and roughly chopped

1 Preheat the oven to 170°C (325°F/Gas 3).
Lightly grease a baking tray.
2 Sift the flour, baking powder and
bicarbonate of soda into a large bowl,
then stir in the sugar.
3 Crack the eggs into another bowl, then
add the orange zest and vanilla and mix
well using a fork. Pour the egg mixture
into the flour mixture and stir until nearly
combined. Using your hands, knead briefly

to form a firm dough. Turn the dough out
onto a lightly floured work surface and
knead the walnuts into the dough.
4 Divide the dough into three equal
portions. Working with one piece at a
time, roll each portion to form a 29 cm
(11½ inch) log. Gently pat the surface to
flatten the log to a 4 cm (1½ inch) width,
then place on the baking tray and bake for
30 minutes, or until the logs are light
golden and firm. Remove from the oven
and allow to cool for 15 minutes.
5 Reduce the oven temperature to 150°C
(300°F/Gas 2). When the biscotti logs are
cool enough to handle, place them on a
chopping board and, using a sharp, serrated
knife, cut them on the diagonal into slices
1 cm (½ inch) thick.
6 Arrange the slices in a single layer on
two lightly greased baking trays. Bake for
15 minutes, or until the biscotti are dry,
swapping the trays around halfway through
baking. Remove from the oven and leave to
cool on a wire rack. Store in an airtight
container for up to 3 weeks.

CASHEW BROWNIES

Makes 25

300 g (10½ oz/2 cups) chopped dark chocolate
175 g (6 oz) unsalted butter, chopped
2 eggs
230 g (8 oz/1¼ cups) soft brown sugar
40 g (1½ oz/⅓ cup) unsweetened cocoa
    powder, sifted
125 g (4½ oz/1 cup) plain (all-purpose) flour, sifted
80 g (2¾ oz/½ cup) unsalted cashew nuts,
    toasted and chopped

Chocolate icing
200 g (7 oz/1⅓ cups) chopped dark chocolate
125 g (4½ oz/½ cup) sour cream
30 g (1 oz/¼ cup) icing (confectioners')
    sugar, sifted

1 Preheat the oven to 160°C (315°F/
Gas 2–3). Lightly grease a 23 cm (9 inch)
square shallow tin and line the base with
baking paper.
2 Put 200 g (7 oz/1⅓ cups) of the chocolate
in a heatproof bowl with the butter. Set the
bowl over a saucepan of simmering water,
ensuring the base of the bowl doesn't touch
the water. Stir until the chocolate and
butter have melted. Allow to cool.
3 Whisk the eggs and sugar in a large bowl
for 5 minutes, or until pale and thick. Fold
the cooled chocolate mixture through, then
the cocoa powder and flour. Fold in the
cashews and remaining chocolate.
4 Pour into the prepared tin, smoothing
the surface. Bake for 30–35 minutes, or
until just firm to the touch (the mixture
will firm on cooling). Remove from the
oven and allow to cool.
5 To make the chocolate icing (frosting),
put the chocolate in a small heatproof
bowl. Set the bowl over a small saucepan
of simmering water, ensuring the base of
the bowl doesn't touch the water. Stir until
the chocolate has melted. Cool slightly,
then mix in the sour cream and icing sugar.
Spread over the cooled brownies.
6 Leave for a few hours or overnight to
firm up, then cut into squares. Store in an
airtight container for up to 5 days.

DATE AND CINNAMON SQUARES

Makes 36

600 g (1 lb 5 oz/3⅓ cups) pitted whole dried
  dates, chopped
1 teaspoon bicarbonate of soda (baking soda)
125 g (4½ oz) unsalted butter, chopped
155 g (5½ oz/heaped ¾ cup) soft brown sugar
2 eggs
125 g (4½ oz/1 cup) plain (all-purpose) flour
60 g (2¼ oz/½ cup) self-raising flour
½ teaspoon ground cinnamon, plus ½ teaspoon,
  extra
60 g (2¼ oz/½ cup) icing (confectioners') sugar

1 Preheat the oven to 180°C (350°F/Gas 4).
Lightly grease a 23 cm (9 inch) square
shallow tin and line the base with
baking paper.
2 Put the dates in a saucepan with 500 ml
(17 fl oz/2 cups) water. Bring to the boil,

then remove from the heat. Stir in the
bicarbonate of soda, mix well, then leave
to cool to room temperature.
3 Using electric beaters, cream the butter
and sugar in a large bowl until light and
fluffy. Add the eggs one at a time, beating
well after each addition.
4 Sift the flours and cinnamon into a bowl,
then fold into the butter mixture alternately
with the date mixture. Spoon the batter into
the prepared tin, smoothing the surface.
5 Bake for 55–60 minutes, or until a skewer
inserted into the centre comes out clean.
Remove from the oven and leave to cool in
the tin for 5 minutes, then turn out onto a
wire rack to cool completely.
6 Cut into 36 pieces and place on a sheet
of baking paper. Just before serving, sift the
combined icing sugar and extra cinnamon
over the squares and toss to coat. Store in
an airtight container (without the sugar
coating) for up to 4 days.

GINGER AND PISTACHIO BISCUITS

Makes about 25

100 g (3½ oz) unsalted butter
125 g (4½ oz/⅔ cup) soft brown sugar
1 teaspoon natural vanilla extract
2 eggs, at room temperature
250 g (9 oz/2 cups) plain (all-purpose) flour
1½ teaspoons baking powder
2 teaspoons ground ginger
100 g (3½ oz/⅔ cup) pistachio nuts, chopped
melted white chocolate, for drizzling

1 Preheat the oven to 170°C (325°F/Gas 3). Line two baking trays with baking paper.
2 Using electric beaters, cream the butter, sugar and vanilla in a bowl until light and fluffy. Add the eggs one at a time, beating well after each addition.
3 Sift the flour, baking powder and ginger into a bowl, then fold into the butter mixture. Stir the pistachios through.
4 Using lightly floured hands, roll tablespoons of the mixture into balls and place on the baking trays, allowing room for spreading. Flatten the biscuits slightly with a lightly floured fork.
5 Bake for 15 minutes, or until crisp and golden, swapping the trays around halfway through baking. Remove from the oven and leave to cool on the trays for 5 minutes, then transfer to a wire rack to cool.
6 Drizzle the cooled biscuits with melted white chocolate. Store in an airtight container for up to 4 days.

PLUM AND CARAWAY BISCUITS

Makes 24

80 g (2¾ oz) unsalted butter, softened
60 g (2¼ oz/¼ cup) cream cheese, chopped
115 g (4 oz/½ cup) caster (superfine) sugar
1 teaspoon natural vanilla extract
2 egg yolks
1½ teaspoons caraway seeds
150 g (5½ oz/1¼ cups) plain (all-purpose) flour
plum jam, for brushing
icing (confectioners') sugar, for dusting

1 Using electric beaters, cream the butter, cream cheese and sugar in a bowl until light and fluffy. Beat in the vanilla and 1 egg yolk. Add the caraway seeds and flour and stir until a dough forms. Turn out onto a lightly floured work surface, form into a flat rectangle, then cover with plastic wrap and refrigerate for 2 hours, or until firm.
2 Preheat the oven to 180°C (350°F/Gas 4). Lightly grease two baking trays. Combine the remaining egg yolk with 2 teaspoons water, mix well and set aside.
3 Cut the dough in half, then roll out each half on a lightly floured work surface to an 18 x 24 cm (7 x 9½ inch) rectangle. Using a lightly floured sharp knife, cut the dough into 6 cm (2½ inch) squares. Place a scant teaspoon of jam diagonally across the centre of each square, then brush all four corners of the square with the egg wash. Take one corner and fold it into the centre. Take the opposite corner and fold it into the centre, overlapping the first corner slightly, to partially enclose the jam.
4 Brush the tops of the biscuits with the egg wash, then place on the baking trays, seam side up. Bake for 10–12 minutes, or until light golden, swapping the trays around halfway through baking.
5 Remove from the oven and leave to cool on the trays for 5 minutes, then transfer to a wire rack to cool completely. Dust with icing sugar before serving. Store in an airtight container for up to 1 week.

OATMEAL AND RASPBERRY MUFFINS

Makes 12

125 g (4½ oz/1 cup) oatmeal
375 ml (13 fl oz/1½ cups) milk
250 g (9 oz/2 cups) plain (all-purpose) flour
1 tablespoon baking powder
115 g (4 oz/heaped ½ cup) soft brown sugar
1 egg, lightly beaten
90 g (3¼ oz/¼ cup) honey
60 g (2¼ oz) unsalted butter, melted
150 g (5½ oz/1¼ cups) raspberries

1 Preheat the oven to 190°C (375°F/Gas 5). Grease a 12-hole standard muffin tin, or line the holes with paper cases.

2 Put the oatmeal in a bowl, stir in the milk and set aside for 5 minutes. Sift the flour and baking powder into a large bowl, then stir in the sugar. Make a well in the centre.
3 Put the egg, honey and butter in a bowl and mix well. Pour the egg mixture and oatmeal mixture into the well in the flour and stir quickly until just combined. Do not overmix—the batter should be slightly lumpy. Gently fold the raspberries through.
4 Spoon the batter into the muffin holes. Bake for 20–25 minutes, or until the muffins are golden and a skewer inserted into the centre comes out clean. Remove from the oven and leave to cool in the tin for 5 minutes, before transferring to a wire rack. Serve warm.

CRANBERRY AND HAZELNUT REFRIGERATOR BISCUITS

Makes about 50

125 g (4½ oz/1 cup) icing (confectioners') sugar
175 g (6 oz) unsalted butter, softened
2 egg yolks
2 teaspoons lemon juice
185 g (6½ oz/1½ cups) plain (all-purpose) flour
110 g (3¾ oz/1 cup) ground hazelnuts
150 g (5½ oz/1½ cups) sweetened dried
   cranberries
80 g (2¾ oz/½ cup) poppy seeds

1 Sift the icing sugar into a bowl and add the butter. Using electric beaters, cream until light and fluffy. Add the egg yolks and lemon juice and beat to combine well. Sift the flour over the top, add the ground hazelnuts and stir to combine well. Stir in the cranberries.
2 Divide the dough in half. Scatter half the poppy seeds over a 30 cm (12 inch) length of foil. Place half the dough on a work surface and form into a sausage shape about 21 cm (8¼ inches) long. Place the dough on the foil, firmly roll it in the poppy seeds to coat, then roll tightly in the foil to form a neat cylinder, twisting the ends tight. Scatter the remaining poppy seeds over another piece of foil and repeat with the remaining dough. Refrigerate for at least 4 hours, or up to 5 days. (The uncooked dough can also be frozen.)
3 Preheat the oven to 170°C (325°F/Gas 3). Lightly grease two baking trays. Unwrap the dough and, using a large serrated knife, cut into slices 8 mm (⅜ inch) thick. Place the rounds on the baking trays and bake for 12–15 minutes, or until firm and lightly coloured, swapping the trays around halfway through baking.
4 Remove from the oven and leave to cool on the trays for 5 minutes, then transfer to a wire rack to cool completely. Store in an airtight container for up to 1 week.

PEACH GALETTES

Makes 12

800 g (1 lb 12 oz) frozen sweet shortcrust (pie) pastry, thawed
600 g (1 lb 5 oz) peaches, pitted and thinly sliced
20 g (¾ oz) unsalted butter, melted
1 tablespoon honey
1 tablespoon caster (superfine) sugar
¼ teaspoon ground nutmeg
1 egg yolk
1 tablespoon milk
80 g (2¾ oz/¼ cup) apricot jam
25 g (1 oz/¼ cup) flaked almonds, toasted

1 Roll the pastry out on a lightly floured work surface to 3 mm (⅛ inch) thick. Cut out twelve 12 cm (4½ inch) rounds.
2 In a bowl, gently toss together the peach slices, butter, honey, sugar and nutmeg.

3 Spoon the peach mixture onto the pastry rounds, leaving a 1 cm (½ inch) border around the edge. Fold the pastry over the filling, leaving the centre uncovered, and pleating the pastry at 1 cm (½ inch) intervals to fit. Place on a lightly greased baking tray and refrigerate for 30 minutes.
4 Meanwhile, preheat the oven to 200°C (400°F/Gas 6). In a small bowl, mix together the egg yolk and milk. Brush the egg wash over the pastry edges, then bake for 30 minutes, or until golden. Remove from the oven and leave on the baking tray to cool slightly.
5 Put the jam and 1 tablespoon water in a small saucepan and stir over low heat until smooth. Brush the jam mixture over the hot galettes, then sprinkle with the flaked almonds. Allow the galettes to cool before serving.

BLUEBERRY SEMOLINA MUFFINS

Makes 12

30 g (1 oz/¼ cup) self-raising flour
40 g (1½ oz/⅓ cup) fine semolina
230 g (8 oz/1 cup) caster (superfine) sugar
25 g (1 oz/¼ cup) ground almonds
½ teaspoon finely grated lemon zest
4 egg whites, lightly beaten
125 g (4½ oz) unsalted butter, melted
80 g (2¾ oz/½ cup) blueberries
45 g (1½ oz/½ cup) flaked almonds

1 Preheat the oven to 170°C (325°F/Gas 3). Line a 12-hole standard muffin tin with paper cases.
2 Sift the flour and semolina into a large bowl. Stir in the sugar, ground almonds and lemon zest.
3 Beat in the egg whites using electric beaters until combined. Pour in the melted butter and beat until smooth. Fold the blueberries through, then spoon the batter into the paper cases.
4 Sprinkle with the flaked almonds and bake for 30 minutes, or until a skewer inserted into the centre comes out clean. Remove from the oven, leave in the tin for a few minutes, then turn out onto a wire rack to cool slightly. Serve warm.

YOGHURT BANANA CAKES WITH HONEY ICING

Makes 2 cakes, each serving 8

180 g (6 oz) unsalted butter, softened
90 g (3¼ oz/¼ cup) honey
230 g (8 oz/1 cup) caster (superfine) sugar
1½ teaspoons natural vanilla extract
3 eggs
360 g (12¾ oz/1½ cups) mashed ripe banana
  (about 4 bananas)
185 g (6½ oz/¾ cup) plain yoghurt
½ teaspoon bicarbonate of soda (baking soda)
375 g (13 oz/3 cups) self-raising flour, sifted

Honey icing
125 g (4½ oz) unsalted butter
90 g (3¼ oz/¼ cup) honey
125 g (4½ oz/1 cup) icing (confectioners') sugar
1 tablespoon milk

1 Preheat the oven to 180°C (350°F/Gas 4). Lightly grease two 15 cm (6 inch) round cake tins and line the bases with baking paper.

2 Using electric beaters, cream the butter, honey, sugar and vanilla in a bowl until light and fluffy. Add the eggs one at a time, beating well after each addition, then beat in the banana.

3 In a small bowl, mix together the yoghurt and bicarbonate of soda. Fold the flour into the banana mixture alternately with the yoghurt mixture. Spoon the batter into the cake tins, smoothing the surface.

4 Bake for 50–60 minutes, or until a skewer inserted into the centre of the cakes comes out clean. Remove from the oven and leave to cool in the tins for 5 minutes, then turn the cakes out onto a wire rack to cool completely.

5 To make the honey icing (frosting), cream the butter and honey in a small bowl using electric beaters until light and fluffy. Gradually add the icing sugar alternately with the milk, beating well until very pale.

6 Spread the icing over the cold cakes, working it into rough peaks. Store in an airtight container for up to 4 days. Un-iced cakes can be frozen for up to 3 months.

CURRANT CREAM SCONES

Makes 12

375 g (13 oz/3 cups) plain (all-purpose) flour
1½ teaspoons bicarbonate of soda (baking soda)
3 teaspoons cream of tartar
1 teaspoon mixed (pumpkin pie) spice
2 teaspoons caster (superfine) sugar,
    plus extra, for sprinkling
50 g (1¾ oz) cold unsalted butter, chopped
150 ml (5 fl oz) pouring (whipping) cream
150 ml (5 fl oz) milk, plus extra, for brushing
125 g (4½ oz/heaped ¾ cup) currants
jam, to serve
thick (double/heavy) cream, to serve

1 Preheat the oven to 220°C (425°F/Gas 7). Grease a baking tray or line the tray with baking paper.

2 Sift the flour, bicarbonate of soda, cream of tartar, mixed spice and sugar into a large bowl. Using your fingertips, lightly rub in the butter until the mixture resembles breadcrumbs.

3 Add the cream, milk and currants and mix with a flat-bladed knife to form a soft dough, adding a little extra flour if the mixture is too sticky.

4 Using floured hands, gently gather the dough together and lift out onto a lightly floured work surface. Pat into a smooth ball, then press out to a 2 cm (¾ inch) thickness. Using a 6 cm (2½ inch) pastry cutter, cut the dough into rounds, or use a knife dipped in flour to cut out 4 cm (1½ inch) squares.

5 Place the scones on the baking tray, brush the tops lightly with a little extra milk and sprinkle with the extra sugar. Bake for 10–12 minutes, or until golden. Transfer to a wire rack lined with a tea towel (dish towel) to cool slightly. Serve warm, with jam and thick cream.

GLACE FRUIT BARS
Makes 24

440 g (15½ oz/2 cups) chopped glacé fruit
2 tablespoons rum, plus 1 teaspoon, extra
90 g (3¼ oz) unsalted butter, softened
80 g (2¾ oz/⅓ cup) caster (superfine) sugar
2 eggs
2 teaspoons natural vanilla extract
140 g (5 oz/1 cup) mixed toasted nuts, chopped
30 g (1 oz/¼ cup) plain (all-purpose) flour, sifted
30 g (1 oz/¼ cup) self-raising flour, sifted
25 g (1 oz/¼ cup) powdered milk
85 g (3 oz/⅔ cup) icing (confectioners') sugar

1 Preheat the oven to 190°C (375°F/Gas 5). Grease a shallow, 28 x 18 cm (11¼ x 7 inch) baking tin and line with baking paper, allowing it to hang over the two long sides.
2 Put the glacé fruit in a bowl and pour the rum over. Set aside.

3 Using electric beaters, cream the butter and sugar in a bowl until light and fluffy. Add the eggs one at a time, beating well after each addition. Beat in the vanilla, then stir in the fruit mixture, nuts, flours and milk powder.
4 Spoon the batter into the baking tin, smoothing the surface. Bake for 15 minutes, then reduce the oven temperature to 180°C (350°F/Gas 4) and bake for a further 10 minutes, or until golden brown. Remove from the oven and leave to cool in the tin until just warm.
5 Put the icing sugar and extra rum in a small bowl. Stir in 1 teaspoon water to make a spreadable but not runny icing (frosting)—if it is too thick, stir in a little more rum or water.
6 Spread the icing over the slice and leave to cool completely. Cut into bars and store in an airtight container for up to 4 days.

GINGER CAKES WITH CHOCOLATE CENTRES

Makes 12

Ginger ganache
100 g (3½ oz/⅔ cup) chopped good-quality dark chocolate
60 ml (2 fl oz/¼ cup) pouring (whipping) cream
1 tablespoon finely chopped glacé ginger

100 g (3½ oz) unsalted butter, softened
125 g (4½ oz/⅔ cup) soft brown sugar
115 g (4 oz/⅓ cup) treacle or dark corn syrup
2 eggs
125 g (4½ oz/1 cup) self-raising flour
85 g (3 oz/⅔ cup) plain (all-purpose) flour
2 teaspoons ground cinnamon
1 tablespoon ground ginger
60 ml (2 fl oz/¼ cup) buttermilk

1 Preheat the oven to 180°C (350°F/Gas 4). Line a 12-hole standard muffin tin with paper cases.

2 To make the ginger ganache, put the chocolate in a small heatproof bowl. Heat the cream until almost boiling, then pour it over the chocolate and stir until melted and smooth. Stir in the ginger. Allow to cool to room temperature, then refrigerate until firm. Divide into 12 equal portions and roll each into a ball. Freeze until required.

3 Using electric beaters, cream the butter, sugar and treacle in a bowl until light and fluffy. Add the eggs one at a time, beating well after each addition. Sift the flours and spices into a bowl, then fold into the butter mixture alternately with the buttermilk.

4 Spoon three-quarters of the batter into the paper cases. Top each with a frozen ganache ball, then spoon the remaining batter over the top. Bake for 25–30 minutes, or until deep golden (don't test the cakes with a skewer—the centres will be molten).

5 Remove from the oven and leave to cool in the tin for 5 minutes before turning out. Remove the paper cases and serve warm.

CHOCOLATE, RAISIN AND PEANUT CLUSTERS

Makes about 40

200 g (7 oz/1⅓ cups) chopped good-quality dark chocolate
60 g (2¼ oz) unsalted butter, chopped
170 g (6 oz/¾ cup) caster (superfine) sugar
1 tablespoon golden syrup or dark corn syrup
1½ teaspoons natural vanilla extract
155 g (5½ oz/1¼ cups) raisins
200 g (7 oz/1¼ cups) peanuts, toasted and roughly chopped
40 g (1½ oz/⅓ cup) plain (all-purpose) flour
2 tablespoons unsweetened cocoa powder

1 Preheat the oven to 170°C (325°F/Gas 3). Lightly grease two baking trays.
2 Put 75 g (2½ oz/½ cup) of the chocolate in a heatproof bowl with the butter, sugar, golden syrup and vanilla. Set the bowl over a small saucepan of simmering water, ensuring the base of the bowl doesn't touch the water. Stir until the chocolate and butter have melted and the mixture is smooth. Allow to cool slightly.
3 Roughly chop the remaining chocolate and place in a large bowl with the raisins and peanuts. Sift the flour and cocoa powder over the peanut mixture and toss to combine. Add the melted chocolate mixture and stir using a wooden spoon until the mixture is well combined and a firm dough forms.
4 Roll tablespoons of the mixture into rough rounds. Place on the baking trays, about 4 cm (1½ inches) apart. Bake for 15 minutes, or until the biscuits are firm and no longer glossy, swapping the trays around halfway through baking.
5 Remove from the oven and leave to cool on the trays for 5 minutes, then carefully transfer to a wire rack to cool completely. Store in an airtight container for up to 1 week, or freeze for up to 8 weeks.

APPLE, BUTTERMILK, MAPLE SYRUP AND BRAN MUFFINS

Makes 12

75 g (2½ oz/1 cup) unprocessed bran
375 ml (13 fl oz/1½ cups) buttermilk
185 ml (6 fl oz/¾ cup) maple syrup
1 egg, lightly beaten
60 ml (2 fl oz/¼ cup) vegetable oil
1 cooking apple (such as granny smith),
   peeled, cored and chopped
70 g (2½ oz/½ cup) hazelnuts, toasted,
   peeled and chopped
250 g (9 oz/2 cups) self-raising flour
1 teaspoon ground cinnamon

1 Preheat the oven to 180°C (350°F/Gas 4). Grease a 12-hole standard muffin tin, or line the holes with paper cases.
2 Put the bran and buttermilk in a bowl, stirring to mix well. Set aside for 5 minutes.
3 Add the maple syrup, egg, oil, apple and hazelnuts and stir to combine well. Sift the flour and cinnamon over the mixture, then gently fold in until just combined. Do not overmix—the batter should be slightly lumpy.
4 Spoon the batter into the muffin holes. Bake for 20–25 minutes, or until the tops are golden and a skewer inserted into the centre comes out clean.
5 Remove from the oven and leave to cool in the tin for 2 minutes before turning out onto a wire rack. Serve warm.

CHOCOLATE BANANA CAKE

Serves 6–8

240 g (8½ oz/1 cup) mashed ripe bananas
(about 3 bananas)
185 g (6½ oz/heaped ¾ cup) caster (superfine)
sugar
185 g (6½ oz/1½ cups) self-raising flour
2 eggs, lightly beaten
60 ml (2 fl oz/¼ cup) light olive oil
60 ml (2 fl oz/¼ cup) milk
100 g (3½ oz/heaped ¾ cup) grated
good-quality dark chocolate (see Note)
90 g (3¼ oz/¾ cup) chopped walnuts
thick (double/heavy) cream, to serve (optional)

1 Preheat the oven to 180°C (350°F/Gas 4). Grease a 20 x 10 cm (8 x 4 inch) loaf (bar) tin and line the base with baking paper.

2 Mix the banana and sugar in a large bowl until just combined. Sift the flour into a bowl, then add to the mixture with the eggs, olive oil and milk. Stir gently for 30 seconds with a wooden spoon, then fold the chocolate and walnuts through.

3 Pour the batter into the loaf tin and bake for 55 minutes, or until a skewer inserted into the centre of the cake comes out clean.

4 Remove from the oven and leave to cool in the tin for 5 minutes before turning onto a wire rack. Serve warm, with cream if desired. **Note** In warm weather, chocolate can be grated more easily if it is left to harden in the freezer for a few minutes first.

CARROT, SPICE AND SOUR CREAM CAKE
Serves 8–10

310 g (11 oz/2½ cups) self-raising flour
2 teaspoons ground cinnamon
1 teaspoon ground nutmeg
150 g (5½ oz/heaped ¾ cup) dark brown sugar
200 g (7 oz/1⅓ cups) grated carrot
4 eggs
250 g (9 oz/1 cup) sour cream
250 ml (9 fl oz/1 cup) vegetable oil

Orange cream icing
60 g (2¼ oz/¼ cup) cream cheese, softened
20 g (¾ oz) unsalted butter, softened
1 teaspoon grated orange zest
2 teaspoons orange juice
125 g (4½ oz/1 cup) icing (confectioners') sugar

1 Preheat the oven to 160°C (315°F/ Gas 2–3). Grease a deep, 22 cm (8½ inch) round cake tin and line the base with baking paper. Sift the flour and spices into a large bowl, then stir in the sugar and carrot and mix well.

2 In another bowl, lightly beat the eggs together with the sour cream and oil. Add to the carrot mixture and stir until well combined. Spoon the batter into the cake tin and smooth the surface.

3 Bake for 1¼ hours, or until a skewer inserted into the centre of the cake comes out clean. Remove from the oven and leave in the tin for 10 minutes before turning out onto a wire rack to cool.

4 To make the orange cream icing (frosting), beat the cream cheese, butter, orange zest and juice in a bowl with electric beaters until light and fluffy. Gradually beat in the icing sugar until smooth. Spread over the cooled cake and store in an airtight container in a cool place for up to 4 days.

FRUIT AND TEA LOAF

Makes 1 loaf

500 g (1 lb 2 oz/2⅔ cups) mixed dried fruit
185 ml (6 fl oz/¾ cup) strong, hot black tea
125 g (4½ oz/⅔ cup) soft brown sugar
1 egg, lightly beaten
125 g (4½ oz/1 cup) plain (all-purpose) flour
¾ teaspoon baking powder
1 teaspoon ground cinnamon
¼ teaspoon ground nutmeg
a large pinch of ground cloves
butter, to serve (optional)

1 Put the fruit in a large bowl and pour the hot tea over. Cover with plastic wrap and leave to stand for 3 hours, or overnight.
2 Preheat the oven to 160°C (315°F/ Gas 2–3). Grease a 25 x 11 cm (10 x 4¼ inch) loaf (bar) tin and line the base with baking paper. Dust the sides with a little flour, shaking off the excess.
3 Stir the sugar and egg into the fruit mixture to combine well. Sift the flour, baking powder and spices into a bowl, then add to the fruit mixture. Using a large slotted spoon, stir together well.
4 Spoon the batter into the loaf tin and bake for 1 hour 35 minutes, covering the top with foil if it browns too quickly. The loaf is cooked when a skewer inserted into the centre comes out clean.
5 Remove from the oven and leave to cool completely in the tin before turning out. Slice and serve with butter, if desired. Store in an airtight container in a cool place, wrapped in plastic wrap, for up to 1 week, or up to 8 weeks in the freezer.

PECAN AND ORANGE LOAF CAKE

Serves 8–10

125 g (4½ oz) unsalted butter, softened
185 g (6½ oz/heaped ¾ cup) caster (superfine) sugar
2 eggs
100 g (3½ oz/¾ cup) ground pecans
3 teaspoons grated orange zest
185 g (6½ oz/1½ cups) self-raising flour, sifted
125 ml (4 fl oz/½ cup) milk

Icing
125 g (4½ oz/1 cup) icing (confectioners') sugar
15 g (½ oz) unsalted butter, softened
1 teaspoon grated orange zest

1 Preheat the oven to 180°C (350°F/Gas 4). Grease a 22 x 12 cm (8½ x 4½ inch) loaf (bar) tin and line the base and two long sides with baking paper.

2 Using electric beaters, cream the butter and sugar in a bowl until light and fluffy. Add the eggs one at a time, beating well after each addition. Add the ground pecans and orange zest. Using a metal spoon, gently fold in the flour alternately with the milk. Spoon the batter into the loaf tin and smooth the surface.

3 Bake for 50–60 minutes, or until a skewer inserted into the centre of the cake comes out clean. Remove from the oven and leave in the tin for 10 minutes before turning out onto a wire rack to cool.

4 Put the icing (frosting) ingredients in a bowl with 1–2 tablespoons hot water and mix until smooth. Spread over the cooled cake and store in an airtight container in a cool place for up to 4 days.

RHUBARB YOGHURT CAKE

Serves 8

150 g (5½ oz/1¼ cups) finely sliced rhubarb
250 g (9 oz/heaped 1 cup) caster (superfine)
  sugar
310 g (11 oz/2½ cups) self-raising flour
1 teaspoon natural vanilla extract
2 eggs, lightly beaten
125 g (4½ oz/½ cup) plain yoghurt
1 tablespoon rosewater
125 g (4½ oz) unsalted butter, melted
yoghurt or cream, to serve (optional)

1 Preheat the oven to 180°C (350°F/Gas 4). Lightly grease a 23 cm (9 inch) round cake tin and line the base with baking paper.
2 In a bowl, mix together the rhubarb and sugar. Sift the flour over the rhubarb and mix it through. Stir in the vanilla, egg, yoghurt, rosewater and butter until just combined.
3 Spoon the batter into the cake tin and bake for 1 hour, or until a skewer inserted into the centre of the cake comes out clean.
4 Remove from the oven and leave in the tin for 15 minutes before turning out onto a wire rack to cool. Serve with yoghurt or cream, if desired. Store in an airtight container in a cool place for up to 4 days.

Sweet tooths, rejoice! Here are your just desserts—a compilation of some of our favourite after-dinner sweets, representing the spectrum from cakey and crumbly to creamy and crunchy and molten and gooey to silky and sticky, with some lighter, fruitier options thrown in for good measure. After all, when the rest of the vegetarian diet is so virtuous, you can afford to reward yourself and sneak in some indulgences now and then... after all, if there's fruit in it, it can't be all bad for you, can it? A little bit of what we fancy—sweetness and light, sugar and spice and all things nice—is what keeps us feeling good, and desserts just have that magical alchemy that keeps on drawing us in. Oh happy day!

DESSERTS

NUTMEG AND SAFFRON PANNA COTTA

Makes 6

500 ml (17 fl oz/2 cups) pouring
(whipping) cream
185 ml (6 fl oz/¾ cup) milk
100 g (3½ oz/scant ½ cup) caster
(superfine) sugar
1 teaspoon ground nutmeg
a pinch of saffron threads
2½ teaspoons powdered gelatine
fresh fruit, to serve

1 Put the cream, milk, sugar, nutmeg and saffron in a saucepan. Heat over low heat until the mixture just comes to the boil. Immediately remove from the heat and leave to cool until lukewarm.

2 Pour 2 tablespoons hot water into a small bowl and sprinkle with the gelatine. Leave to stand for a few minutes to soften, then whisk with a fork to dissolve. Stir into the cream mixture and leave to cool.

3 Strain the mixture and pour into six 125 ml (4 fl oz/½ cup) ramekins or dariole moulds. Refrigerate overnight to set.

4 Just before serving, dip a blunt knife into warm water and run the tip around the edge of each mould. Dip the moulds in a bowl of warm water for a few seconds, shaking slightly to loosen. Place a serving plate over each mould, then invert and remove the mould. Serve with fresh fruit.

RED FRUIT SALAD WITH BERRIES

Serves 6

55 g (2 oz/¼ cup) caster (superfine) sugar
125 ml (4 fl oz/½ cup) dry red wine
1 star anise
1 teaspoon finely chopped lemon zest
250 g (9 oz/1⅔ cups) strawberries,
  hulled and halved
150 g (5½ oz/1 cup) blueberries
150 g (5½ oz/1¼ cups) raspberries, mulberries
  or other red berries
250 g (9 oz) cherries
5 small red plums, about 250 g (9 oz) in total,
  pitted and quartered
yoghurt or thick (double/heavy) cream, to serve

1 Put the sugar, wine, star anise, lemon zest and 125 ml (4 fl oz/½ cup) water in a small saucepan. Bring to the boil over medium heat, stirring to dissolve the sugar. Boil for 3 minutes, then set aside to cool for 30 minutes. When cool, strain the syrup.
2 Mix the fruit together in a large bowl and pour the syrup over. Mix well to coat the fruit, then cover with plastic wrap and refrigerate for 1½ hours.
3 Divide the fruit among serving bowls and drizzle with some of the syrup. Serve with a dollop of yoghurt or cream.

BAKED PASSIONFRUIT CHEESECAKE

Serves 6–8

60 g (2¼ oz/½ cup) plain (all-purpose) flour
30 g (1 oz/¼ cup) self-raising flour
50 g (1¾ oz) unsalted butter
2 tablespoons caster (superfine) sugar
grated zest of 1 lemon
2 tablespoons lemon juice

Filling

600 g (1 lb 5 oz) cream cheese, at room
    temperature
170 g (6 oz/¾ cup) caster (superfine) sugar
30 g (1 oz/¼ cup) plain (all-purpose) flour
125 ml (4 fl oz/½ cup) strained passionfruit juice
4 eggs
170 ml (5½ fl oz/⅔ cup) pouring (whipping) cream

1 Put the flours, butter, sugar and lemon zest in a food processor. Add the lemon juice and, using the pulse button, process until a dough forms. Turn out onto a lightly floured surface and gently press together into a ball. Cover with plastic wrap and refrigerate for 1 hour.

2 Meanwhile, preheat the oven to 180°C (350°F/Gas 4). Grease a 22 cm (8½ inch) round spring-form cake tin.

3 Roll out the pastry on a lightly floured surface to a 5 mm (¼ inch) thickness. Roll the pastry around the rolling pin, then lift and ease it into the tin, gently pressing to fit the side. Trim the edges, then refrigerate for 10 minutes.

4 Bake the pastry for 15–20 minutes, or until golden. Remove from the oven and leave to cool. Reduce the oven temperature to 150°C (300°F/Gas 2).

5 To make the filling, beat the cream cheese and sugar using electric beaters until smooth. Add the flour and passionfruit juice and beat until combined. Add the eggs one at a time, beating well after each addition. Stir in the cream, then pour the mixture over the cooled pastry base.

6 Bake for 50 minutes, then cover the cheesecake with foil and move to the lowest shelf of the oven. Bake for a further 10 minutes, or until the centre is just firm to the touch. Remove from the oven and leave to cool in the tin completely before serving.

ROASTED SPICED PEARS AND STRAWBERRIES

Serves 4

170 g (6 oz/¾ cup) caster (superfine) sugar
2 vanilla beans, split lengthways
2 star anise
1 cinnamon stick, broken in half
4 firm pears, peeled and cut into quarters
250 g (9 oz/1⅔ cups) strawberries, hulled,
   then cut in half if large
Greek-style yoghurt, to serve

1 Preheat the oven to 170°C (325°F/Gas 3). Pour 310 ml (10¾ fl oz/1¼ cups) water into a baking dish and add the sugar, vanilla beans, star anise and cinnamon. Stir to dissolve the sugar, then bake for 10 minutes.

2 Add the pears to the syrup. Cover with foil and bake for 35–45 minutes, or until the pears are almost tender, turning once.

3 Add the strawberries and turn to coat them in the syrup. Cover with foil again and bake for a further 5 minutes, or until the strawberries soften.

4 Set aside to cool to room temperature. Serve with a dollop of yoghurt.

STRAWBERRY AND STAR ANISE SORBET

Serves 4

115 g (4 oz/½ cup) caster (superfine) sugar
3 star anise
750 g (1 lb 10 oz) strawberries
60 ml (2 fl oz/¼ cup) lime juice

1 Pour 250 ml (9 fl oz/1 cup) water into a small saucepan and add the sugar and star anise. Stir over low heat until the sugar has dissolved, then increase the heat and allow to boil for 1 minute. Set the syrup aside to cool completely. Discard the star anise.
2 Hull and purée the strawberries. Pour the strawberry purée into a bowl, add the lime juice and cold sugar syrup and stir until well combined.

3 Pour the mixture into an ice cream maker and churn according to the manufacturer's instructions until the sorbet is just firm. Spoon into an airtight container and freeze until ready to serve. Alternatively, pour the mixture into a shallow metal tray and freeze for 2 hours, or until frozen around the edges. Transfer to a food processor and process until just smooth, or transfer to a bowl and beat with a wooden spoon until smooth. Return to the tray and freeze for another 2 hours, then process or beat again. Repeat this process two more times, then spoon into an airtight container and freeze until ready to serve.

GINGERBREAD AND APRICOT UPSIDE DOWN CAKE

Serves 6

180 g (6 oz/¾ cup) glacé apricots
185 g (6½ oz) unsalted butter
35 g (1¼ oz/⅓ cup) pecans, finely chopped
140 g (5 oz/¾ cup) light brown sugar
90 g (3¼ oz/¼ cup) golden syrup or
  dark corn syrup
185 g (6½ oz/1½ cups) self-raising flour
3 teaspoons ground ginger
½ teaspoon ground nutmeg
custard, to serve (optional)

1 Preheat the oven to 180°C (350°F/Gas 4). Grease and flour the base of a deep, 20 cm (8 inch) round cake tin, shaking out the excess flour. Arrange the apricots around the bottom of the tin, cut side up.

2 Melt the butter in a small saucepan over low heat. Transfer 1 tablespoon of the melted butter to a small bowl. Add the pecans and 45 g (1½ oz/¼ cup) of the sugar and mix well. Sprinkle the mixture over the apricots.

3 Add the golden syrup and 125 ml (4 fl oz/ ½ cup) water to the remaining melted butter and stir together over medium heat.

4 Sift the flour and spices into a bowl, then stir in the remaining sugar. Pour in the golden syrup mixture and mix well. Spoon the mixture over the apricots and smooth the surface.

5 Bake for 35–40 minutes, or until a skewer inserted into the centre of the cake comes out clean. Leave the cake in the tin for 15 minutes before turning it out of the tin and setting it on a wire rack to cool. Serve with custard, if desired.

WHITE CHOCOLATE, ALMOND AND CRANBERRY TORTE

Serves 8–10

8 egg whites

200 g (7 oz/scant 1 cup) caster (superfine) sugar

250 g (9 oz/1⅔ cups) chopped good-quality white chocolate

200 g (7 oz/1¼ cups) blanched almonds, toasted, then chopped

200 g (7 oz/1½ cups) sweetened dried cranberries

40 g (1½ oz/⅓ cup) self-raising flour

1 Preheat the oven to 180°C (350°F/Gas 4). Lightly grease a 24 cm (9½ inch) round spring-form cake tin and line the base with baking paper. Dust the side of the tin with a little flour, shaking out the excess.

2 Whisk the egg whites in a clean, dry bowl until stiff peaks form. Gradually add the sugar, whisking well after each addition. Whisk until the mixture is stiff and glossy and the sugar has dissolved.

3 Put the chocolate, almonds and cranberries in a bowl, add the flour and toss to combine.

4 Gently fold the chocolate mixture into the egg whites. Spoon the batter into the cake tin and gently tap the base to remove any air bubbles.

5 Bake for 1 hour, covering the cake with foil if it begins to brown too quickly. Turn off the oven, open the door slightly and leave the torte to cool completely in the oven.

6 Run a knife around the edge of the tin to loosen the torte, then remove the tin. Cut into wedges to serve.

CINNAMON AND ORANGE MINI PAVLOVAS WITH BERRIES

Serves 4

2 egg whites
125 g (4½ oz/heaped ½ cup) caster (superfine)
  sugar
2 teaspoons ground cinnamon
1 teaspoon finely grated orange zest
3 teaspoons cornflour (cornstarch)
1 teaspoon white vinegar
125 ml (4 fl oz/½ cup) pouring (whipping) cream
fresh berries, to serve

1 Preheat the oven to 140°C (275°F/Gas 1). Line a baking tray with baking paper and mark four 10 cm (4 inch) circles on the baking paper. Turn the paper upside down so the marks don't stain the meringues.

2 Beat the egg whites in a clean, dry bowl using electric beaters until soft peaks form. Gradually add the sugar, beating well after each addition. Continue to beat for a further 4–5 minutes, or until the sugar has dissolved and the meringue is thick and glossy. Gently fold in the cinnamon, orange zest, cornflour and vinegar.

3 Place 2 tablespoons of the mixture into each circle, gently spreading it out to the edges with the back of a spoon. Hollow out the centres to make nest shapes.

4 Bake for 10 minutes, then turn the tray around and bake for a further 30–35 minutes, or until pale and crisp. Turn the oven off, open the door slightly and leave the pavlovas in the oven to cool completely. They may crack slightly on cooling.

5 Whip the cream and spoon a little into each pavlova. Top with berries and serve.

GRILLED FIGS WITH RICOTTA

Serves 4

2 tablespoons honey
1 cinnamon stick
25 g (1 oz/¼ cup) flaked almonds
4 large or 8 small fresh figs
2 tablespoons icing (confectioners') sugar
125 g (4½ oz/½ cup) ricotta cheese
½ teaspoon natural vanilla extract
a pinch of ground cinnamon
½ teaspoon finely grated orange zest

1 Put the honey and cinnamon stick in a small saucepan with 80 ml (2½ fl oz/⅓ cup) water. Bring to the boil, then reduce the heat and simmer gently for 6 minutes, or until the syrup has thickened and reduced by half. Discard the cinnamon stick and stir in the almonds.

2 Preheat the grill to medium–high and grease a shallow baking dish large enough to fit all the figs side by side. Slice the figs into quarters from the top to within 1 cm (½ inch) of the bottom, keeping them attached at the base. Arrange in the dish.

3 Sift the icing sugar into a small bowl. Add the ricotta, vanilla, ground cinnamon and orange zest and mix well. Divide the filling among the figs, spooning it into the cavities. Spoon the honey syrup over the top.

4 Grill the figs for 3–4 minutes, or until the juices start to ooze out and the almonds are lightly toasted. Allow to cool slightly, then spoon the juices from the dish over the figs and serve.

PRUNE AND ALMOND CLAFOUTIS

Serves 6

250 ml (9 fl oz/1 cup) pouring (whipping) cream
100 ml (3½ fl oz) milk
1 teaspoon natural vanilla extract
3 eggs
80 g (2¾ oz/⅓ cup) caster (superfine) sugar
80 g (2¾ oz/¾ cup) ground almonds
350 g (12 oz/scant 1⅔ cups) pitted prunes
icing (confectioners') sugar, for dusting
custard, to serve
whipped cream, to serve (optional)

1 Preheat the oven to 180°C (350°F/Gas 4). Lightly grease a shallow 750 ml (26 fl oz/ 3 cup) baking dish.
2 Pour the cream, milk and vanilla into a saucepan and stir together well. Bring to a simmer over low heat, then remove from the heat and allow to cool slightly.
3 In a bowl, whisk together the eggs, sugar and ground almonds. Stir in the cream mixture until well combined.
4 Arrange the prunes in the baking dish. Pour the batter over the prunes and bake for 35–40 minutes, or until golden. Serve dusted with icing sugar, with custard and whipped cream if desired.

STICKY BLACK RICE PUDDING

Serves 6–8

400 g (14 oz/2 cups) black rice
3 pandan leaves
500 ml (17 fl oz/2 cups) coconut milk
80 g (2¾ oz/⅔ cup) grated palm sugar (jaggery)
   or soft brown sugar
55 g (2 oz/¼ cup) caster (superfine) sugar
coconut cream, to serve
diced mango or papaya, to serve

1 Put the rice in a large non-metallic bowl and cover with water. Leave to soak for at least 8 hours, or preferably overnight.
2 Drain the rice, then place in a saucepan with 1 litre (35 fl oz/4 cups) water and slowly bring to the boil. Cook at a low boil, stirring frequently, for 20 minutes, or until tender. Drain.
3 Pull your fingers through the pandan leaves to shred them, then tie them into a knot. Pour the coconut milk into a large saucepan and heat until almost boiling. Add the pandan leaves, palm sugar and caster sugar and stir until all the sugar has dissolved.
4 Add the rice and cook, stirring often, for 8 minutes without boiling. Turn off the heat, then cover and leave for 15 minutes for all the flavours to absorb into the rice. Remove the pandan leaves.
5 Spoon into bowls and serve warm, with coconut cream and diced fruit.

BANANA FRITTERS IN COCONUT BATTER

Serves 6

100 g (3½ oz/½ cup) glutinous rice flour (see Note)
100 g (3½ oz/1 cup) freshly grated coconut, or 60 g (2¼ oz/⅔ cup) desiccated coconut
55 g (2 oz/¼ cup) sugar
1 tablespoon sesame seeds
60 ml (2 fl oz/¼ cup) coconut milk
6 sugar bananas
vegetable oil, for deep-frying
ice cream, to serve

1 Put the flour, coconut, sugar, sesame seeds and coconut milk in a bowl. Add 60 ml (2 fl oz/¼ cup) water and whisk to a smooth batter, adding more water if the batter is too thick. Cover and leave to stand for 1 hour.

2 Peel the bananas and cut them in half lengthways (cut each portion in half crossways if the bananas are large).
3 Fill a wok or deep heavy-based saucepan one-third full of oil and heat to 180°C (350°F), or until a cube of bread dropped into the oil browns in 15 seconds. Working in batches, dip the bananas into the batter, then gently drop into the hot oil and cook for 4–6 minutes, or until golden brown all over. Remove with a slotted spoon and drain on paper towels. Serve hot, with ice cream.
Note Glutinous rice flour, also known as sweet rice flour or sweet rice powder, is not to be confused with regular rice flour. Very fine and powdery, glutinous rice flour is made from a short-grained glutinous rice and is sold in Asian grocery stores. Regular rice flour cannot be substituted as it will not give the same chewy, sticky result.

RHUBARB SLICE

Makes about 25 pieces

300 g (10½ oz) rhubarb, trimmed and
   cut into 5 mm (¼ inch) slices
345 g (12 oz/1½ cups) caster (superfine) sugar
185 g (6½ oz) unsalted butter, chopped
½ teaspoon natural vanilla extract
3 eggs
90 g (3¼ oz/¾ cup) plain (all-purpose) flour
¾ teaspoon baking powder
1 tablespoon sugar
icing (confectioners') sugar, for dusting
thick (double/heavy) cream, to serve

1 Put the rhubarb in a bowl and add 115 g
(4 oz/½ cup) of the sugar. Mix well, then
cover and leave to stand for 1 hour, or until
the rhubarb has released its juices and the
sugar has dissolved, stirring occasionally.
Strain well, discarding the liquid.

2 Preheat the oven to 180°C (350°F/Gas 4).
Lightly grease a 20 x 30 cm (8 x 12 inch)
rectangular shallow tin with butter. Line
the base with baking paper, leaving the
paper hanging over the two long sides
of the tin.

3 Put the butter, vanilla and remaining
sugar in a bowl and cream using electric
beaters until pale and fluffy. Add the eggs
one at a time, beating well after each
addition. Sift the flour and baking powder
over the mixture, then stir to combine.

4 Spoon the batter into the prepared tin,
then arrange the rhubarb over the top in a
single layer. Sprinkle with the sugar and
bake for 40–45 minutes, or until golden.
Remove from the oven and leave to cool
slightly in the tin, then carefully lift out
and cut into squares.

5 Dust with icing sugar and serve warm,
with thick cream.

PEAR TARTE TATIN

Serves 8

145 g (5 oz/⅔ cup) caster (superfine) sugar
50 g (1¾ oz) unsalted butter, chopped
½ teaspoon ground ginger
½ teaspoon ground cinnamon
3 beurre bosc pears, peeled, cored and
    cut into wedges
450 g (1 lb) block of frozen butter puff
    pastry, thawed
thick (double/heavy) cream, to serve

1 Preheat the oven to 220°C (425°F/Gas 7).
2 Put a 22 cm (8½ inch) heavy-based frying pan with an ovenproof handle over medium heat. Add the sugar and heat, shaking the pan constantly, until the sugar is a dark caramel colour.
3 Add the butter, ginger and cinnamon and stir until well combined. Add the pears and spoon the caramel all over them. Reduce the heat to low, then cover and cook for 5 minutes, or until the pears just begin to soften.
4 Remove the frying pan from the heat and arrange the pears over the base of the pan, overlapping the wedges neatly to make a decorative finish when the dish is turned out. Leave to cool slightly.
5 Roll the pastry out on a lightly floured work surface to a 24 cm (9½ inch) round. Place the pastry over the pears in the frying pan, tucking the edges around the pears so they are enclosed in pastry.
6 Bake for 20–25 minutes, or until the pastry is golden and puffed. Remove the tart from the oven and leave to rest in the pan for 10 minutes.
7 Run a knife around the edge of the pan to loosen the tart. Invert onto a serving plate and serve warm, with thick cream.

BAKED ALMOND AND MARZIPAN PEACHES

Serves 6

3 large ripe, firm peaches
50 g (1¾ oz/⅓ cup) roughly chopped dark
    chocolate
50 g (1¾ oz/⅓ cup) whole blanched almonds,
    toasted and chopped
2½ tablespoons marzipan, chopped
2 tablespoons caster (superfine) sugar
1½ tablespoons unsalted butter, softened
1 egg yolk, lightly beaten
thick (double/heavy) cream or crème anglaise,
    to serve

1 Preheat the oven to 170°C (325°F/Gas 3). Lightly grease a roasting tin or a large baking dish.
2 Cut the peaches in half and remove the stones. Remove and finely chop any flesh remaining on the stones, then place in a bowl. Add the chocolate, almonds, marzipan, sugar, butter and egg yolk and mix well.
3 Place the peaches, skin side down, in the roasting tin. Divide the stuffing among the peaches, pressing it firmly onto each peach and heaping it slightly if necessary. Bake for 30 minutes, or until the peaches have softened and the filling is bubbling.
4 Remove from the oven and leave to cool slightly. Serve warm or at room temperature, with thick cream or crème anglaise.

CITRUS DELICIOUS

Serves 4–6

60 g (2¼ oz) unsalted butter, softened
170 g (6 oz/¾ cup) caster (superfine) sugar
3 eggs, separated
125 ml (4 fl oz/½ cup) citrus juice
250 ml (9 fl oz/1 cup) milk
60 g (2¼ oz/½ cup) self-raising flour
2 tablespoons finely grated citrus zest
ice cream, to serve

1 Preheat the oven to 180°C (350°F/Gas 4). Lightly grease a 1.25 litre (44 fl oz/5 cup) baking dish.
2 Cream the butter and sugar in a bowl using electric beaters until pale and fluffy. Add the egg yolks one at a time, beating well after each addition. Stir in the citrus juice, milk, flour and zest, mixing well.
3 Whisk the egg whites in a clean, dry bowl until stiff peaks form, then gently fold them into the batter. Spoon the mixture into the baking dish. Put the dish in a large roasting tin and pour in enough hot water to come halfway up the side of the dish.
4 Bake for 40–45 minutes, or until golden (cover the top with foil if it browns too quickly). Serve hot or warm, with ice cream.

BANANA AND PLUM CRUMBLE

Serves 4–6

30 g (1 oz/¼ cup) plain (all-purpose) flour
50 g (1¾ oz/½ cup) rolled (porridge) oats
30 g (1 oz/½ cup) shredded coconut
45 g (1½ oz/¼ cup) soft brown sugar
finely grated zest of 1 lime
100 g (3½ oz) unsalted butter, chopped
2 bananas
4 plums, halved and pitted
60 ml (2 fl oz/¼ cup) lime juice
ice cream or whipped cream, to serve

1 Preheat the oven to 180°C (350°F/Gas 4). Put the flour, oats, coconut, sugar and lime zest in a small bowl and mix together well. Using your fingertips, rub the butter into the flour mixture until crumbly.
2 Peel the bananas, cut them in half lengthways and place in a 1.25 litre (44 fl oz/ 5 cup) baking dish. Add the plums, pour the lime juice over and toss to coat all the fruit in the juice. Sprinkle the crumble mixture evenly over the top.
3 Bake for 25–30 minutes, or until the crumble is golden. Serve hot, with ice cream or whipped cream.

SUNKEN CHOCOLATE DESSERT CAKES

Serves 4

1 tablespoon melted butter
115 g (4 oz/½ cup) caster (superfine) sugar,
    plus extra, for sprinkling
150 g (5½ oz/1 cup) chopped good-quality
    dark chocolate
125 g (4½ oz) unsalted butter
3 eggs
30 g (1 oz/¼ cup) plain (all-purpose) flour
ice cream, to serve (optional)
icing (confectioners') sugar, to serve (optional)

1 Preheat the oven to 180°C (350°F/Gas 4). Brush four 250 ml (9 fl oz/1 cup) ramekins or dariole moulds with the melted butter and coat lightly with some caster sugar, shaking out the excess.

2 Put the chocolate and butter in a small heatproof bowl. Set the bowl over a small saucepan of simmering water, ensuring the base of the bowl doesn't touch the water. Stir until the chocolate and butter have melted, then remove from the heat.
3 In a bowl, whisk the eggs and caster sugar using electric beaters until pale and thick. Sift the flour over the top, then fold it through. Whisk in the melted chocolate.
4 Pour the batter into the ramekins and set on a baking tray. Bake for 30–35 minutes, or until the cakes are firm to touch. Remove from the oven and leave to cool in the ramekins for 10 minutes before turning out—you may need to run a knife around the inside edge to loosen them.
5 Serve warm, with ice cream. Alternatively, serve them in the ramekins, dusted with icing sugar.

MIXED BERRY SPONGE PUDDINGS

Serves 6

1 tablespoon melted butter
125 g (4½ oz) unsalted butter, softened
115 g (4 oz/½ cup) caster (superfine) sugar,
   plus 6 teaspoons extra
2 eggs
165 g (5¾ oz/1⅓ cups) self-raising flour, sifted
60 ml (2 fl oz/¼ cup) milk
200 g (7 oz) mixed fresh or frozen berries
custard or ice cream, to serve

1 Preheat the oven to 180°C (350°F/Gas 4). Brush six 125 ml (4 fl oz/½ cup) ramekins or dariole moulds with the melted butter.
2 Cream the butter and sugar in a bowl using electric beaters until pale and fluffy. Add the eggs one at a time, beating well after each addition. Gently fold in the flour alternately with the milk.
3 Divide the berries among the moulds and top each with a teaspoon of the extra caster sugar. Spoon the batter over the berries. Sit the moulds in a large roasting tin and pour in enough hot water to come halfway up the side of the moulds. Cover the roasting tin with a sheet of baking paper, then cover with a sheet of foil, pleating two sheets of foil together if necessary. Fold the foil tightly around the edges of the tin to seal.
4 Bake for 35–40 minutes, or until the puddings spring back when touched. Remove the puddings from their water bath and leave to cool in the moulds for 5 minutes. Run a small knife around the inside edge of each mould and turn out onto serving plates. Serve warm, with custard or ice cream.

CARDAMOM, ORANGE AND PLUM DESSERT CAKES

Makes 8

185 g (6½ oz) unsalted butter, chopped
95 g (3¼ oz/½ cup) soft brown sugar
115 g (4 oz/½ cup) caster (superfine) sugar
3 eggs
1 teaspoon finely grated orange zest
310 g (11 oz/2½ cups) self-raising flour, sifted
1 teaspoon ground cardamom
185 ml (6 fl oz/¾ cup) milk
4 tinned plums, drained and patted dry,
  then cut in half
1 tablespoon raw (demerara) sugar
thick (double/heavy) cream, to serve

1 Preheat the oven to 180°C (350°F/Gas 4). Lightly grease eight 250 ml (9 fl oz/1 cup) ceramic ramekins or dariole moulds and dust with flour, shaking out the excess.
2 Put the butter, brown sugar and caster sugar in a bowl. Cream using electric beaters until pale and fluffy. Add the eggs one at a time, beating well after each addition. Stir in the orange zest. Fold the flour and cardamom through the mixture alternately with the milk until combined and smooth.
3 Spoon the batter into the ramekins and place a plum half, cut side down, on top of each. Sprinkle with the raw sugar, then place the ramekins on a baking tray.
4 Bake for 30–35 minutes, or until the cakes are golden and firm to the touch. Serve warm or at room temperature, with cream.

SPICED QUINCE CHARLOTTE

Serves 4–6

460 g (1 lb/2 cups) caster (superfine) sugar
1 vanilla bean
1 cinnamon stick
1 teaspoon allspice
1.5 kg (3 lb 5 oz) quinces
2 loaves of brioche
unsalted butter, for spreading
crème anglaise or custard, to serve

1 Preheat the oven to 180°C (350°F/Gas 4).
2 Put the sugar in a saucepan, pour in
1 litre (35 fl oz/4 cups) water and stir over
medium heat until the sugar has dissolved.
Split the vanilla bean down the middle and
scrape the seeds into the saucepan. Add the
vanilla bean, cinnamon stick and allspice.
Stir and remove from the heat.
3 Peel the quinces, cut them into quarters
and remove the cores. Place in a roasting

tin or baking dish and pour the syrup over.
Cover with foil and bake for 2 hours, or
until the quince is very tender. Drain well.
4 Thinly slice the brioche and spread with
butter. Cut out a semi-circle from two slices
of brioche, to make a circle large enough
to fit the base of a 2 litre (70 fl oz/8 cup)
charlotte mould or ovenproof bowl.
Reserving four slices of brioche for the
top, cut the remainder into 2 cm (¾ inch)
wide fingers, long enough to fit the height
of the mould. Press the brioche vertically
around the side of the dish, overlapping
the strips slightly.
5 Place the quince quarters in the brioche-
lined mould and cover with the reserved
slices of brioche. Place on a baking tray
and bake for 25–30 minutes.
6 Remove from the oven and leave to cool
for 10 minutes, then unmould the charlotte
onto a serving plate. Serve warm, with
crème anglaise or custard.

RHUBARB AND BERRY CRUMBLE

Serves 4

850 g (1 lb 14 oz) rhubarb, cut into 2.5 cm
  (1 inch) lengths
150 g (5½ oz/1¼ cups) blackberries
1 teaspoon grated orange zest
250 g (9 oz/heaped 1 cup) caster
  (superfine) sugar
125 g (4½ oz/1 cup) plain (all-purpose) flour
100 g (3½ oz/1 cup) ground almonds
½ teaspoon ground ginger
150 g (5½ oz) cold unsalted butter,
  chopped
cream or ice cream, to serve

1 Preheat the oven to 180°C (350°F/Gas 4).
Grease a deep, 1.5 litre (52 fl oz/6 cup)
baking dish.
2 Bring a saucepan of water to the boil.
Add the rhubarb and cook over high heat
for 2 minutes, or until just tender. Drain
well and place in a bowl.
3 Add the blackberries, orange zest and
80 g (2¼ oz/⅓ cup) of the sugar and gently
mix together. Taste and add a little more
sugar if needed. Spoon the rhubarb mixture
into the baking dish.
4 In a bowl, mix together the flour,
ground almonds, ginger and remaining
sugar. Using your fingertips, rub the butter
into the flour mixture until it resembles
coarse breadcrumbs. Sprinkle the crumble
mixture over the fruit, pressing down
lightly—don't press it down too firmly, or
the topping will become flat and dense.
5 Place the dish on a baking tray and bake
for 25–30 minutes, or until the crumble
topping is golden and the fruit is bubbling
underneath.
6 Remove from the oven and leave to stand
in the dish for 5 minutes. Serve warm, with
cream or ice cream.

Published in 2008 by Murdoch Books Pty Limited.

Murdoch Books Australia
Pier 8/9
23 Hickson Road
Millers Point NSW 2000
Phone: + 61 (0) 2 8220 2000
Fax: + 61 (0) 2 8220 2558
www.murdochbooks.com.au

Murdoch Books UK Limited
Erico House, 6th Floor
93–99 Upper Richmond Road
Putney, London SW15 2TG
Phone: + 44 (0) 20 8785 5995
Fax: + 44 (0) 20 8785 5985
www.murdochbooks.co.uk

Chief Executive: Juliet Rogers
Publishing Director: Kay Scarlett

Design manager: Vivien Valk
Project manager and editor: Katri Hilden
Design concept: Annette Fitzgerald
Designer: Jo Yuen
Cover photography: Tanya Zouev
Cover styling: Katy Holder
Production: Kita George
Recipes developed by the Murdoch Books Test Kitchen

National Library of Australia Cataloguing-in-Publication Data:
  A commonsense guide to vegetarian cooking. Includes index.
  ISBN 9781741961232.
  1. Vegetarian cookery. (Series : A commonsense guide).
  641.5636

A catalogue record for this book is available from the British Library

Printed by Phoenix Offset in 2008. PRINTED IN CHINA.

IMPORTANT: Those who might be at risk from the effects of salmonella poisoning
(the elderly, pregnant women, young children and those suffering from immune
deficiency diseases) should consult their doctor with any concerns about eating raw eggs.

CONVERSION GUIDE: You may find cooking times vary depending on the oven you
are using. For fan-forced ovens, as a general rule, set the oven temperature to 20°C (35°F)
lower than indicated in the recipe.

VEGETARIAN
COOKING

A COMMONSENSE GUIDE